LANGUAGE AS A COMPLEX ADAPTIVE SYSTEM

Nick C. Ellis and Diane Larsen-Freeman, Editors

D1547429

© 2009 Language Learning Research Club, University of Michigan

Blackwell Publishing was acquired by John Wiley & Sons in February 2007. Blackwell's publishing program has been merged with Wiley's global Scientific, Technical, and Medical business to form Wiley-Blackwell.

Registered Office
John Wiley & Sons Ltd, The Atrium, Southern Gate, Chichester, West Sussex, PO19 8SQ, United Kingdom

Editorial Offices
350 Main Street, Malden, MA 02148-5020, USA
9600 Garsington Road, Oxford, OX4 2DQ, UK
The Atrium, Southern Gate, Chichester, West Sussex, PO19 8SQ, UK

For details of our global editorial offices, for customer services, and for information about how to apply for permission to reuse the copyright material in this book please see our website at www.wiley.com/wiley-blackwell.

The right of Nick C. Ellis and Diane Larsen-Freeman to be identified as the authors of the editorial material in this work has been asserted in accordance with the Copyright, Designs and Patents Act 1988.

All rights reserved. No part of this publication may be reproduced, stored in a retrieval system, or transmitted, in any form or by any means, electronic, mechanical, photocopying, recording or otherwise, except as permitted by the UK Copyright, Designs and Patents Act 1988, without the prior permission of the publisher.

Wiley also publishes its books in a variety of electronic formats. Some content that appears in print may not be available in electronic books.

Designations used by companies to distinguish their products are often claimed as trademarks. All brand names and product names used in this book are trade names, service marks, trademarks or registered trademarks of their respective owners. The publisher is not associated with any product or vendor mentioned in this book. This publication is designed to provide accurate and authoritative information in regard to the subject matter covered. It is sold on the understanding that the publisher is not engaged in rendering professional services. If professional advice or other expert assistance is required, the services of a competent professional should be sought.

Library of Congress Cataloging-in-Publication Data

Language as a complex adaptive system / Nick C. Ellis and Diane Larsen-Freeman, editors.
  p. cm.
"In celebration of Language Learning's 60th anniversary in 2008, the journal hosted a conference at the University of Michigan on the theme of "Language as a Complex Adaptive System"."
ISBN 978-1-4443-3400-5
1. Language acquisition–Research. 2. Second language acquisition research. 3. Language and languages–Study and teaching. I. Ellis, Nick C. II. Larsen-Freeman, Diane. III. Research Club in Language Learning (Ann Arbor, Mich.)
P118.L2576 2009
407'.2–dc22

                                        2009045865

A catalogue record for this book is available from the British Library.

Set in 10/13 pt TimesNRPS by Aptara

01—2009

Language as a Complex Adaptive System

Contents

Nick C. Ellis and Diane Larsen-Freeman
Editorial and Dedications .... v–vii

*The "Five Graces Group" (Clay Beckner, Richard Blythe,
Joan Bybee, Morten H. Christiansen, William Croft,
Nick C. Ellis, John Holland, Jinyun Ke,
Diane Larsen-Freeman, and Tom Schoenemann)*
Language Is a Complex Adaptive System: Position
Paper 1–26

Clay Beckner and Joan Bybee
A Usage-Based Account of Constituency
and Reanalysis 27–46

Richard A. Blythe and William A. Croft
The Speech Community in Evolutionary Language
Dynamics 47–63

Jeremy K. Boyd, Erin A. Gottschalk, and Adele E. Goldberg
Linking Rule Acquisition in Novel Phrasal
Constructions 64–89

Nick C. Ellis with Diane Larsen-Freeman
Constructing a Second Language: Analyses and
Computational Simulations of the Emergence of Linguistic
Constructions From Usage 90–125

Morten H. Christiansen and Maryellen C. MacDonald
A Usage-Based Approach to Recursion in Sentence
Processing 126–161

P. Thomas Schoenemann
Evolution of Brain and Language 162–186

Hannah Cornish, Monica Tamariz, and Simon Kirby
Complex Adaptive Systems and the Origins of Adaptive
Structure: What Experiments Can Tell Us 187–205

Christian M. I. M. Matthiessen
Meaning in the Making: Meaning Potential Emerging
From Acts of Meaning 206–229

Zoltán Dörnyei
Individual Differences: Interplay of Learner
Characteristics and Learning Environment 230–248

Robert J. Mislevy and Chengbin Yin
If Language Is a Complex Adaptive System, What
Is Language Assessment? 249–267

Subject Index 268–275

Language Learning   ISSN 0023-8333

Editorial and Dedications

Our 60th Anniversary

Language Learning was first published from the University of Michigan in 1948. Its subtitle then was "A Quarterly Journal of Applied Linguistics"; indeed the beginnings of "Applied Linguistics" have been attributed to this usage. In the 60 years since, our subtitle has evolved to become "A Journal of Research in Language Studies," reflecting our mission:

> *Language Learning* is a scientific journal dedicated to the understanding of language learning broadly defined. It publishes research articles that systematically apply methods of inquiry from disciplines including psychology, linguistics, cognitive science, educational inquiry, neuroscience, ethnography, sociolinguistics, sociology, and semiotics. It is concerned with fundamental theoretical issues in language learning such as child, second, and foreign language acquisition, language education, bilingualism, literacy, language representation in mind and brain, culture, cognition, pragmatics, and intergroup relations.

This supplement celebrates our 60th anniversary, our remarkable success toward these ends, and our realization that an understanding of language learning can only come from such integrated interdisciplinary inquiry.

The value of a journal lies in the quality of the articles it publishes. First and foremost, this comes from our submitting authors and from the scholars who voluntarily give many hours of their time and their expertise reviewing these submissions, thus to shape our discipline. There is a considerable investment from our Editors, our Board, and our Publishers too. Finally, there are you, our readers, who appreciate this work, cite it, and build upon it. Our first dedication, then, is to all who have made this journal what it is over the last 60 years.

Language as a Complex Adaptive System

To celebrate our anniversary, members of the Board, past Editors, our associates at Wiley-Blackwell, and friends and confederates in this enterprise, held a conference at the University of Michigan from November 7 to 9, 2008. The subject of the event was "Language as a Complex Adaptive System." Leading researchers in linguistics, psychology, anthropology, and complex systems discussed the path-breaking significance of this perspective for their understanding of language learning.

This theme built upon foundations laid by colleagues at a meeting at the Santa Fe Institute in March 2007. As a result of that workshop, the "Five Graces Group" (named after their rather special accommodations there) authored a position paper, *Language as a Complex Adaptive System*, which was circulated to 10 invited speakers who were asked to focus upon the issues presented here when considering their particular areas of language in the 60th anniversary conference and in their papers in this special issue of *Language Learning*.

The authors of these 10 papers are active in their recognition of complexity in their respective areas, ranging from language usage, structure, and change, to sociolinguistics, cognitive linguistics, anthropology, language evolution, first language acquisition, second language acquisition, psycholinguistics and language processing, language education, individual differences, and language testing. After their presentations at the conference, the discussion of these papers was led by members of the Board of *Language Learning* in order to contextualize these influences within Applied Linguistics and the Language Sciences more generally.

The conference was recorded. The podcast records of the main presentations from the conference are free to download at http://www.wiley.com/bw/podcast/lang.asp. We thank our publishers Wiley-Blackwell, for sponsoring this.

After the conference, the speakers submitted written versions of their papers, revised in the light of the discussions there. All of these underwent the standard review process. The results are gathered here as a special issue of *Language Learning* (Vol. 59, Supplement 1, December 2009), beginning with the Five Graces position paper.

The study of Complex Adaptive Systems, Emergentism, and Dynamic System Theory is a relatively recent phenomenon, yet it is revolutionizing our understanding of the natural, physical, and social worlds. Our beginnings here in considering *Language as a Complex Adaptive System* rest on the foundational research in this area, much of it from the Santa Fe Institute (SFI). One of the founding fathers at SFI was John Holland. His work on CAS and genetic algorithms, including his two key books *Hidden Order: How Adaptation Builds Complexity* (1995) and *Emergence: From Chaos to Order* (1998), pioneered the study of complex systems and nonlinear science. We are lucky to have him at the University of Michigan and as a member of the Five Graces group. John is 80 years old this year. Our second dedication, therefore, is to him.

Nick C. Ellis, General Editor, *Language Learning*
Diane Larsen-Freeman, Member, Board of Directors
Editors of this 60th Anniversary Issue
University of Michigan July 9, 2009

Language Learning ISSN 0023-8333

Language Is a Complex Adaptive System: Position Paper

The "Five Graces Group"

Clay Beckner
University of New Mexico

Nick C. Ellis
University of Michigan

Richard Blythe
University of Edinburgh

John Holland
Santa Fe Institute; University of Michigan

Joan Bybee
University of New Mexico

Jinyun Ke
University of Michigan

Morten H. Christiansen
Cornell University

Diane Larsen-Freeman
University of Michigan

William Croft
University of New Mexico

Tom Schoenemann
Indiana University

Language has a fundamentally social function. Processes of human interaction along with domain-general cognitive processes shape the structure and knowledge of language. Recent research in the cognitive sciences has demonstrated that patterns of use strongly affect how language is acquired, is used, and changes. These processes are not independent of one another but are facets of the same *complex adaptive system* (CAS). Language as a CAS involves the following key features: The system consists of multiple agents (the speakers in the speech community) interacting with one another.

This paper, our agreed position statement, was circulated to invited participants before a conference celebrating the 60th Anniversary of *Language Learning*, held at the University of Michigan, on the theme *Language is a Complex Adaptive System*. Presenters were asked to focus on the issues presented here when considering their particular areas of language in the conference and in their articles in this special issue of *Language Learning*. The evolution of this piece was made possible by the Sante Fe Institute (SFI) though its sponsorship of the "Continued Study of Language Acquisition and Evolution" workgroup meeting, Santa Fe Institute, 1–3 March 2007.

Correspondence concerning this article should be addressed to Nick C. Ellis, University of Michigan, 500 E. Washington Street, Ann Arbor, MI 48104. Internet: ncellis@umich.edu

The system is adaptive; that is, speakers' behavior is based on their past interactions, and current and past interactions together feed forward into future behavior. A speaker's behavior is the consequence of competing factors ranging from perceptual constraints to social motivations. The structures of language emerge from interrelated patterns of experience, social interaction, and cognitive mechanisms. The CAS approach reveals commonalities in many areas of language research, including first and second language acquisition, historical linguistics, psycholinguistics, language evolution, and computational modeling.

Introduction: Shared Assumptions

Language has a fundamentally social function. Processes of human interaction along with domain-general cognitive processes shape the structure and knowledge of language. Recent research across a variety of disciplines in the cognitive sciences has demonstrated that patterns of use strongly affect how language is acquired, is structured, is organized in cognition, and changes over time. However, there is mounting evidence that processes of language acquisition, use, and change are not independent of one another but are facets of the same system. We argue that this system is best construed as a *complex adaptive system* (CAS). This system is radically different from the static system of grammatical principles characteristic of the widely held generativist approach. Instead, language as a CAS of dynamic usage and its experience involves the following key features: (a) The system consists of multiple agents (the speakers in the speech community) interacting with one another. (b) The system is adaptive; that is, speakers' behavior is based on their past interactions, and current and past interactions together feed forward into future behavior. (c) A speaker's behavior is the consequence of competing factors ranging from perceptual mechanics to social motivations. (d) The structures of language emerge from interrelated patterns of experience, social interaction, and cognitive processes.

The advantage of viewing language as a CAS is that it allows us to provide a unified account of seemingly unrelated linguistic phenomena (Holland, 1995, 1998; Holland, Gong, Minett, Ke, & Wang, 2005). These phenomena include the following: variation at all levels of linguistic organization; the probabilistic nature of linguistic behavior; continuous change within agents and across speech communities; the emergence of grammatical regularities from the interaction of agents in language use; and stagelike transitions due to underlying nonlinear processes. We outline how the CAS approach reveals commonalities in many areas of language research, including cognitive linguistics, sociolinguistics, first and second language acquisition, psycholinguistics, historical linguistics, and language evolution. Finally, we indicate how the CAS approach provides new directions for future research involving converging evidence from multiple methods, including corpus analysis, crosslinguistic comparisons, anthropological and historical studies of grammaticalization, psychological and neuroscience experimentation, and computational modeling.

Language and Social Interaction

Language is shaped by human cognitive abilities such as categorization, sequential processing, and planning. However, it is more than their simple product. Such cognitive abilities do not require language; if we had only those abilities, we would not need to talk. Language is used for human social interaction, and so its origins and capacities are dependent on its role in our social life (Croft, 2009; Tomasello, 2008). To understand how language has evolved in the human lineage and why it has the properties we can observe today, we need to look at the combined effect of many interacting constraints, including the structure of thought processes, perceptual and motor biases, cognitive limitations, and socio-pragmatic factors (Christiansen & Chater, 2008; Clark, 1996).

Primate species are particularly socially interactive mammals, but humans appear to have emphasized this type of social interaction to an even greater extent. This means that language evolved in the context of an already highly interactive social existence. This intensive interaction suggests that the evolution of language cannot be understood outside of a social context. Language plays a fundamental role in human society and culture, providing the central means by which cultural knowledge is transmitted, elaborated, and reformed over time. Culture itself is at least partly to be understood as a reflection of what humans find interesting and important, which in turn reflects a complex interplay of both evolved biological biases (e.g., we find pleasure in satiating biological desires) as well as cultural biases (e.g., styles of clothing, etc.). Thus, both language and culture are emergent phenomena of an increasingly complex social existence.

The nature of language follows from its role in social interaction. Although social interactions can sometimes be uncooperative and characterized by conflict, they are often characterized by what philosophers of action call shared cooperative activity (Bratman, 1992, 1993, 1997) or joint actions (Clark, 1996). Joint actions are dependent on what might be broadly called *shared cognition*, a human being's recognition that she can share beliefs and intentions with other humans. Joint action involves (among other things) individuals performing individual actions that are intended to carry out a jointly intended shared action, such as moving a piano or performing in a string quartet. Bratman enumerated several mental attitudes for shared cooperative activity, including meshing of subplans to carry out the joint action, a commitment to help out the other, and shared belief of all of the above.

Finally, Bratman also pointed out that the individual actions that form the joint action must be coordinated for the joint action to be carried out successfully (imagine what would happen if the movers of the piano or the performers in the string quartet did not coordinate their actions). This is where language ultimately comes in. Joint actions pose coordination problems (Lewis, 1969) between the participants. There are various coordination devices that solve the coordination problems of joint actions, of which the simplest is joint attention to jointly salient properties of the environment (Lewis, 1969; Tomasello, 1999). However, by far the most effective coordination device is, of course, for the participants to communicate with each other. However, communication is a joint action: The speaker and hearer must converge on a recognition of the speaker's intention by the hearer (Grice, 1948/1989). Humans have developed a powerful coordination device for communication—that is, convention or, more precisely, a conventional signaling system (Clark, 1996, 1999; Lewis, 1969). Convention is a regularity of behavior (producing an utterance of a particular linguistic form) that is partly arbitrary and entrenched in the speech community. As a coordination device, it solves a recurring coordination problem, namely the joint action of communication. Additionally, communication is in turn a coordination device for any joint action (or other type of interaction) that human beings wish to perform or have happen. On this basis, human culture is built.

Language is a two-level system embedded in the two higher levels of communication (i.e., meaning in the Gricean sense) and joint action (which illocutionary acts are really a simplified example of; see Austin, 1962; Searle, 1969). Language involves the production of signals in a medium such as speech, sign, or writing. This is the regularity of behavior to which the interlocutors jointly attend, called an *utterance act* by Austin. However, these signals are formulated into what Searle called propositional acts and what linguists call words and grammatical constructions. Thus, there are finally four levels in which language operates: producing and attending to the utterance; formulating and identifying the proposition; signaling and recognizing the communicative intention; and proposing and taking up the joint action (Clark, 1992, 1996).

This complex model is in fact fragile, as everyone who has misunderstood someone or has been misunderstood knows. However, there are fundamental reasons why the communicative process is fragile and, therefore, introduces variation, the substrate for change in language. First, of course, is that we cannot read each other's minds. Equally important is that convention is not airtight as a coordination device (Croft, 2000, 2009). A speaker chooses the words and constructions—the linguistic conventions—to communicate a situation based on the prior use of these conventions in similar situations. The hearer does the same—but the hearer's knowledge of prior uses of the conventions is not the same as the speaker's. Finally, the new situation being communicated is unique and subject to different construals. Although we must not overstate the impossibility of communication—after all, vast civilizations have been constructed on its basis—we cannot deny the indeterminacy of communication, whose product is the ubiquity of language change.

Usage-Based Grammar

We adopt here a usage-based theory of grammar in which the cognitive organization of language is based directly on experience with language. Rather than being an abstract set of rules or structures that are only indirectly related to experience with language, we see grammar as a network built up from the categorized instances of language use (Bybee, 2006; Hopper, 1987). The basic units of grammar are constructions, which are direct form-meaning pairings that range from the very specific (words or idioms) to the more general (passive construction, ditransitive construction), and from very small units (words with affixes, *walked*) to clause-level or even discourse-level units (Croft, 2001; Goldberg, 2003, 2006).

Because grammar is based on usage, it contains many details of co-occurrence as well as a record of the probabilities of occurrence and co-occurrence. The evidence for the impact of usage on cognitive organization includes the fact that language users are aware of specific instances of constructions that are conventionalized and the multiple ways in which frequency of use has an impact on structure. The latter include speed of access related to token frequency and resistance to regularization of high-frequency forms (Bybee, 1995, 2001, 2007); it also includes the role of probability in syntactic and lexical processing (Ellis, 2002; Jurafsky, 2003; MacDonald & Christiansen, 2002) and the strong role played by frequency of use in grammaticalization (Bybee, 2003).

A number of recent experimental studies (Saffran, Aslin, & Newport, 1996; Saffran, Johnson, Aslin, & Newport, 1999; Saffran & Wilson, 2003) show that both infants and adults track co-occurrence patterns and statistical regularities in artificial grammars. Such studies indicate that subjects learn patterns even when the utterance corresponds to no meaning or communicative intentions. Thus, it is not surprising that in actual communicative settings, the co-occurrence of words has an impact on cognitive representation. Evidence from multiple sources demonstrates that cognitive changes occur in response to usage and contribute to the shape of grammar. Consider the following three phenomena:

1. Speakers do not choose randomly from among all conceivable combinatorial possibilities when producing utterances. Rather there are conventional ways of expressing certain ideas (Sinclair, 1991). Pawley and Syder (1983) observed that "nativelike selection" in a language requires knowledge of expected speech patterns, rather than mere generative rules. A native English speaker might say *I want to marry you*, but would not say *I want marriage with you* or *I desire you to become married to me*, although these latter utterances do get the point across. Corpus analyses in fact verify that communication largely consists of prefabricated sequences, rather than an "open choice" among all available words (Erman & Warren, 2000). Such patterns could only exist if speakers were registering instances of co-occurring words, and tracking the contexts in which certain patterns are used.

2. Articulatory patterns in speech indicate that as words co-occur in speech, they gradually come to be retrieved as chunks. As one example, Gregory, Raymond, Bell, Fossler-Lussier, & Jurafsky (1999) find that the degree of reduction in speech sounds, such as word-final "flapping" of English [t], correlates with the "mutual information" between successive words (i.e., the probability that two words will occur together in contrast with a chance distribution) (see also Bush, 2001; Jurafsky, Bell, Gregory, & Raymond, 2001). A similar phenomenon happens at the syntactic level, where frequent word combinations become encoded as chunks that influence how we process sentences on-line (Ellis, 2008b; Ellis, Simpson-Vlach, & Maynard, 2008; Kapatsinski & Radicke, 2009; Reali & Christiansen, 2007a, 2007b).

3. Historical changes in language point toward a model in which patterns of co-occurrence must be taken into account. In sum, "items that are used together fuse together" (Bybee, 2002). For example, the English contracted forms (*I'm, they'll*) originate from the fusion of co-occurring forms (Krug, 1998). Auxiliaries become bound to their more frequent collocate, namely the preceding pronoun, even though such developments run counter to a traditional, syntactic constituent analysis.

Such detailed knowledge of the interactions of grammar and lexicon in usage, which includes knowledge of which words commonly go into which constructions, leads to a conception of lexicon and grammar as highly intertwined rather than separate (Bybee, 1998a; Ellis, 2008b; Goldberg, 2006; Halliday, 1994; Langacker, 1987). The cognitive representations underlying language use are built up by the categorization of utterances into exemplars and exemplar clusters based on their linguistic form as well as their meaning and the context in which they have been experienced (Pierrehumbert, 2001). Because this categorization is ongoing during language use, even adult grammars are not fixed and static but have the potential to change as experience changes (e.g., MacDonald & Christiansen, 2002; Sankoff & Blondeau, 2007; Wells, Christiansen, Race, Acheson, & MacDonald, 2009).

Language change proceeds gradually via localized interactions, but this is not to say that there are no generalizations within or across languages. General properties of language that are both formal and substantive come about in language as in any CAS—through the repeated application of general processes of change. Because the same processes apply in all languages, general resemblances develop; however, the trajectories of change (such as paths of grammaticalization) are much more similar than the resulting states (Bybee, Perkins, & Pagliuca, 1994; Greenberg, 1978).

In the usage-based framework, we are interested in emergent generalizations across languages, specific patterns of use as contributors to change and as indicators of linguistic representations, and the cognitive underpinnings of language processing and change. Given these perspectives, the sources of data for usage-based grammar are greatly expanded over that of structuralist or generative grammar: Corpus-based studies of either synchrony or diachrony as well as experimental and modeling studies are considered to produce valid data for our understanding of the cognitive representation of language.

The Development of Grammar out of Language Use

The mechanisms that create grammar over time in languages have been identified as the result of intense study over the last 20 years (Bybee et al., 1994; Heine, Claudi, & Hünnemeyer, 1991; Hopper & Traugott, 2003). In the history of well-documented languages it can be seen that lexical items within constructions can become grammatical items and loosely organized elements within and across clauses come to be more tightly joined. Designated "grammaticalization," this process is the result of repetition across many speech events, during which sequences of elements come to be automatized as neuromotor routines, which leads to their phonetic reduction and certain changes in meaning (Bybee, 2003; Haiman, 1994). Meaning changes result from the habituation that follows from repetition, as well as from the effects of context. The major contextual effect comes from co-occurring elements and from frequently made inferences that become part of the meaning of the construction.

For example, the recently grammaticalized future expression in English *be going to* started out as an ordinary expression indicating that the subject is going somewhere to do something. In Shakespeare's English, the construction had no special properties and occurred in all of the plays of the Bard (850,000 words) only six times. In current English, it is quite frequent, occurring in one small corpus of British English (350,000 words) 744 times. The frequency increase is made possible by changes in function, but repetition is also a factor in the changes that occur. For instance, it loses its sense of movement in space and takes on the meaning of "intention to do something," which was earlier only inferred. With repetition also comes phonetic fusion and reduction, as the most usual present-day pronunciation of this phrase is *(be) gonna*. The component parts are no longer easily accessible.

The evidence that the process is essentially the same in all languages comes from a crosslinguistic survey of verbal markers and their diachronic sources in 76 unrelated languages (Bybee et al., 1994). This study demonstrated that markers of tense, aspect, and modality derive from very similar semantic sources crosslinguistically. For instance, of the 76 languages, 10 were found to have a future that developed from a verb meaning "go," 10 languages develop a similar meaning from a verb meaning "come," and some languages use a verb meaning "want" (an example is English *will*, which formerly meant "want").

Thus, grammatical categories develop in all languages in this way, but not all of the categories turn out the same. Categories from different lexical sources may have different nuances of meaning; categories that are more or less grammaticalized have different meanings and range of usage. Some rare lexical sources also exist. As odd as it may seem, using a temporal adverb such as "soon" or "by and by" to form a future is rare but does occur.

Given that grammaticalization can be detected as ongoing in all languages at all times, it is reasonable to assume that the original source of grammar in human language was precisely this process: As soon as humans were able to string two words together, the potential for the development of grammar exists, with no further mechanisms other than sequential processing, categorization, conventionalization, and inference-making (Bybee, 1998b; Heine & Kuteva, 2007).

Language change is a cultural evolutionary process (Christiansen & Chater, 2008; Croft, 2000). According to the General Analysis of Selection (Hull, 1988, 2001), evolutionary processes take place at two linked levels: replication and selection. Replicators are units such as a gene, a word, or the practice of marriage that are replicated with some chance for innovation and variation. Selection is a process by which individuals—organisms, or humans as speakers or cultural beings—interacting with their environment cause replication of the replicators to be differential; that is, some replicators are replicated more than others, which in the extreme case leads to fixation of the former and extinction of the latter. In language, linguistic structures—sounds, words, and constructions— are replicated in utterances every time we open our mouths; that is, replication, and variation, occurs when we use language in the service of joint actions between human beings in a community. Due in part to the indeterminacy of communication described earlier, this replication process produces variation. Speakers differentially replicate certain structures through interaction with their environment, namely the situations being communicated and their interlocutors. In the former case, changes in lifestyles lead to the rise and fall of words and constructions associated with those lifestyles (e.g., the rise of *cell* [*phone*] and the fall of *harquebus*). In the latter case, the social identity and the social contexts of interaction lead to the rise and fall of linguistic forms that are associated with various social values by speakers.

First and Second Language Acquisition

Usage-based theories of language acquisition (Barlow & Kemmer, 2000) hold that we learn constructions while engaging in communication, through the "interpersonal communicative and cognitive processes that everywhere and always shape language" (Slobin, 1997). They have become increasingly influential in the study of child language acquisition (Goldberg, 2006; Tomasello, 2003). They have turned upside down the traditional generative assumptions of innate language acquisition devices, the continuity hypothesis, and top-down, rule-governed processing, replacing these with data-driven, emergent accounts of linguistic systematicities. Constructionist analyses chart the ways in which children's creative linguistic ability—their language system—emerges from their analyses of the utterances in their usage history using general cognitive abilities and from their abstraction of regularities within them. In this view, language acquisition is a sampling problem, involving the estimation of the population norms from the learner's limited sample of experience as perceived through the constraints and affordances of their cognitive apparatus, their human embodiment, and the dynamics of social interaction. The complete body of psycholinguistic research, which demonstrates language users' exquisite sensitivity to the frequencies of occurrence of different constructions in the language input (Gernsbacher, 1994; Reali & Christiansen, 2007a, 2007b) and to the contingencies of their mappings of form and meaning (MacWhinney, 1987), is clear testament to the influence of each usage event, and the processing of its component constructions, on the learner's system (Bybee & Hopper, 2001; Ellis, 2002).

Input and interaction have long been at the center of accounts of second language (L2) learning (Gass, 1997; Larsen-Freeman & Long, 1991). Co-occurrence patterns and their probabilities shape L2 interlanguage (Selinker, 1972) as learners engage in online processing of linguistic stimuli. Initially, these constructions exhibit mutual exclusion (the one-to-one principle; Andersen, 1984). Later, they are categorized, generalized, and, ultimately, analyzed into constitutive forms, although, as in the first language (L1), constructions may simultaneously be represented and stored at various levels of abstraction. L2 developmental sequences are reflective of the linguistic input (Collins & Ellis, 2009; Ellis & Cadierno, 2009)—including Zipfian profiles of construction token and type frequencies (Ellis, 2002; Larsen-Freeman, 1976), cue reliabilities (MacWhinney, 1997), and the salience of the cue and the importance of its outcome in the interpretation of the utterance as a whole (Ellis, 2006; Goldschneider & DeKeyser, 2001). L2 constructions are sensitive to the usual trinity of determinants of associative learning: frequency, recency and context. As with the L1, learners do not merely conform to the L2; they go beyond it, constructing novel forms through analogizing and recombining the patterns (Larsen-Freeman, 1997). Their acquisition of schematic, productive constructions follows the general principles of category learning (Robinson & Ellis, 2007).

Yet despite these similarities, first and second language acquisition differ in significant ways. First, L2 learners come to L2 learning with firmly entrenched L1 patterns (MacWhinney, 1997). Neural commitment to these patterns results in crosslinguistic influence, which manifests itself in a number of ways: the pace at which developmental sequences are traversed, relexification, overgeneralization, avoidance, overproduction, and hypercorrection (Odlin, 1989). The L1 also tunes the learners' perceptual mechanisms so that their learned attention blocks them from perceiving differences in the L2. Second, constructions, as conventionalized linguistic means for presenting different construals of an event, structure concepts and window attention to aspects of experience through the options that specific languages make available to speakers

(Talmy, 2000). Crosslinguistic research shows how different languages lead speakers to prioritize different aspects of events in narrative discourse (Berman & Slobin, 1994). Thus, the conceptual patterns derived from the L1 shape the way that constructions are put together, leading to nonnative categorization and "thinking for speaking" (Slobin, 1996). Third, although both L1 and L2 acquisition are sociocognitive processes (Kramsch, 2002; Larsen-Freeman, 2002), because L2 learners are normally more cognitively mature, the social environment/conditions of learning are significantly different from those of a child acquiring an L1. Thus, understanding the cognitive linguistics of the L2 (Robinson & Ellis, 2007), the psycholinguistics of the L2 (Kroll & De Groot, 2005), and the sociolinguistics of the L2 (Lantolf, 2006) all involve extra layers of complexity beyond those of the L1.

These various factors interact dynamically (de Bot, Lowie, & Verspoor, 2007; Ellis & Larsen Freeman, 2006) to result in a level of ultimate attainment for even the most diligent L2 learner that is usually considerably below what a child L1 acquirer achieves, with some naturalistic L2 acquirers only acquiring a "Basic Variety" characterized by pragmatic word order and minimal morphology (Klein & Purdue, 1992). Usage patterns for grammatical functors in the L1 impede their L2 acquisition because of the shortening that takes place for frequently occurring forms, limiting their perceptual saliency (Ellis, 2006). This is especially true, for example, with bound morphemes. To assist learners in learning these forms, their consciousness must be recruited and their attention directed at these forms through explicit instruction (Ellis, 2005; Larsen-Freeman, 2003). Without such explicit instruction, language use by a high proportion of adult language learners typically means simplification, most obviously manifested in a loss of redundancy and irregularity, and an increase in transparency (McWhorter, 2003; Trudgill, 2001). The emergence of new languages in the form of pidgins and creoles is a more dramatic case of language change, and there are many parallels between the grammatical structures of creoles and the Basic Variety of interlanguage of L2 learners (Becker & Veenstra, 2003; Schumann, 1978). Yet rather than entertaining a deficit view of L2 learning, think instead of adult learners as being multicompetent (Cook, 1991), with different levels of mastery to satisfice (Simon, 1957) in accomplishing what they intend for a variety of languages.

Thus, a CAS perspective on the limited end state typical of adult L2 learners suggests that this results from dynamic cycles of language use, language change, language perception, and language learning in the interactions of members of language communities (Ellis, 2008a). In summary, we have the following: (a) *Usage leads to change*: High-frequency use of grammatical functors causes their phonological erosion and homonymy. (b) *Change affects perception:* Phonologically reduced cues are hard to perceive. (c) *Perception affects learning:* Low-salience cues are difficult to learn, as are homonymous/polysemous constructions because of the low contingency of their form-function association. (d) *Learning affects usage:* (i) Where language is predominantly learned naturalistically by adults without any form-focus, a typical result is a Basic Variety of interlanguage, low in grammatical complexity but communicatively effective. Because *usage leads to change,* in cases in which the target language is not available from the mouths of L1 speakers, maximum contact languages learned naturalistically can thus simplify and lose grammatical intricacies. Alternatively, (ii) where there are efforts promoting formal accuracy, the attractor state of the Basic Variety can be escaped by means of dialectic forces, socially recruited, involving the dynamics of learner consciousness, form-focused attention, and explicit learning. Such influences promote language maintenance.

Modeling Usage-Based Acquisition and Change

In the various aspects of language considered here, it is always the case that form, user, and use are inextricably linked. However, such complex interactions are difficult to investigate *in vivo.* Detailed, dense longitudinal studies of language use and acquisition are rare enough for single individuals over a time course of months. Extending the scope to cover the community of language users, and the timescale to that for language evolution and change, is clearly not feasible. Thus, our corpus studies and psycholinguistic investigations try to sample and focus on times of most change and interactions of most significance. However, there are other ways to investigate how language might emerge and evolve as a CAS. A valuable tool featuring strongly in our methodology is mathematical or computational modeling.

Given the paucity of relevant data, one might imagine this to be of only limited use. We contend that this is not the case. Because we believe that many properties of language are emergent, modeling allows one to prove, at least *in principle,* that specific fundamental mechanisms can combine to produce some observed effect (Holland, 1995, 1998, 2006a, 2006b; Holland et al., 2005). Although this may also be possible through an entirely verbal argument, modeling provides additional quantitative information that can be used to locate and revise shortcomings. For example, a mathematical model constructed by Baxter et al. (2009) within a usage-based theory for new-dialect formation (Trudgill, 2004) was taken in conjunction with empirical data (Gordon et al., 2004) to show that although the model predicted a realistic dialect, its formation time was much longer than that observed. Another example comes from the work of Reali and Christiansen (2009), who demonstrated how the impact of cognitive constraints on sequential learning across many generations of learners could give rise to consistent word order regularities.

Modeling can also be informative about which mechanisms most strongly affect the emergent behavior and which have little consequence. To illustrate, let us examine our view that prior experience is a crucial factor affecting an individual speaker's linguistic behavior. It is then natural to pursue this idea within an *agent-based* framework, in which different speakers may exhibit different linguistic behavior and may interact with different members of the community (as happens in reality). Even in simple models of imitation, the probability that a cultural innovation is adopted as a community norm, and the time taken to do so, is very strongly affected by the social network structure (Castellano, Fortunato, & Loreto, 2007, give a good overview of these models and their properties). This formal result thus provides impetus for the collection of high-quality social network data, as their empirical properties appear as yet poorly established. The few cases that have been discussed in the literature—for example, networks of movie co-stars (Watts & Strogatz, 1998), scientific collaborators (Newman, 2001), and sexually-active high school teens (Bearman, Moody, & Stovel, 2004)—do not have a clear relevance to language. We thus envisage a future in which formal modeling and empirical data collection mutually guide one another.

The fact that modeling is a quantitative enterprise obscures the fact that it is as much an art as a science. This is partly because social force laws are not mathematically well established and experimentally confirmed in the way their physical counterparts are. However, the view that language is a CAS, and, in particular, the usage-based framework, does place some constraints on the way that a mathematical or computational model of language use, variation, and change should be constructed.

Clearly, speakers need to be equipped with a prescription for producing utterances that may vary between speakers (a grammar). The unit of variation depends on what is being modeled; for example, in models of language competition (see, e.g., Abrams & Strogatz, 2003; Minnet & Wang, 2008; Reali & Christiansen, 2009; Schulze, Stauffer, & Wichmann, 2008), it is natural to define speakers by the languages they speak. In other cases, a concrete mapping between objects (or concepts) and sounds is appropriate (Hurford, 1989; Nowak, Komaraova, & Niyogi, 2002; Steels, 2000). A more flexible approach adopts abstract units of variation—termed *linguemes* by Croft (2000)—that encapsulate all types of linguistic variations, from single vowel sounds up to sentence structure (e.g., Baxter, Blythe, Croft, & McKane, 2006; Oudeyer & Kaplan, 2007).

Above all, a usage-based model should provide insight into the frequencies of variants within the speech community. The rules for producing utterances should then be inducted from this information by general mechanisms. This approach contrasts with an approach that has speakers equipped with fixed, preexisting grammars.

We have already argued for the need for an agent-based model that allows for variation in exposure history (perhaps by occupying different positions in a social network structure) and the behavior that results from it. An important point here is that the interactions that mold a speaker's grammar continue throughout her lifetime (for examples of this approach in modeling research, see Baxter et al., 2009; Wedel, 2006). This idea contrasts with approaches in which vertical transmission from fixed speakers in one generation to fluid learners in the next is the dominant mechanism for change (Nowak et al., 2002; Smith, Kirby, & Brighton, 2003). The dynamics in the population of linguistic utterances is therefore not connected in a simple way to that of the underlying human population; hence, the role of natural selection in shaping languages is likely to be diminished compared to what has sometimes been assumed elsewhere (Croft, 2002; Nowak et al., 2002).

Despite these observations, many details of the linguistic interactions remain unconstrained and one can ask whether having a model reproduce observed phenomena proves the specific set of assumptions that went into it. The answer is, of course, negative. However, greater confidence in the assumptions can be gained if a model based on existing data and theories makes new, testable predictions. In the event that a model contains ad hoc rules, one must, to be consistent with the view of language as a CAS, be able to show that these are emergent properties of more fundamental, general processes for which there is independent support.

Characteristics of Language as a Complex Adaptive System

We now highlight seven major characteristics of language as a CAS, which are consistent with studies in language change, language use, language acquisition, and computer modeling of these aspects.

Distributed Control and Collective Emergence
Language exists both in individuals (as idiolect) and in the community of users (as communal language). Language is emergent at these two distinctive but

interdependent levels: An idiolect is emergent from an individual's language use through social interactions with other individuals in the communal language, whereas a communal language is emergent as the result of the interaction of the idiolects. Distinction and connection between these two levels is a common feature in a CAS. Patterns at the collective level (such as bird flocks, fish schools, or economies) cannot be attributed to global coordination among individuals; the global pattern is emergent, resulting from long-term local interactions between individuals. Therefore, we need to identify the level of existence of a particular language phenomenon of interest. For example, language change is a phenomenon observable at the communal level; the mechanisms driving language change, such as production economy and frequency effects that result in phonetic reduction, may not be at work in every individual in the same way or at the same time. Moreover, functional or social mechanisms that lead to innovation in the early stages of language change need not be at work in later stages, as individuals later may acquire the innovation purely due to frequency when the innovation is established as the majority in the communal language. The actual process of language change is complicated and interwoven with a myriad of factors, and computer modeling provides a possible venue to look into the emergent dynamics (see, e.g., Christiansen & Chater, 2008, for further discussion).

Intrinsic Diversity

In a CAS, there is no ideal representing agent for the system. Just as in an economy, there is no ideal representative consumer; similarly, there is no ideal speaker-hearer for language use, language representation, or language development. Each idiolect is the product of the individual's unique exposure and experiences of language use (Bybee, 2006). Sociolinguistics studies have revealed the large degree of orderly heterogeneity among idiolects (Weinreich, Labov, & Herzog, 1968), not only in their language use but also in their internal organization and representation (Dąbrowska, 1997). Mindfulness of intrinsic diversity is helpful for theory construction. As the quest for top-down principles and parametric constraints on linguistic universals stagnates, cognitive linguistics instead turns to the investigation of universals that emerge from the interactions of lower level representations, such as those described in construction-based grammars, and the general cognitive abilities, such as sociability, joint attention, pattern extraction, imitation, and so on, which underlie their acquisition.

Perpetual Dynamics

Both communal language and idiolects are in constant change and reorganization. Languages are in constant flux, and language change is ubiquitous

(Hopper, 1987). At the individual level, every instance of language use changes an idiolect's internal organization (Bybee, 2006). As we define language primarily through dynamism, rather than by forces designed to pull it to a static equilibrium, it shares, along with almost all complex systems, a fundamentally far-from-equilibrium nature (Holland, 1995). An open system continues to change and adapt as its dynamics are "fed" by energy coming into the system, whereas a closed system will reduce to a stable state or equilibrium (Larsen-Freeman & Cameron, 2008).

Adaptation Through Amplification and Competition of Factors

Complex adaptive systems generally consist of multiple interacting elements, which may amplify and/or compete with one another's effects. Structure in complex systems tends to arise via positive feedback, in which certain factors perpetuate themselves, in conjunction with negative feedback, in which some constraint is imposed—for instance, due to limited space or resources (Camazine et al., 2001; Steels, 2006). Likewise in language, all factors interact and feed into one another. For instance, language may change in the tug-of-war of conflicting interests between speakers and listeners: Speakers prefer production economy, which encourages brevity and phonological reduction, whereas listeners want perceptual salience, explicitness, and clarity, which require elaboration (Christiansen & Chater, 2008; Cooper, 1999; DuBois, 1985; Lindblom, 1990; Zipf, 1949). Language may evolve for altruistic information sharing and social coordination, or for competition for relevance and for status between coalitions (Dessalles, 2000).

Nonlinearity and Phase Transitions

In complex systems, small quantitative differences in certain parameters often lead to phase transitions (i.e., qualitative differences). Elman (2005) pointed out that multiple small phenotypic differences between humans and other primates (such as in degree of sociability, shared attention, memory capacity, rapid sequencing ability, vocal tract control, etc.) may in combination result in profound consequences, allowing means of communication of a totally different nature. Additionally, in a dynamic system, even when there is no parametric change, at a certain point in a continuous dynamic system, behavior can change dramatically, going through a phase transition. For example, constant heating of water leads to a transition from liquid to gas, without having any parametric change. In language development, such phase transitions are often observed. Developmental "lexical spurts" often lead to rapid grammatical development (Bates & Goodman, 1997). The S-curve shape of dynamics in language change is also a kind of phase transition. Several computer models of language origin have demonstrated this feature (Ke, Minett, Au, & Wang, 2002; Kirby, 2000). Grammaticalization as a result of language use may be another example of such phase transitions, in which lexical items become grammatical items. For instance, in the history of English we may observe that the main verb *cunnan* "to know" underwent incremental changes that resulted in a qualitative difference, so that *can* now functions as an auxiliary expressing root possibility (Bybee, 2003). Such changes accumulate gradually as the result of individual speaker utterances and inferences. Yet at a certain point in the shift, processes of change may seem to escalate one another: As the meaning of *can* becomes more abstract and general, the item increases further in frequency, which further drives forward the development of grammatical status.

Sensitivity to and Dependence on Network Structure

Network studies of complex systems have shown that real-world networks are not random, as was initially assumed (Barabási, 2002; Barbarási & Albert, 1999; Watts & Strogatz, 1998), and that the internal structure and connectivity of the system can have a profound impact on system dynamics (Newman, 2001; Newman, Barabási, & Watts, 2006). Similarly, linguistic interactions are not via random contacts; they are constrained by social networks. The social structure of language use and interaction has a crucial effect in the process of language change (Milroy, 1980) and language variation (Eckert, 2000), and the social structure of early humans must also have played important roles in language origin and evolution. An understanding of the social network structures that underlie linguistic interaction remains an important goal for the study of language acquisition and change. The investigation of their effects through computer and mathematical modeling is equally important (Baxter et al., 2009).

Change Is Local

Complexity arises in systems via incremental changes, based on locally available resources, rather than via top-down direction or deliberate movement toward some goal (see, e.g., Dawkins, 1985). Similarly, in a complex systems framework, language is viewed as an extension of numerous domain-general cognitive capacities such as shared attention, imitation, sequential learning, chunking, and categorization (Bybee, 1998b; Ellis, 1996). Language is emergent from ongoing human social interactions, and its structure is fundamentally molded by the preexisting cognitive abilities, processing idiosyncrasies and limitations, and general and specific conceptual circuitry of the human brain.

Because this has been true in every generation of language users from its very origin, in some formulations, language is said to be a form of cultural adaptation to the human mind, rather than the result of the brain adapting to process natural language grammar (Christiansen, 1994; Christiansen & Chater, 2008; Deacon, 1997; Schoenemann, 2005). These perspectives have consequences for how language is processed in the brain. Specifically, language will depend heavily on brain areas fundamentally linked to various types of conceptual understanding, the processing of social interactions, and pattern recognition and memory. It also predicts that so-called "language areas" should have more general, prelinguistic processing functions even in modern humans and, further, that the homologous areas of our closest primate relatives should also process information in ways that makes them predictable substrates for incipient language. Further, it predicts that the complexity of communication is to some important extent a function of social complexity. Given that social complexity is, in turn, correlated with brain size across primates, brain size evolution in early humans should give us some general clues about the evolution of language (Schoenemann, 2006). Recognizing language as a CAS allows us to understand change at all levels.

Conclusions

Cognition, consciousness, experience, embodiment, brain, self, human interaction, society, culture, and history are all inextricably intertwined in rich, complex, and dynamic ways in language. Everything is connected. Yet despite this complexity, despite its lack of overt government, instead of anarchy and chaos, there are patterns everywhere. Linguistic patterns are not preordained by God, genes, school curriculum, or other human policy. Instead, they are emergent—synchronic patterns of linguistic organization at numerous levels (phonology, lexis, syntax, semantics, pragmatics, discourse, genre, etc.), dynamic patterns of usage, diachronic patterns of language change (linguistic cycles of grammaticalization, pidginization, creolization, etc.), ontogenetic developmental patterns in child language acquisition, global geopolitical patterns of language growth and decline, dominance and loss, and so forth. We cannot understand these phenomena unless we understand their interplay. The individual focus articles that follow in this special issue illustrate such interactions across a broad range of language phenomena, and they show how a CAS framework can guide future research and theory.

Revised version accepted 14 May 2009

References

Abrams, D. M., & Strogatz, S. H. (2003). Modelling the dynamics of language death. *Nature, 424*, 900.

Andersen, R. W. (1984). The one to one principle of interlanguage construction. *Language Learning, 34*, 77–95.

Austin, J. L. (1962). *How to do things with words.* Cambridge, MA: Harvard University Press.

Barabási, A.-L. (2002). *Linked: The new science of networks.* Cambridge, MA: Perseus Books.

Barbarási, A.-L., & Albert, R. (1999). Emergence of scaling in random networks. *Science, 286*, 509–511.

Barlow, M., & Kemmer, S. (Eds.). (2000). *Usage based models of language.* Stanford, CA: CSLI Publications.

Bates, E., & Goodman, J. C. (1997). On the inseparability of grammar and the lexicon: Evidence from acquisition, aphasia and real-time processing. *Language and Cognitive Processes, 12*, 507–586.

Baxter, G. J., Blythe, R. A., Croft, W., & McKane, A. J. (2006). Utterance selection model of language change. *Physical Review E, 73*, 046118.

Baxter, G. J., Blythe, R. A., Croft, W., & McKane, A. J. (2009). Modeling language change: An evaluation of Trudgill's theory of the emergence of New Zealand English. *Language Variation and Change, 21*(2), 257–296.

Bearman, P. S., Moody, J., & Stovel, K. (2004). Chains of affection: The structure of adolescent romantic and sexual networks. *American Journal of Sociology, 110*, 44–92.

Becker, A., & Veenstra, T. (2003). Creole prototypes as basic varieties and inflectional morphology. In C. Dimroth & M. Starren (Eds.), *Information structure and the dynamics of language acquisition* (pp. 235–264). Amsterdam: Benjamins.

Berman, R. A., & Slobin, D. I. (Eds.). (1994). *Relating events in narrative: A crosslinguistic developmental study.* Hillsdale, NJ: Lawrence Erlbaum.

Bratman, M. (1992). Shared cooperative activity. *The Philosophical Review, 101*, 327–341.

Bratman, M. (1993). Shared intention. *Ethics, 104*, 97–113.

Bratman, M. (1997). I intend that we. In G. Holmström-Hintikka & R. Tuomela (Eds.), *Contemporary action theory* (Vol. 2, pp. 49–63). Dordrecht: Kluwer.

Bush, N. (2001). Frequency effects and word-boundary palatalization in English. In J. Bybee & P. Hopper (Eds.), *Frequency and the emergence of linguistic structure* (pp. 255–280). Amsterdam: Benjamins.

Bybee, J. (1995). Regular morphology and the lexicon. *Language and Cognitive Processes, 10*, 425–455.

Bybee, J. (1998a). The emergent lexicon. In M. C. Gruber, D. Higgins, K. S. Olson, and T. Wysocki (Eds.), *CLS 34: The panels* (pp. 421–435). University of Chicago: Chicago Linguistic Society.

Bybee, J. (1998b). A functionalist approach to grammar and its evolution. *Evolution of Communication, 2*, 249–278.

Bybee, J. (2001). *Phonology and language use.* Cambridge: Cambridge University Press.

Bybee, J. (2002). Sequentiality as the basis of constituent structure. In T. Givón & B. F. Malle (Eds.), *The evolution of language out of pre-language* (pp. 109–132). Amsterdam: Benjamins.

Bybee, J. (2003). Mechanisms of change in grammaticalization: The role of frequency. In R. D. Janda & B. D. Joseph (Eds.), *Handbook of historical linguistics* (pp. 602–623). Oxford: Blackwell.

Bybee, J. (2006). From usage to grammar: The mind's response to repetition. *Language, 82*, 711–733.

Bybee, J. (2007). *Frequency of use and the organization of language.* Oxford: Oxford University Press.

Bybee, J., & Hopper, P. (Eds.). (2001). *Frequency and the emergence of linguistic structure.* Amsterdam: Benjamins.

Bybee, J., Perkins, R., & Pagliuca, W. (1994). *The evolution of grammar: Tense, aspect, and modality in the languages of the world.* Chicago: University of Chicago Press.

Camazine, S., Deneubourg, J.-L., Franks, N. R., Sneyd, J., Theraulaz, G., & Bonabeau, E. (2001). *Self-organization in biological systems.* Princeton, NJ: Princeton University Press.

Castellano, C., Fortunato, S., & Loreto, V. (2007, June 7). Statistical physics of social dynamics. Online preprint. Retrieved from http://arxiv.org/abs/0710.3256.

Christiansen, M. H. (1994). *Infinite languages, finite minds: Connectionism, learning and linguistic structure.* Unpublished doctoral dissertation, University of Edinburgh, Edinburgh.

Christiansen, M. H., & Chater, N. (2008). Language as shaped by the brain. *Behavioral & Brain Sciences, 31*, 489–509.

Clark, H. H. (1992). *Arenas of language use.* Chicago: University of Chicago Press/Stanford, CA: Center for the Study of Language and Information.

Clark, H. H. (1996). *Using language.* Cambridge: Cambridge University Press.

Clark, H. H. (1999). On the origins of conversation. *Verbum, 21*, 147–161.

Collins, L., & Ellis, N. C. (Eds.). (2009). Input and second language construction learning: frequency, form, and function [Special issue]. *Modern Language Journal, 93*(2).

Cook, V. (1991). The poverty-of-the-stimulus argument and multi-competence. *Second Language Research, 7*, 103–117.

Cooper, D. (1999). *Linguistic attractors: The cognitive dynamics of language acquisition and change.* Amsterdam: Benjamins.

Croft, W. (2000). *Explaining language change: An evolutionary approach.* London: Longman.

Croft, W. (2001). *Radical construction grammar: Syntactic theory in typological perspective.* Oxford: Oxford University Press.

Croft, W. (2002). The Darwinization of linguistics. *Selection, 3,* 75–91.

Croft, W. (2009). Towards a social cognitive linguistics. In V. Evans & S. Pourcel (Eds.), *New directions in cognitive linguistics* (pp. 395–420). Amsterdam: Benjamins.

Dąbrowska, E. (1997). The LAD goes to school: A cautionary tale for nativists. *Linguistics, 35,* 735–766.

Dawkins, R. (1985). *The blind watchmaker.* New York: Norton.

de Bot, K., Lowie, W., & Verspoor, M. (2007). A dynamic systems theory to second language acquisition. *Bilingualism: Language and Cognition, 10,* 7–21.

Deacon, T. W. (1997). *The symbolic species: The co-evolution of language and the brain.* New York: W.W. Norton.

Dessalles, J.-L. (2000). *Aux origines du langage: Une histoire naturelle de la parole.* Paris: Hermès.

DuBois, J. A. (1985). Competing motivations. In J. Haiman (Ed.), *Iconicity in syntax* (pp. 343–366). Amsterdam: Benjamins.

Eckert, P. (2000). *Linguistic variation as social practice: The linguistic construction of identity in Belten High.* Oxford: Blackwell.

Ellis, N. C. (1996). Sequencing in SLA: Phonological memory, chunking, and points of order. *Studies in Second Language Acquisition, 18*(1), 91–126.

Ellis, N. C. (2002). Frequency effects in language processing: A review with implications for theories of implicit and explicit language acquisition. *Studies in Second Language Acquisition, 24*(2), 143–188.

Ellis, N. C. (2005). At the interface: Dynamic interactions of explicit and implicit language knowledge. *Studies in Second Language Acquisition, 27,* 305–352.

Ellis, N. C. (2006). Selective attention and transfer phenomena in SLA: Contingency, cue competition, salience, interference, overshadowing, blocking, and perceptual learning. *Applied Linguistics, 27*(2), 1–31.

Ellis, N. C. (2008a). The dynamics of language use, language change, and first and second language acquisition. *Modern Language Journal, 41*(3), 232–249.

Ellis, N. C. (2008b). Phraseology: The periphery and the heart of language. In F. Meunier & S. Grainger (Eds.), *Phraseology in language learning and teaching* (pp. 1–13). Amsterdam: Benjamins.

Ellis, N. C., & Cadierno, T. (Eds.). (2009). Constructing a second language. [Special Section]. *Annual Review of Cognitive Linguistics, 7,* 113–292.

Ellis, N. C., & Larsen-Freeman, D. (Eds.). (2006). Language emergence: Implications for Applied Linguistics [Special issue]. *Applied Linguistics, 27*(4).

Ellis, N. C., Simpson-Vlach, R., & Maynard, C. (2008). Formulaic language in native and second-language speakers: Psycholinguistics, corpus linguistics, and TESOL. *TESOL Quarterly, 42*(3), 375–396.

Elman, J. L. (2005). Connectionist views of cognitive development: Where next? *Trends in Cognitive Science, 9*, 111–117.

Erman, B., & Warren, B. (2000). The idiom principle and the open choice principle. *Text, 20*, 29–62.

Gass, S. (1997). *Input, interaction, and the development of second languages.* Mahwah, NJ: Lawrence Erlbaum.

Gernsbacher, M. A. (1994). *A handbook of psycholinguistics.* San Diego, CA: Academic Press.

Goldberg, A. E. (2003). Constructions: A new theoretical approach to language. *Trends in Cognitive Science, 7*, 219–224.

Goldberg, A. E. (2006). *Constructions at work: The nature of generalization in language.* Oxford: Oxford University Press.

Goldschneider, J. M., & DeKeyser, R. (2001). Explaining the "natural order of L2 morpheme acquisition" in English: A meta-analysis of multiple determinants. *Language Learning, 51*, 1–50.

Gordon, E., Campbell, L., Hay, J., Maclagen, M., Sudbury, A., & Trudgill, P. (2004). *New Zealand English: Its origins and evolution.* Cambridge: Cambridge University Press.

Greenberg, J. (1978). Diachrony, synchrony and language universals. In J. H. Greenberg, C. A. Ferguson, & E. A. Moravcsik (Eds.), *Universals of human language: Vol. 1. Method and theory* (pp. 61–92). Stanford, CA: Stanford University Press.

Gregory, M., Raymond, W. D., Bell, A., Fossler-Lussier, E., & Jurafsky, D. (1999). The effects of collocational strength and contextual predictability in lexical production. *Chicago Linguistic Society, 35*, 151–166.

Grice, H. P. (1948/1989). *Meaning: Studies in the way of words.* Cambridge, MA: Harvard University Press.

Haiman, J. (1994). Ritualization and the development of language. In W. Pagliuca (Ed.), *Perspectives on grammaticalization* (pp. 3–28). Amsterdam: Benjamins.

Halliday, M. A. K. (1994). *An introduction to functional grammar* (2nd ed.). London: Edward Arnold.

Heine, B., Claudi, U., & Hünnemeyer, F. (1991). *Grammaticalization: A conceptual framework.* Chicago: University of Chicago Press.

Heine, B., & Kuteva, T. (2007). *The genesis of grammar.* Oxford: Oxford University Press.

Holland, J. H. (1995). *Hidden order: How adaption builds complexity.* Reading, MA: Addison-Wesley.

Holland, J. H. (1998). *Emergence: From chaos to order.* Oxford: Oxford University Press.

Holland, J. H. (2006a). A cognitive model of language acquisition. *Journal of Bio-Education, 1*, 79–83.

Holland, J. H. (2006b). Studying complex adaptive systems. *Journal of Systems Science and Complexity, 19*, 1–8.

Holland, J. H., Gong, T., Minett, J. W., Ke, J., & Wang, W. S.-Y. (2005). Language acquisition as a complex adaptive system. In J. W. Minett & W. S.-Y. Wang (Eds.), *Language acquisition, change and emergence* (pp. 411–435). Hong Kong: City University of Hong Kong Press.

Hopper, P. J. (1987). Emergent grammar. *Berkeley Linguistics Society, 13*, 139–157.

Hopper, P. J., & Traugott, E. C. (2003). *Grammaticalization* (2nd ed.). Cambridge: Cambridge University Press.

Hull, D. L. (1988). *Science as a process: An evolutionary account of the social and conceptual development of science.* Chicago: University of Chicago Press.

Hull, D. L. (2001). *Science and selection: Essays on biological evolution and the philosophy of science.* Cambridge: Cambridge University Press.

Hurford, J. (1989). Biological evolution of the Saussurean sign as a component of the language acquisition device. *Lingua, 77*, 187–222.

Jurafsky, D. (2003). Probabilistic modeling in psycholinguistics: Linguistic comprehension and production. In R. Bod, J. Hay, & S. Jannedy (Eds.), *Probabilistic linguistics* (pp. 39–95). Cambridge, MA: MIT Press.

Jurafsky, D., Bell, A., Gregory, M., & Raymond, W. D. (2001). Probabilistic relations between words: Evidence from reduction in lexical production. In J. Bybee & P. Hopper (Eds.), *Frequency and the emergence of linguistic structure* (pp. 229–254). Amsterdam: Benjamins.

Kapatsinski, V., & Radicke, J. (2009). Frequency and the emergence of prefabs: Evidence from monitoring. In R. Corrigan, E. A. Moravcsik, H. Ouali, & K. M. Wheatley (Eds.), *Formulaic language: Volume 2. Acquisition, loss, psychological reality, functional explanation* (pp. 499–520). Amsterdam: Benjamins.

Ke, J.-Y., Minett, J., Au, C.-P., & Wang, W. S.-Y. (2002). Self-organization and natural selection in the emergence of vocabulary. *Complexity, 7*, 41–54.

Kirby, S. (2000). Syntax without Natural Selection: How compositionality emerges from vocabulary in a population of learners. In C. Knight (Ed.), *The evolutionary emergence of language: Social function and the origins of linguistic form* (pp. 303–323). Cambridge: Cambridge University Press.

Klein, W., & Purdue, C. (1992). *Utterance structure: Developing grammars again.* Amsterdam: Benjamins.

Kramsch, C. (Ed.). (2002). *Language acquisition and language socialization: Ecological perspectives.* London: Continuum.

Kroll, J. F., & De Groot, A. M. B. (Eds.). (2005). *Handbook of bilingualism: Psycholinguistic approaches.* Oxford: Oxford University Press.

Krug, M. (1998). String frequency: A cognitive motivating factor in coalescence, language processing and linguistic change. *Journal of English Linguistics, 26*, 286–320.

Langacker, R. W. (1987). *Foundations of cognitive grammar: Vol. 1. Theoretical prerequisites*. Stanford, CA: Stanford University Press.

Lantolf, J. (2006). Sociocultural theory and L2: State of the art. *Studies in Second Language Acquisition, 28*, 67–109.

Larsen-Freeman, D. (1976). An explanation for the morpheme acquisition order of second language learners. *Language Learning, 26*, 125–134.

Larsen-Freeman, D. (1997). Chaos/complexity science and second language acquisition. *Applied Linguistics, 18*, 141–165.

Larsen-Freeman, D. (2002). Language acquisition and language use from a chaos/complexity theory perspective. In C. Kramsch (Ed.), *Language acquisition and language socialization*. London: Continuum.

Larsen-Freeman, D. (2003). *Teaching language: From grammar to grammaring*. Boston: Heinle & Heinle.

Larsen-Freeman, D., & Cameron, L. (2008). *Complex systems and applied linguistics*. Oxford: Oxford University Press.

Larsen-Freeman, D., & Long, M. (1991). *An introduction to second language acquisition research*. New York: Longman.

Lewis, D. (1969). *Convention*. Cambridge, MA: MIT Press.

Lindblom, B. (1990). Explaining phonetic variation: A sketch of the H & H theory. In W. Hardcastle & A. Marchal (Eds.), *Speech production and speech modeling* (pp. 403–439). Dordrecht: Kluwer Academic.

MacDonald, M. C., & Christiansen, M. H. (2002). Reassessing working memory: Comment on Just and Carpenter (1992) and Waters and Caplan (1996). *Psychological Review, 109*, 35–54.

MacWhinney, B. (1997). Second language acquisition and the Competition Model. In A. M. B. De Groot & J. F. Kroll (Eds.), *Tutorials in bilingualism: Psycholinguistic perspectives* (pp. 113–142). Mahwah, NJ: Lawrence Erlbaum.

MacWhinney, B. (Ed.). (1987). *Mechanisms of language acquisition*. Hillsdale, NJ: Lawrence Erlbaum.

McWhorter, J. (2003). Pidgins and creoles as models of language change: The state of the art. *Annual Review of Applied Linguistics, 23*, 202–212.

Milroy, J. (1980). *Language and social networks*. Oxford: Blackwell.

Minnet, J. W., & Wang, W. S.-Y. (2008). Modelling endangered languages: The effects of bilingualism and social structure. *Lingua, 118*(1), 19–45.

Newman, M. E. J. (2001). Scientific collaboration networks. I. Network construction and fundamental results. *Physics Review, E 64*, 016131.

Newman, M. E. J., Barabási, A.-L., & Watts, D. J. (Eds.). (2006). *The structure and dynamics of networks*. Princeton, NJ: Princeton University Press.

Nowak, M. A., Komaraova, N. L., & Niyogi, P. (2002). Computational and evolutionary aspects of language. *Nature, 417*, 611–617.

Odlin, T. (1989). *Language transfer*. New York: Cambridge University Press.

Oudeyer, P.-Y., & Kaplan, F. (2007). Language evolution as a Darwinian process: Computational studies. *Cognitive Processing, 8*, 21–35.

Pawley, A., & Syder, F. H. (1983). Two puzzles for linguistic theory: Nativelike selection and nativelike fluency. In J. C. Richards & R. W. Schmidt (Eds.), *Language and communication* (pp. 191–225). London: Longman.

Pierrehumbert, J. (2001). Exemplar dynamics: Word frequency, lenition, and contrast. In J. Bybee & P. Hopper (Eds.), *Frequency and the emergence of linguistic structure* (pp. 137–157). Amsterdam: Benjamins.

Reali, F., & Christiansen, M. H. (2007a). Processing of relative clauses is made easier by frequency of occurrence. *Journal of Memory and Language, 57*, 1–23.

Reali, F., & Christiansen, M. H. (2007b). Word chunk frequencies affect the processing of pronomial object-relative clauses. *Quarterly Journal of Experimental Psychology, 60*, 161–170.

Reali, F., & Christiansen, M. H. (2009). Sequential learning and the interaction between biological and linguistic adaptation in language evolution. *Interaction Studies, 10*, 5–30.

Robinson, P., & Ellis, N. C. (Eds.). (2007). *A handbook of cognitive linguistics and SLA.* Mahwah, NJ: Lawrence Erlbaum.

Saffran, J. R., Aslin, R. N., & Newport, E. L. (1996). Statistical learning by 8-month-old infants. *Science, 274*, 1926–1928.

Saffran, J. R., Johnson, E. K., Aslin, R. N., & Newport, E. L. (1999). Statistical learning of tone sequences by human infants and adults. *Cognition, 70*, 27–52.

Saffran, J. R., & Wilson, D. P. (2003). From syllables to syntax: Multilevel statistical learning by 12-month-old infants. *Infancy, 4*, 273–284.

Sankoff, G., & Blondeau, H. (2007). Language change across the lifespan: /r/ in Montreal French. *Language, 83*, 560–614.

Schoenemann, P. T. (2005). Conceptual complexity and the brain: Understanding language origins. In W. S.-Y. Wang & J. W. Minett (Eds.), *Language acquisition, change and emergence: Essays in evolutionary linguistics* (pp. 47–94). Hong Kong: City University of Hong Kong Press.

Schoenemann, P. T. (2006). Evolution of the size and functional areas of the human brain. *Annual Review of Anthropology, 35*, 379–406.

Schulze, C., Stauffer, D., & Wichmann, S. (2008). Birth, survival and death of languages by Monte Carlo simulation. *Communications in Computational Physics, 3*, 271–294.

Schumann, J. H. (1978). *The pidginisation process: A model for second language acquisition.* Rowley, MA: Newbury House.

Searle, J. R. (1969). *Speech acts: An essay in the philosophy of language.* Cambridge: Cambridge University Press.

Selinker, L. (1972). Interlanguage. *IRAL, 10*, 209–231.

Simon, H. A. (1957). *Models of man: Social and rational*. New York: Wiley and Sons.

Sinclair, J. (1991). *Corpus, concordance, collocation*. Oxford: Oxford University Press.

Slobin, D. I. (1996). From "thought and language" to "thinking for speaking." In J. J. Gumperz & S. C. Levinson (Eds.), *Rethinking linguistic relativity* (pp. 70–96). Cambridge: Cambridge University Press.

Slobin, D. I. (1997). The origins of grammaticizable notions: Beyond the individual mind. In D. I. Slobin (Ed.), *The crosslinguistic study of language acquisition* (Vol. 5, pp. 265–323). Mahwah, NJ: Lawrence Erlbaum.

Smith, K., Kirby, S., & Brighton, H. (2003). Iterated learning: A framework for the evolution of language. *Artificial Life, 9*, 371–386.

Steels, L. (2000). Language as a complex adaptive system. In M. Schoenauer, K. Deb, G. Rudolph, X. Yao, E. Lutton, J. J. Merelo, & H.-P. Schwefel (Eds.), *Parallel problem solving from nature—PPSN VI*, Lecture Notes in Computer Science Vol. 1917 (pp. 17–26). Berlin: Springer.

Steels, L. (2006). How to do experiments in artificial language evolution and why. In *Proceedings of the 6th International Conference on the Evolution of Language*, pp. 323–332.

Talmy, L. (2000). *Toward a cognitive semantics: Concept structuring systems*. Cambridge MA: MIT Press.

Tomasello, M. (1999). *The cultural origins of human cognition*. Boston: Harvard University Press.

Tomasello, M. (2003). *Constructing a language*. Boston: Harvard University Press.

Tomasello, M. (2008). *The origins of human communication*. Cambridge, MA: MIT Press.

Trudgill, P. (2001). Contact and simplification: Historical baggage and directionality in linguistic change. *Language Typology, 5*, 371–374.

Trudgill, P. (2004). *New-dialect formation: The inevitability of colonial Englishes*. Edinburgh: Edinburgh University Press.

Watts, D. J., & Strogatz, S. H. (1998). Collective dynamics of "small-world" networks. *Nature, 393*, 440–442.

Wedel, A. B. (2006). Exemplar models, evolution and language change. *The Linguistic Review, 23*, 247–274.

Weinreich, U., Labov, W., & Herzog, M. I. (1968). Empirical foundations for a theory of language change. In W. P. Lehmann & Y. Malkiel (Eds.), *Directions for historical linguistics* (pp. 95–195). Austin: University of Texas Press.

Wells, J., Christiansen, M. H., Race, D. S., Acheson, D., & MacDonald, M. C. (2009). Experience and sentence processing: Statistical learning and relative clause comprehension. *Cognitive Psychology, 58*, 250–271.

Zipf, G. K. (1949). *Human behaviour and the principle of least effort: An introduction to human ecology*. Cambridge, MA: Addison-Wesley.

Language Learning ISSN 0023-8333

A Usage-Based Account of Constituency and Reanalysis

Clay Beckner

University of New Mexico

Joan Bybee

University of New Mexico

Constituent structure is considered to be the very foundation of linguistic competence and often considered to be innate, yet we show here that it is derivable from the domain-general processes of chunking and categorization. Using modern and diachronic corpus data, we show that the facts support a view of constituent structure as gradient (as would follow from its source in chunking and categorization) and subject to gradual changes over time. Usage factors (i.e., repetition) and semantic factors both influence chunking and categorization and, therefore, influence constituent structure. We take as our example the complex prepositions of English, for instance, *on top of*, *in back of*, and *in spite of*, whose internal constituent structure has been much debated. From observing strong (but not absolute) usage trends in the corpus data, we find that these complex preposition sequences display varying degrees of emerging constituency. We conclude that constituent reanalysis, like language change generally, proceeds gradually.

Introduction

Most theories of language take the categories of grammar and their hierarchical relations (i.e., constituent structures) as givens. Constituent structure, such as might be formalized with phrase structure rules or syntactic trees, typically takes a prominent place as a substantive universal in theories of Universal Grammar and is thus held to be innate and domain-specific (Chomsky, 1965; Jackendoff, 2002). We take the view, in contrast, that no part of grammar needs to be given a priori (Hopper, 1987); rather we follow Lindblom, MacNeilage,

---

Correspondence concerning this article should be addressed to Clay Beckner, Department of Linguistics, University of New Mexico, MSC 03 2130, Albuquerque, NM 87131. Internet: coogle@unm.edu

and Studdert-Kennedy (1984) in their plea for explanations for linguistic structures and universals. They specifically incite us to "DERIVE LANGUAGE FROM
NON-LANGUAGE!" (emphasis in the original). Thus, in this article we propose
to derive constituent structure from the domain-general processes of chunking
and categorization within the storage network for language. Because language
is a dynamic system, an important part of our argument will rest on the idea
that constituent structure, like all of grammar, is constantly undergoing gradual change. Thus, structural reanalysis, as often discussed in the context of
grammaticalization, will be pivotal to our argument and exposition.

We mean by *structural reanalysis* a change in constituent structure, as when
to as an earlier allative or infinitive marker with a verb as its complement fuses
with *going* in the future expression *be going to* (*going* [*to see*] > [*going to*]
see). Indicators of reanalysis include changes in distribution, such as the fact
that selectional restrictions in a clause with *be going to* are determined by what
is now the main verb, and phonological changes, such as the reduction of *going*
to to *gonna*.

Are such changes abrupt or gradual? In generative models of syntax (see,
e.g., Lightfoot, 1979; Roberts & Roussou, 2003), structural reanalysis is necessarily abrupt, because it is held that a sequence of words has a unique, discrete
constituent analysis.[1] In this view, constituents are clearly defined and do not
overlap; in a sequence such as *going to VERB*, *to* must be grouped either with
the following verb, or with *going*, with no intermediate stages. The only way
for discrete constituent boundaries to shift is via abrupt means—specifically,
via the mechanism of language acquisition, when children misinterpret the constituents they hear in adult language and assign a different structural analysis
than the previous generation.

However, because most linguistic change appears to be quite gradual, with
slowly changing meanings and distributions and overlapping stages, a problem
arises for a theory with discrete constituent structure. Evidence from the grad-
ualness of change has led some researchers to doubt discrete categories and
structures (Haspelmath, 1998; Hoffmann, 2005; Quirk, Greenbaum, Leech, &
Svartvik, 1985).

Continuing from Bybee and Scheibman (1999), we join these researchers in
proposing that constituent structure can change gradually. We take the view that
it is altogether common even for an individual speaker to have nondiscrete syntactic representations for the same word sequence. Taking a complex systems-
based perspective, we hold that syntactic structure is in fact much richer than the
discrete constituency view would indicate. There are multiple overlapping and,
at times, competing influences on the shape of units in the grammar, and these

multiple factors have an ongoing effect on each speaker's synchronic representations of syntactic structure. Specifically, syntactic constituents are subject to ongoing influence from general, abstract patterns in language, in addition to more localized, item-specific usage patterns. The foregoing perspective makes it possible that the same word sequence may be characterized by multiple constituent structures and that these structures have gradient strengths rather than discrete boundaries. Our position in this article is thus that constituency may change in a gradual fashion via usage, rather than via acquisition, and that structural reanalysis need not be abrupt.

As a case study of shifting constituent boundaries, we focus on the semantic and syntactic analysis of English complex prepositions (i.e., multiword sequences that function prepositionally, such as *on top of* or *in spite of*). Complex prepositions often may be replaced by a single word (a preposition), such as *The car is in back of the house/The car is behind the house*. This replaceability hints that certain complex sequences have formed (or have started to form) into new prepositions (see Quirk et al., 1985; Quirk & Mulholland, 1964). Complex prepositions are also quite often unpredictable in meaning and, as such, are taught as noncompositional units to second language learners. For example, the English Preposition-Preposition sequence *out of* has multiple meanings that cannot be predicted from the component words, even accounting for the fact that the component prepositions are themselves polysemous: *We are out of milk again*; *I've been out of town*; *The storm came out of the west*; *They made a decision out of desperation*.

A large number of English sequences (among them, *because of, according to, by dint of, due to*) exhibit the above traits and/or other syntactic characteristics that imply that they are constituents (Quirk et al., 1985, pp. 669–673). Despite such evidence, the syntactic status of complex prepositions has been a matter of some debate. We enter this debate in this article from the viewpoint that constituent structure is gradient, mutable, and emergent from domain-general processes. In the next section, we describe the way chunking and categorization together provide constituency analyses of phrases and utterances for speakers. In the third section, we describe how the model proposed in the second section accounts for reanalysis, using the case of the complex preposition *in spite of* whose development in terms of both meaning and syntax is discussed. In the fourth section, we respond to objections by critics who argue against assigning constituent status to complex prepositions, based on the discrete constituency view. We argue that our view, which references meaning as well as gradual change in cohesiveness and autonomy, provides a better explanation for the problems raised by the analysis of complex prepositions.

Constituent Structure as Emergent From Chunking, Categorization, and Generalization

Bybee (2002, in press) discusses the nature of sequential learning and chunking as it applies to the formation of constituents. Because members of the same constituent appear in a linear sequence with some frequency, these items are subject to chunking, by which sequences of repeated behavior come to be stored and processed as a single unit. Ellis (1996) gave the following quote from Newell (1990), which emphasizes the domain-general application of chunking:

> A chunk is a unit of memory organization, formed by bringing together a set of already formed chunks in memory and welding them together into a larger unit. Chunking implies the ability to build up such structures recursively, thus leading to a hierarchical organization of memory. Chunking appears to be a ubiquitous feature of human memory.[2] (p. 7)

Chunking occurs automatically as behaviors are repeated in the same order, whether they are motor activities such as driving a car or cognitive tasks such as memorizing a list. Repetition is the factor that leads to chunking, and chunking is the response that allows repeated behaviors to be accessed more quickly and produced more efficiently (Haiman, 1994). Chunking has been shown to be subject to The Power Law of Practice (Anderson, 1993), which stipulates that performance improves with practice, but the amount of improvement decreases as a function of increasing practice or frequency. Thus, once chunking occurs after several repetitions, further benefits or effects of repetition accrue much more slowly.

Chunked elements in language are oft-repeated sequences such as determiner plus noun, preposition plus noun phrase, verb plus object, and so on. Specific lexemes that are used together, as in formulas or prefabs (e.g., *dark night, salt and pepper,* or *take a break*), also constitute chunks. The formation of chunks produces hierarchical structure in language, as smaller chunks will be more frequent, will have undergone more practice, and will therefore be more cohesive than larger ones. As smaller chunks appear within larger ones, a nested structure emerges.

Chunking is also responsible for the fact that some sequences of linguistic units show formal cohesion in the absence of semantic cohesion. Bybee (2002) gave as an example auxiliary contraction in English. Whereas most chunks have some semantic coherence, the English auxiliary is chunked with the subject, usually a pronoun (e.g., *I'm*), resulting in a formal unit that crosses a traditional constituent boundary (between NP and VP) and that does not result in a semantically coherent unit. Another example is the common fusion of prepositions with definite articles in French, Spanish, German, and other European languages. However, because elements that are semantically related tend to occur together, most chunks are also semantically coherent and therefore considered to be constituents in most theories of grammar.

The second domain-general process that contributes to the formation of constituent structure is categorization. We propose conceiving of cognitive representations as a network of exemplars that undergoes change as language is used. An incoming token of linguistic experience, such as a word, is mapped onto an identical or similar stored exemplar, strengthening it. For the purposes of this article we will assume familiarity with exemplar models and not provide the evidence and arguments for them here (but see Bybee, 2001, 2006, in press; Pierrehumbert, 2001). Instead, we will concentrate on the relationship between chunking and categorization.

Mapping experienced tokens onto stored exemplars is an act of categorization. For instance, deciding that *pull* in the idiom *pull strings* is the same verb as that occurring in other expressions (e.g., *pull the trigger*, *pull someone's leg*) is an act of categorization. It is based on phonetic and semantic similarity as well as morpho-syntactic distribution. In the network model first proposed in Bybee (1985), the categorization by similarity would be represented as in Figure 1.

In Figure 1, the sequence *pull strings* is represented as a consecutive string because the two words have been used together enough to constitute a chunk. It might also be argued on the basis of idiomaticity alone that *pull strings* has unitary status, but note that even semantically compositional sequences can become chunks as a result of usage. For example, compositional sequences such as *for some reason* and *dark night* represent the conventional way of expressing certain notions, in contrast with semantically plausible (but unlikely)

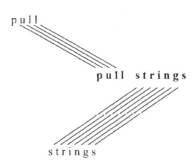

Figure 1 The connections between an idiom and its component words (Bybee, 1998).

sequences like *from some reason* or *black night.* A fully realized exemplar model proposes that each of the conventionalized sequences has an independent mental representation: The conventionality of *pull strings, for some reason,* and *dark night* arises because our cognitive systems track the usage of these specific sequences in language.

However, even when a sequence of words is chunked together, the components of the chunk may remain identifiable in both form and meaning (Nunberg, Sag, & Wasow, 1994). As shown in Figure 1, the representation for *pull strings* maintains connections to other instances of the component words *pull* and *strings.* In Langacker's (1987) terms, the chunk is analyzable. Note that the categorization of the parts of the chunk provides an internal constituent structure. In our view, categorization within a network architecture is the mechanism that creates abstract syntactic patterns—those regularities that would be represented via phrase structure rules in a generative model. Because certain words have similar distributions and may be categorized together, generalizations emerge across recurrent categories of items, resulting in abstract constituent patterns. For instance, *the charming dog* is a constituent (labeled NP by linguists) because it fits into a general pattern in which phrases may consist of Determiner plus Adjective plus Noun.[3]

In sum, we find that the constituency of a sequence of words is best characterized by appealing to both "local" (item-specific) and "global" (general, type-based) influences. Local influences can chunk a specific, recurrent word sequence into a constituent—a constituent that nevertheless maintains a limited internal structure due to the way component words are categorized following global patterns. On the other hand, constituency is often determined largely via global influences, as words in a sequence are each categorized following general patterns and chunked together according to a recurrent type-based generalization. A complete syntactic model will recognize that local and global influences may oppose one another and that in different cases they will affect constituency to varying degrees. Given these multiple factors, chunking and categorizability are *gradient* properties of sequences and they may change over time with usage.

Changes in Constituent Structure

In grammaticalization it often happens that grammaticalizing expressions change their constituent structure. Thus, it is often said that grammaticalization is the reanalysis of a lexical item as a grammatical item. As Haspelmath (1998) pointed out, often the change can be thought of as a simple change in a category status. Thus, a verb becomes an auxiliary; a serial verb becomes an adposition or a complementizer; a noun becomes a conjunction or adposition. In some cases, however, shifts in constituent boundaries do occur; in particular, it is common to lose some internal constituent boundaries. A prominent example of such a change involves complex prepositions. Many complex prepositions start out as a sequence of two prepositional phrases (e.g., *on top of* NP) but evolve into a kind of intermediate structure in some analyses—the complex preposition—and eventually they can even develop further into simple prepositions, as has occurred with *beside, behind, and among* (Hopper & Traugott, 2003; König & Kortmann, 1991; Svorou, 1994).

In Spite of: from P NP P to Prepositional Unit

A typical example of a complex preposition in English, *in spite of,* was originally constituted of a preposition *in,* whose object was the noun phrase headed by *spite.* A traditional phrase structure analysis of the earlier, analyzable sequence has a nested structure such as the following:

(1) [in [spite [of [the king]$_{NP}$]$_{PP}$]$_{NP}$]$_{PP}$

Basically, the starting point for reanalysis is a hierarchical constituent structure in which *spite* is an ordinary noun meaning "defiance, contempt, scorn," and there are two prepositional phrases with *in* and *of.* Note, however, that the most frequently recurring part of the structure is *in spite of,* as the object of *of* is highly variable and the rest of the expression is fixed. This means that *in spite of* can become a chunk.

The hierarchical analysis, as in (1), will remain only as long as the phrase remains analyzable—that is, as long as *spite* within the phrase continues to be categorized as a noun and as the same item as the noun *spite* that occurs in other expressions, and as long as the prepositions are associated with other instances of these same prepositions. Because not much phonetic change is observed in this phrase, two factors are important to the change in analyzability. One is the effect of frequency of use, which leads to the access of the phrase as a unit; as Hay (2001) pointed out, each time the sequence is processed as a unit that increases its sequential cohesion. The second factor in reducing analyzability is semantic change, which, of course, interacts with frequency of use; the semantic change weakens the association of the noun *spite* with its lexical counterparts, leading to a loss of analyzability and also categoriality (Hopper, 1991; Hopper & Traugott, 2003). As the noun *spite* within the phrase becomes disassociated from the independent noun, it loses its nounlike behavior—that is, it ceases to take determiners or modifiers.[4]

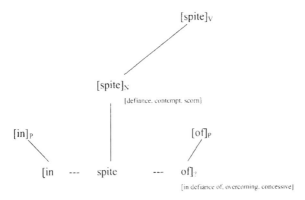

Figure 2 Exemplar representation of *in spite of* and some of its lexical connections.

Figure 2 helps us visualize how gradual reanalysis can be modeled over time. A number of morphological models have been proposed in which morphologically complex words can be accessed in two ways: either directly, already composed, or from the component parts via a compositional mechanism. Some of these models (Baayen, 1993; Hay, 2001) propose to consider any accessing event as a combination of the two mechanisms in which one or the other may be prominent. As this is not an either-or situation, the extent to which the component parts are activated may vary. When each part is accessed and then combined, the connecting lines to the parts are strengthened. When the multiword sequence is accessed without activating the parts, the whole sequence is strengthened. Thus, given the network in Figure 2, over accessing events, the vertical connection lines (indicating categorization of the individual words) become relatively weaker while the sequential connections (indicating the formation of a multiword chunk) become relatively stronger.

The noun *spite* has a set of meanings and contexts of use; the phrase *in spite of* as an exemplar develops its own meanings and contexts of use. As the phrase becomes less associated with its component parts, it also becomes more autonomous pragmatically and semantically and begins to take on meanings inferred from the context, such as concessive meaning. Moreover, the increasing autonomy and fixedness of *in spite of* develop in tandem with a particular syntactic distribution, which is essentially the distribution of a preposition; that is, *in spite of* occurs as a chunk in similar environments as other English prepositions: We may say [*in spite of*] *resistance* or [*without*] *resistance* (see additional discussion in the fourth section). With respect to the formation of global, category-based generalizations, such a distributional pattern would then gradually encourage classification of *in spite of* as a prepositional unit.

Given the above proposed model, Hay (2001) reasoned that if the complex unit is more frequent than its parts, it is more likely to be accessed as a unit, leading to the loss of analyzability that comes about through categorization. Applied to *in spite of*, we would predict that as the complex phrase becomes more frequent than the simple noun *spite*, it would also become more autonomous and less analyzable. In Shakespeare's comedies (written at the end of the 16th century) we find 20 occurrences of *spite*; only 6 of them are in the phrase *in spite of*. In Modern American English, over 90% of the occurrences of *spite* are in that phrase (see the Corpus of Contemporary American English [COCA], Davies, 2008).

Consider also some of the examples from Shakespeare's usage. In the next section we will discuss semantic change in more detail, but note here that in both (2) and (3) the meaning of *in spite of* invokes *spite* in its original meaning of defiance. Note also that in (2) Beatrice uses *spite* as a verb after using it in the phrase *in spite of*. This suggests analyzability of the phrase. In (3) Ulysses interrupts the phrase with a modifier, *very*, which is here used as an adjective meaning "true." The added modifier gives evidence that *spite* is being categorized as a noun, and the sequence is analyzable; such uses are very rare today.

(2) (*Much Ado About Nothing*):

> BENEDICK: Suffer love! a good epithet! I do suffer love indeed, for I love thee against my will.

> BEATRICE *In spite of* your heart, I think; alas, poor heart! If you spite it for my sake, I will spite it for yours; for I will never love that which my friend hates.

(3) (*Troilus & Cressida*):

> ULYSSES: Ajax hath lost a friend
> And foams at mouth, and he is arm'd and at it,
> Roaring for Troilus, who hath done to-day
> Mad and fantastic execution,
> Engaging and redeeming of himself
> With such a careless force and forceless care
> As if that luck, in very *spite of* cunning,
> Bade him win all.

In the next section, we look briefly at the gradual progression of the semantic change.

The Semantic Development of *in Spite of*

Paralleling the morpho-syntactic and usage changes we have documented, developing complex prepositions undergo semantic change typical of grammaticalization. Hoffmann (2005) showed that each complex preposition follows its own trajectory and pointed out further that a strict chronology may not be possible, given the paucity of surviving early examples. Here, we focus on *in spite of* and sketch the general picture of the emergence of concessive meaning for that complex preposition.

In spite of appears to have been first used with a literal interpretation of the noun *spite*, which meant "scorn, contempt, or defiance." The most literal of uses are those that indicate an explicit defiance of an enemy, as in the following 15th century examples:

(4) c1400 *Destr. Troy* 1968. But for noy of my nobilte & my nome gret, I shuld..spede the to spille *in spite of* þi kynge.

    If it were not for the risk to my nobility and my reputation, I would hasten to kill you in spite of your king. (Translation from Hoffmann, 2005)

(5) 1400–1482 *The Brut* The Erle þen, with his pepill, drove ouer þe havon of Gravenyng thaire pray of bestes, att lowe water, *in spite of* al þe Flemmynges, and brought hem with al thaire prisoners to Caleis, and lost neuer a man; thonket be God!

    Then the Earl, with his people, drove over the inlet at Gravening their herd of animals, at low water, in spite of the Flemish, and them with all their prisoners to Calais, and never lost a man; thanks be to God!

Later examples show a generalization of the object of *in spite of* to include obstacles of various sorts—for instance, authority figures, rules of law, or culture—as shown in the following examples taken from the *Oxford English Dictionary*, spanning the 16th to the 19th centuries.

(6) 1581 G. PETTIE tr. *Guazzo's Civ. Conv.* III. (1586) 129b, The wife *in spight of* the husband, gave halfe the meate . . . to a poore bodie.

(7) 1617 MORYSON *Itin.* I. 232 They . . said, that the Scripture must be beleeved, *in spite of* all Cosmographers and Philosophers.

(8) 1711 E. WARD *Quix.* I. 158 Who would *in Spite of* Wedlock Run To Cuddle with the Emp'rour's Son.

(9) 1853 KINGSLEY *Misc.* (1859) I. 15 The English are attacked treacherously *in spite of* solemn compacts.

At about the same time, examples appear in which the opposing force is the effort of someone, which, alas, is not successful. In some cases, the efforts are exerted by the same person who puts forth or undergoes the main action. Examples (10) and (11) show that such usage continues; the expression *in spite of oneself* is still in use today.

(10) 1765 *Museum Rust.* IV. 266 They grow poor, *in spite of* all possible industry.

(11) 1818 SCOTT *Br. Lamm.* xx, The tears, *in spite of* her, forced their way between her fingers.

Example (12) is also an instance in which the object of *in spite of* is someone's effort, but in this case, it is the effort of another actor.

(12) 1782 COWPER *Gilpin* xxii, That trot became a gallop soon *in spite of* curb and rein.

All of these examples carry a discourse-based inference of counterexpectation, which is the seed of the concessive meaning. The object of *in spite of* expresses an obstacle that is overcome or not overcome in the physical and social world, so it also sets up the expectation that the situation expressed in the clause is not to be expected. As uses with this inference of counterexpectation become more common, the concessive inference can become part of the meaning of the phrase (Traugott & Dasher, 2002). This leads to examples that are ambiguous between a reading in which the speaker/writer is describing counterforces in the real world and a reading in which the speaker/writer is expressing counterexpectation. Example (13) seems ambiguous, as does (14).

(13) 1859 *Bentley's Q. Rev.* No. 3. 26 *In spite of* this aimlessness the wealth and empire of England are constantly increasing.

(14) *In spite of* the rough conditions, travel advisories and the war on terrorism, scores of older Americans are uprooting their lives to help needy nations improve their living conditions. (*Time* Magazine Corpus, [Davies, 2007], 2003)

In the final development, tokens in which only the concessive meaning of counter-expectation is discernible arise, as in (15) and (16):

(15) Yet *in spite of* music's remarkable influence on the human psyche, scientists have spent little time attempting to understand why it possesses such potency. (*Time* Corpus, 2000)

(16) The condition of accelerated puberty in girls is more of a hypothesis than a widely observed phenomenon—*in spite of* anecdotal reports. (*Time Corpus*, 2000)

Along with these purely concessive meanings — in which the *in spite of* phrase simply marks a counter-to-expectation condition—some of the older uses continue. Example (17) shows the older, more literal meaning of overcoming opposing forces.

(17) I saw the pictures of the Iraqi people walking to the polls to exercise their right to vote in the face of death threats, bombs and with entire families in jeopardy. To vote *in spite of* all that takes courage above and beyond what most Americans would show today. The Iraqis expressed the true spirit of democracy. (*Time* Corpus, 2005)

Although it is difficult to establish a reliable chronology, due to the paucity of early examples, the indications are that the true concessive use has only become common recently, perhaps in the last century and a half. It is thus important to note that the uses of *in spite of* do not change abruptly nor does one use replace another. A range of uses is maintained in the current language. However, we take the emergence of concessive meaning as a sure indicator of unithood for the phrase *in spite of*. As the phrase develops a weakened association with the semantics of *spite*, not coincidentally, the internal constituent structure of the phrase also weakens. We consider a study of the semantic change necessary for determining when a change in constituency occurs, as a sequence may begin to be extended to new semantic contexts only when loss of analyzability has occurred. In addition, we believe that the semantic changes are also necessary for understanding *why* reanalysis takes place, as no change occurs in isolation, but in a particular semantic-pragmatic context.

In the next section we turn to the traditional morpho-syntactic diagnostics of constituency, which we argue are epi-phenomena (Hopper, 1987), as the most basic determinants of constituency are usage and cognitive association of the phrase with its component parts in their other uses.

Syntactic Diagnostics and Usage Data in Identifying Constituents

As we have noted, several traditionally oriented analysts have objected that it is incorrect to assign constituent status to *in spite of* and other complex prepositions that have been proposed for English (see Huddleston & Pullum, 2002; Pullum, 2006; Seppänen, Bowen, & Trotta, 1994). In this section, we briefly characterize the nature of such objections, with a particular focus on *in spite of*.[5] We provide a response from our gradient constituency perspective and provide some usage data to contrast with introspective diagnostics.

First, we note that in traditional discussions of constituent status, there is a tendency to favor evidence based on introspective syntactic tests to the exclusion of any other types of evidence. Thus, in Seppänen et al. (1994, p. 4) and Huddleston and Pullum (2002, p. 621), semantics is explicitly rejected as a factor in determining constituency, on the assumption that syntax provides a more systematic and rigorous testing ground. Our view, however, is that the most thorough assessment of constituency will consider *all* evidence (semantic, pragmatic, morpho-syntactic, and phonetic). As we will see in this section, even the syntactic criteria do not all uniformly point in the same direction.

Huddleston and Pullum (2002, p. 620) wrote that some multiword sequences have a "close semantic relation" to single-word prepositional items, such as *in front of/behind, on top of/underneath*, and *in spite of/despite*. These semantic similarities also have correspondences in (purportedly more rigorous) syntactic constituency tests. Syntactic tests such as the "Coordination" test hint that single-word and multiword prepositional forms in fact have similar syntactic distributions and seem to constitute similar types of units:

(18) Scorsese's strongest works are fictions of formation, in which a religious conviction comes *with* or *in spite of* a vocation. (COCA, 1991)

More importantly, it turns out that syntactic criteria give conflicting results. For instance, taking *in spite of*, it is found that *of* cannot be fronted in the constructed example **Of what obstacles did he say he would do it in spite?* (Seppänen et al., 1994). This would suggest that *in spite of* is a unit. Seppänen et al. argued, however, that the sequence is not a constituent because it fails tests for Coordination and Interpolation (Interruption).[6] With respect to Co-ordination, it is indeed the case that users of English sometimes coordinate *in spite of* in a way that indicates an awareness of internal structure for this sequence. In the 385-million-word COCA, we located 7 instances in which writers conjoined *in spite of* with other *of* sequences in the following pattern:

(19) The prime minister remains unable to reap the credit for economic success, which is perceived to have occurred *in spite*, not *because*, *of* his policies ... (COCA, 1995)

(20) ... a lesson in how Congress makes politically expedient decisions *at the expense* (or *in spite*) *of* the constitutional implications of their actions (COCA, 2002)

It is perhaps surprising that writers of English would conjoin *in spite of* in a way that reveals awareness of the individual status of *of*. Yet our position predicts that a word sequence may gradually form a unitary status even while component words are partially activated on each use. To return to Figure 2, note that even as *in spite of* strengthens in constituency, it does not instantaneously become fused into an indivisible unit. The sequence continues to maintain some connections to the separate words *in*, *spite*, and (most importantly here) *of*.

If we look at the full range of usage data, it is in fact unquestionable that *in spite of* has a mostly fixed status, and this fixedness must be acknowledged by a complete theory of constituency. Despite the occurrences of sentences like (19) and (20), it is far more common for English speakers to avoid splitting up *in spite of*, even when they could easily do so. In the COCA, we located 35 such instances. Two of these examples are as follows:

(21) ... the dogma of self-expression says that the gifted child can flower *in the absence of* or *in spite of* art education. (COCA, 1995)

(22) ... in this allegedly anti-American country Sarkozy would be elected (as early as the spring of 2007) either *because of* or *in spite of* the public perception that he is somehow "American." (COCA, 2005)

Even more striking are usage patterns with respect to multiple instances of *in spite of* that are conjoined. English speakers strongly prefer to present multiple instances of *in spite of* as an uninterrupted sequence; (23) is one characteristic example:

(23) *In spite of* motorbikes, *in spite of* karaoke music, *in spite of* the stink of gasoline fumes that seeps into each kitchen. (COCA, 2005)

There are 43 examples of this type in COCA. The corpus does contain two counterexamples in which only subparts of *in spite of* are conjoined, but neither instance occurs in very recent usage.[7] Given a traditional syntactic analysis, we might expect speakers to separate *in spite* and *of* in conjoined uses, assuming that a constituent boundary exists at that juncture. Instead, what we find is that speakers typically repeat this entire three-word sequence without interruption, providing evidence that *in spite of* is produced in a single, formulaic chunk (see Wray, 2006).

Of course, we must also consider the possibility that the unit status of a complex preposition can be questioned if interruptions are permitted by other words (for instance, by hesitations or discourse markers). Seppänen et al. (1994, p. 22) pursue this line of thought also, arguing that *in spite of* retains an internal constituent structure because it can be interpolated in speech. The constructed example they provided is *The morning air was clear and clean, in spite, one might add, of the traffic and crowds.*

In response, we note first that interpolation is not very reliable as a test of constituency, because discourse markers, hesitations, and parenthetical asides may be inserted into speech in many positions, including in the middle of traditional constituents (e.g., into a VP in *It is, however, a profitable company*; McCawley, 1982; see also Hoffmann, 2005, p. 34).

Moreover, with respect to *in spite of*, notwithstanding the constructed example by Seppänen et al. (1994), it seems that speakers very seldom interpolate any material into this sequence. Our corpus search yielded only one attested example, which occurred in a Robert Ingersoll quote from 1877:

(24) The religionists of our time are occupying about the same ground occupied by heretics and infidels of one hundred years ago. The church has advanced *in spite*, as it were, *of* itself. (COCA, 1999)

Example (24) is striking because Ingersoll interrupts *in spite of* precisely for the purpose of calling attention to the component words in the sequence, as he intends to revive the original semantics of *spite.*

Thus, although we concede that it may be possible for speakers to add asides to *in spite of*, it is worth noting how truly rare such interruptions are. Of particular interest in *in spite of* is the transition between *spite* and *of*, because Seppänen et al. (1994) focused on the constituent boundary that they maintained remains active in that juncture. In the COCA, we find 6254 tokens of *in spite.* Out of these instances, 6241 are *also* tokens of *in spite of*. What this means is that in the corpus data, the transitional probability between *in spite* and *of* (the likelihood of following *in spite* with *of*) is 99.5. We find that this fact provides overwhelming evidence that *in spite of* constitutes a single constituent, with only a very weak association of *of* with this preposition elsewhere. We claim that it is difficult to maintain that there is an immutable constituent boundary before *of*, given that people quickly learn transitional patterns on the basis of very limited data (Saffran, Aslin, & Newport, 1996, and related studies), and the usage patterns for *in spite of* would encourage speakers to group *of* with *in spite*, rather than with the following noun phrase.

Conclusion

We have taken stock here of the traditional discrete constituency view that holds that a word sequence either has a holistic structure or a unique, nested hierarchical structure. The accounts we have examined ultimately reject usage as an indicator of constituent structure—discarding evidence from semantics and any usage data that might be countered by partial evidence from introspective syntactic tests. Such a conservative approach rejects even the possibility of finding evidence that particular sequences may have reached an intermediate stage of constituency. Moreover, the discrete constituency view would seem to hold that grammar is driven only by abstract syntactic generalizations and is immune to any gradual effects from item-specific usage patterns.

In contrast, as we do not take constituent structure as given innately, we do not give priority to syntactic tests. Rather we consider data from usage, semantics, and language change. Indeed, we have shown that chunking and categorization have semantic effects and change incrementally over time.

Moreover, in keeping with the theory of complex adaptive systems, we consider constituent structure to be emergent from the domain-general processes of chunking and categorization. Human minds track multiple factors related to constituency, and this complex processing correlates with a rich and dynamic structural representation for word sequences. In our model, constituency is the result of interacting influences that are both local and global in nature. The *global* influences that help shape constituents correspond to general patterns in usage. On the other hand, constituency may also be shaped *locally* by item-specific forces over time. If a sequence is consistently used in a particular context (with complex prepositions like *in spite of* as a case in point), that sequence will gradually form into a unit, overriding general patterns elsewhere in usage. In this regard, we embrace Bolinger's early complex systems view of language as a "jerry-built" and heterogeneous structure that is also intricate and tightly organized (1976, p. 1). Rather than assuming that structure is given a priori via top-down blueprints, we agree with Bolinger (1976) and Hopper (1987) that structure emerges locally and is subject to ongoing revision, even while general patterns exhibit apparent stability.

Revised version accepted 9 June 2009

Notes

1 We recognize that there are some generative syntacticians who have adopted nondiscrete or multifaceted models of constituent structure (for one review, see Carnie, 2007). Our views in the present article may be compatible with such approaches, although we would emphasize that proposals for particular constituent structures should be grounded in usage rather than being postulated ad hoc. Despite recent broadening in generative models, the discrete constituency view remains the

norm in much of linguistic theory, as reflected in descriptive grammars such as Huddleston and Pullum (2002).

2 One reviewer objects that Newell's quote would predict an infinite regress of chunking in cognition. It is indeed the case that multiword chunks consist of words that are themselves chunks, and these chunks are, in turn, made up of phonetic chunks. However, the human perceptual system is not infinitely fine-grained and thus the nested chunking "bottoms out" on just-noticeable-differences in acoustics (see Pierrehumbert, 2001, p. 141). Regarding an emergentist account of linguistic units, see also Bybee and Beckner (2009).

3 Of course, the constituency of *the charming dog* would also be reinforced by a functional unity for the sequence that arises from semantics.

4 Note that because *spite* is a mass noun, we cannot observe any neutralization of number developing for *in spite of*. However, in grammaticalizing complex prepositions, it is common for count nouns to lose plural markers as another indicator of decategorialization. For example, one would say [*on top of*] *the houses*, rather than *on tops of the houses* (DeLancey, 1994). It is possible to say *on the tops of the houses*, but only if the speaker is using *tops* referentially, rather than relationally as part of a preposition.

5 Our discussion in this section is paralleled by a broader corpus study in Chapter 3 of Hoffmann (2005), which examines 30 frequent Preposition-Noun-Preposition sequences in British English. Hoffmann similarly found that in actual usage, complex prepositions are unlikely to undergo the syntactic modifications proposed by Seppänen et al. (1994). Further, Hoffmann (2005, pp. 45–46) found compelling evidence that complex prepositions are retrieved as uninterrupted wholes, based on the distribution of filled pauses in speech.

6 We do not discuss at length here an additional test Seppänen et al. (1994) mentioned, namely Ellipsis, which they illustrated with the following constructed example: *Speaker A: He did it in spite of John and the auditor. Speaker B: Of what auditor? I didn't know they had one in this firm* (p. 22). Such a usage strikes us as unacceptable, and it is unattested in the corpora we have reviewed. Similarly, after doing a search of the British National Corpus involving 30 complex preposition sequences, Hoffmann (2005, pp. 48–49) found only one instance of ellipsis that crossed a complex preposition boundary (*with respect to*).

7 Both counterexamples are quotes in academic prose from older sources. One quote is from Henry James (1903) and the other is from Emily Ruete (English translation, 1888): "In spite of her very small size, and of her plain exterior, she possessed an immense power . . . ."

References

Anderson, J. R. (1993). *Rules of the mind*. Hillsdale, NJ: Lawrence Erlbaum.

Baayen, H. (1993). On frequency, transparency and productivity. In G. Booij & J. van Marle (Eds.), *Yearbook of morphology 1992* (pp. 181–208). Dordrecht: Kluwer Academic.

Bolinger, D. (1976). Meaning and memory. *Forum Linguisticum, 1*(1), 1–14.

Bybee, J. (1985). *Morphology: A study of the relation between meaning and form.* Philadelphia: Benjamins.

Bybee, J. (1998). The emergent lexicon. In M. C. Gruber, D. Higgins, K. S. Olson, & T. Wysocki (Eds.), *CLS 34: The Panels* (pp. 421–435). University of Chicago: Chicago Linguistic Society.

Bybee, J. (2001). *Phonology and language use.* Cambridge: Cambridge University Press.

Bybee, J. (2002). Sequentiality as the basis of constituent structure. In T. Givon & B. Malle (Eds.), *The evolution of language from pre-language* (pp. 109–132). Philadelphia: Benjamins.

Bybee, J. (2006). From usage to grammar: The mind's response to repetition. *Language, 82*, 711–733.

Bybee, J. (in press). *Language, usage and cognition.* Cambridge: Cambridge University.

Bybee, J., & Beckner, C. (2009). Usage-based theory. In B. Heine & H. Narrog (Eds.), *The Oxford handbook of linguistic analysis* (pp. 827–855). Oxford: Oxford University Press.

Bybee, J., & Scheibman, J. (1999). The effect of usage on degree of constituency: The reduction of *don't* in English. *Linguistics, 37*, 575–596.

Carnie, A. (2007). *Constituent structure.* Oxford: Oxford University Press.

Chomsky, N. (1965). *Aspects of the theory of syntax.* Cambridge, MA: MIT Press.

Davies, M. (2007). *Time* Magazine Corpus (100 million words, 1920s–2000s). Retrieved July 1, 2008, from http://corpus.byu.edu/time

Davies, M. (2008). The Corpus of Contemporary American English (COCA): 385 million words, 1990–present. Retrieved November 5, 2008, from http://www.americancorpus.org

DeLancey, S. (1994). Grammaticalization and linguistic theory. *Proceedings of the 1993 Mid-America linguistics conference and conference on Siouan/Caddoan languages* (pp. 1–22). Boulder: University of Colorado Department of Linguistics.

Ellis, N. C. (1996). Sequencing in SLA: Phonological memory, chunking and points of order. *Studies in Second Language Acquisition, 18*, 91–126.

Haiman, J. (1994). Ritualization and the development of language. In W. Pagliuca (Ed.), *Perspectives on grammaticalization* (pp. 3–28). Amsterdam: Benjamins.

Haspelmath, M. (1998). Does grammaticalization need reanalysis? *Studies in Language, 22*, 315–351.

Hay, J. (2001). Lexical frequency in morphology: Is everything relative? *Linguistics, 39*(6), 1041–1070.

Hoffmann, S. (2005). *Grammaticalization and English complex prepositions: A corpus-based study* (Routledge Advances in Corpus Linguistics 7). London: Routledge.

Hopper, P. J. (1987). Emergent grammar. In J. Aske, N. Beery, L.. Michaelis, & H. Filip (Eds.), *Proceedings of the 13th annual meeting of the Berkeley Linguistic Society* (pp. 139–157). Berkeley: University of California at Berkeley.

Hopper, P. J. (1991). On some principles of grammaticization. In E. C. Traugott & B. Heine (Eds.), *Approaches to grammaticalization* (Vol. 1, pp. 17–35). Amsterdam: Benjamins.

Hopper, P. J., & Traugott, E.C. (2003). *Grammaticalization* (2nd ed.). Cambridge: Cambridge University Press.

Huddleston, R. D., & Pullum, G. K. (2002). *The Cambridge grammar of the English language*. Cambridge: Cambridge University Press.

Jackendoff, R. (2002). *Foundations of language: Brain, meaning, grammar, evolution.* Oxford: Oxford University Press.

König, E., & Kortmann, B. (1991). On the reanalysis of verbs as prepositions. In G. Rauh (Ed.), *Approaches to prepositions* (pp. 109–125). Tübingen: Gunter Narr.

Langacker, R. W. (1987). *Foundations of cognitive grammar* (Vol. 1). Stanford, CA: Stanford University Press.

Lightfoot, D. (1979). *Principles of diachronic syntax*. Cambridge: Cambridge University Press.

Lindblom, B., MacNeilage, P., & Studdert-Kennedy, M. (1984). Self-organizing processes and the explanation of phonological universals. In B. Butterworth, B. Comrie, & Ö. Dahl (Eds.), *Explanations for language universals* (pp. 181–203). New York: Mouton.

McCawley, J. (1982). Parentheticals and discontinuous constituents. *Linguistic Inquiry, 13*, 91–106.

Newell, A. (1990). *Unified theories of cognition*. Cambridge, MA: Harvard University Press.

Nunberg, G., Sag, I. A., & Wasow, T. (1994). Idioms. *Language, 70*, 491–538.

Pierrehumbert, J. (2001). Exemplar dynamics: Word frequency, lenition, and contrast. In J. Bybee & P. Hopper (Eds.), *Frequency and the emergence of linguistic structure* (pp. 137–157). Amsterdam: Benjamins.

Pullum, G. (2006). Phrasal prepositions in a civil tone. In M. Liberman & G. Pullum (Eds.), *Far from the madding gerund and other dispatches from Language Log* (pp. 41–45). Wilsonville, OR: William James & Company.

Quirk, R, Greenbaum, S., Leech, G., & Svartvik, J. (1985). *A concise grammar of contemporary English*. New York: Harcourt Brace Jovanovich.

Quirk, R., & Mulholland, J. (1964). Complex prepositions and related sequences. *English Studies, 45*, 64–73.

Roberts, I., & Roussou, A. (2003). *Syntactic change: A minimalist approach to grammaticalization*. Cambridge: Cambridge University Press.

Saffran, J. R., Aslin, R. N., & Newport, E. L. (1996). Statistical learning by 8-month-old infants. *Science, 274*, 1926–1928.

Seppänen, A., Bowen, R., & Trotta, J. (1994). On the so-called complex prepositions. *Studia Anglia Posnaniensia, 29*, 3–29.

Svorou, S. (1994). *The grammar of space*. Amsterdam: Benjamins.

Traugott, E. C., & Dasher, R. (2002). *Regularity in semantic change*. Cambridge: Cambridge University Press.

Wray, A. (2006). Formulaic language. In K. Brown (Ed.), *Encyclopedia of language and linguistics* (Vol. 4, pp. 590–597). Oxford: Elsevier.

Language Learning   ISSN 0023-8333

The Speech Community in Evolutionary Language Dynamics

Richard A. Blythe

University of Edinburgh

William A. Croft

University of New Mexico

Language is a complex adaptive system: Speakers are agents who interact with each other, and their past and current interactions feed into speakers' future behavior in complex ways. In this article, we describe the social cognitive linguistic basis for this analysis of language and a mathematical model developed in collaboration between researchers in linguistics and statistical physics. The model has led us to posit two mechanisms of selection—neutral interactor selection and weighted interactor selection—in addition to neutral evolution and replicator selection (fitness). We describe current results in modeling language change in terms of neutral interactor selection and weighted interactor selection.

Introduction

The idea that language should be analyzed as a complex adaptive system is gaining currency, particularly among those researchers who are developing models of language behavior (e.g., Smith, Kirby, & Brighton, 2003; Steels, 2000). Research groups that have come together in the Five Graces group share this view (e.g., Baxter, Blythe, Croft, & McKane, 2006; Ellis & Larsen-Freeman, 2006; Ke & Holland, 2006). The Five Graces group defines a complex adaptive system as follows:

- The system consists of multiple agents interacting with one another.
- The system is adaptive—that is, agents' behavior is based on their past interactions, and current and past interactions together feed back into future behavior.

Correspondence concerning this article should be addressed to Richard A. Blythe, SUPA, School of Physics and Astronomy, University of Edinburgh, Mayfield Rd., Edinburgh, EH9 3JZ, UK. Internet: R.A.Blythe@ed.ac.uk

- An agent's behavior is the consequence of competing factors from a wide range of environmental affordances and constraints.

The premier example of a model of a complex adaptive system is the evolutionary model originally developed and refined in biology by Charles Darwin and his successors. In this article, we describe the theoretical basis of an application of this model to language behavior—in particular, the language change that naturally emerges from language behavior (Croft, 2000). A language is a complex adaptive system because of the way it is situated in its social context. A language is traditionally treated as a static, fixed system of symbols organized into a grammar. This view has been challenged from several directions, most notably in sociolinguistics, cognitive linguistics, and the usage-based model. Although the approaches to language just mentioned have been quite independent, the complex adaptive systems approach unifies them (see Croft, 2000, 2009).

The linguistic system in the traditional sense is a description of the linguistic structures used in a speech community. The speech community corresponds, of course, to the first characteristic of a complex adaptive system: multiple interacting agents. Speakers/agents produce tokens of linguistic structure in their interactions; that is, speakers *replicate* linguistic structures they have heard previously in their utterances, albeit in novel combinations and sometimes in altered form. This linguistic behavior clearly originates in past interactions— the process of learning a language. Much recent research in the usage-based model (e.g., Bybee, 2001, 2007; Langacker, 1988) demonstrates that linguistic behavior continues to change as a result of current and past interactions. Finally, the behavior is also influenced by a wide range of environmental affordances and constraints, in particular: the conceptual structure of the experience to be communicated; the organization of memory (storage of linguistic knowledge); the processes of production and perception/comprehension at multiple linguistic levels; the social status of the interlocutors relative to each other; and the sociocultural context of the utterance situation.

All of these factors lead to a high degree of variability in the replication of linguistic forms for a particular communicative purpose by speakers (Croft, 2000, 2009, 2010). This generation of variation via replication is the first step in the two-step evolutionary process (Dawkins, 1989; Hull, 1988, 2001). The second step is the selection of variants by speakers, via a range of selection mechanisms.

In this article, we present some forthcoming results about the general properties of an evolutionary model of language as a complex adaptive system. We describe two types of selection mechanisms in addition to the widely accepted mechanisms of neutral evolution (genetic drift) and selection via fitness, and we outline the mathematical model in which all of the selection mechanisms are implemented. Subsequent sections summarize the results we have obtained so far in our investigation of these two types of selection mechanisms, and we conclude with a discussion of the role of fitness in language change.

Overview of Selection Mechanisms

In the classical evolutionary selection model, variant replicators differ in fitness, a value associated with each replicator; differences in fitness result in differential replication. We will call this classical selection model *replicator selection*: There is a value directly associated with the replicator that leads to its differential replication.

In language change, replicator selection corresponds to the traditional sociohistorical linguistic model. Different variants have different social values associated with them (prestige, stigma, identity, etc.—not necessarily consciously, of course). By virtue of the social values associated with the variable, some variants are propagated at the expense of other variants.

However, change by replication can happen without (replicator) selection. Because there is a degree of randomness in the replication process, there will be random fluctuations in replicator frequencies, as reproduction takes place in a finite population. If the fluctuation happens to hit zero, then the replicator goes extinct. Thus, change takes place in the population simply by virtue of random processes; no selection has taken place. This process is called *genetic drift* (Crow & Kimura, 1970); genetic drift is very different from linguistic drift. The process is also called *neutral evolution*, and we will use this term in order to avoid confusion. A significant property of neutral evolution models is that the probability of fixation—fully successful propagation of a variant—is a function of the frequency of the variant. Hence, neutral evolution appears to be a manifestation of the frequency effects in language change identified by the usage-based model.

Another process that can affect changes in replicator frequencies is the nature of the interactions between the interactors in the replication process. In Hull's General Analysis of Selection, this process is a type of selection: Interaction of an interactor with its environment causes replication to be differential. What is unusual is that the environment in this case is another interactor. We will call this process *interactor selection*, to differentiate it from classical replicator selection.

In language change, structured social networks mean that a speaker is more likely to interact with certain speakers rather than others. Because the interaction results in the replication of some linguistic variants (replicators) over others in language use by virtue of the frequency of interactions between specific speakers, it can bring about differential replication. We will call this type of interactor selection *neutral interactor selection*, in that the only factor that influences replication is the frequency of interaction with the interactor.

There is another type of interactor selection that is possible in language change. In this type of interactor selection, interactors (interlocutors) are preferred or dispreferred by a speaker regardless of how frequently or infrequently the speaker interacts with them, and their linguistic replications (utterances) are weighted accordingly. Thus, variants of a speaker whose productions are weighted more heavily will be differentially replicated. We will call this *weighted interactor selection*. Weighted interactor selection implies that a speaker's linguistic behavior is influenced not just by frequency of interaction but also a differential social valuation of particular speakers, possibly because of the social group to which they belong.

Mathematical Models

We now embark on a more quantitative exploration of these different selection mechanisms. Using mathematical models, we will discuss consequences of their predictions for theories of the propagation of new cultural conventions. As we have formulated a series of successively stronger selection mechanisms ranging from pure drift (no selection) through neutral and weighted interactor selection to replicator selection (classical fitness), our methodology is to ask whether empirical observations can be explained by a subset of these mechanisms or whether a certain "strength" of selection is necessary. We begin by reviewing the modeling approach for those who may not be familiar with it and then introduce the utterance selection model (USM) that we have developed for this purpose.

The mathematical aspects of this model were put together by researchers in statistical physics (Baxter et al., 2006) and were thus guided by intuition gained from the modeling of complex interacting systems in the physical sciences. Core among these is the fact that in physical systems, large-scale regularities (such as an ordered structure of atoms or molecules) that arise from the interactions between components turn out to be not too strongly sensitive to the *details* of those interactions. Rather the presence or absence of generic mechanisms for generating these regularities is of greater consequence. The hope is that this is a property of interacting systems in general—even those that lack the deterministic, nonintentional nature of physical systems.

A number of large-scale regularities observed in human populations have been quantitatively reproduced within this statistical mechanical approach (sometimes under the guise of *agent-based modeling*, which is essentially the same thing; see the Introduction). As just three recent examples, we cite flow properties of highway traffic (Knospe, Santen, Schadschneider, & Schreckenberg, 2004), escape of pedestrians from confined spaces in a panic scenario (Helbing, Johansson, & Al-Abideen, 2007), and the way various properties of firms are distributed within an economy (Delli Gatti et al., 2007).

The statistical mechanics community itself has recently been host to a burst of activity in modeling cultural change. For a comprehensive technical review of these preliminary (but nevertheless numerous) developments we defer to Castellano, Fortunato, and Loreto (2007). In general terms, the USM (Baxter et al., 2006) is representative of this large class of models. It has, however, three distinctive features that we feel make it appropriate as a tool to develop a quantitative understanding of language change. (a) Speakers maintain a *distribution* over forms associated with a meaning. This means that speakers may exhibit variability in the form used to express a given target meaning, a variability that is observed in human speech (see the introduction). This contrasts with more simplistic models, such as the *voter model* (Clifford & Sudbury, 1973), in which agents exhibit only the behavior they most recently adopted from other agents. (b) Speakers monitor and reinforce their own linguistic behavior. (c) Both the frequency with which speakers interact and the weight they ascribe to other speaker's utterances are explicit, independently controllable parameters, rather than entering implicitly through ad hoc rules for choosing and modifying the states of agents.

Specifically, the USM is defined as follows. A community of speakers is connected by a social network as shown in Figure 1a. A parameter G_{ij} specifies the frequency with which speakers i and j meet. Variation in these parameters between different pairs corresponds to neutral interactor selection. Each speaker maintains a store that reflects her perception of the frequency with which different variants of a linguistic variable are used within her community. In an interaction, both speakers sample from their store; that is, each produces a sequence of tokens and the probability that any given token is an instance of a particular variant is equal to the corresponding stored frequency. Concretely, one might think of the store as being a bag containing a large number of balls, with different colors representing different variants. To produce a token,

(a)

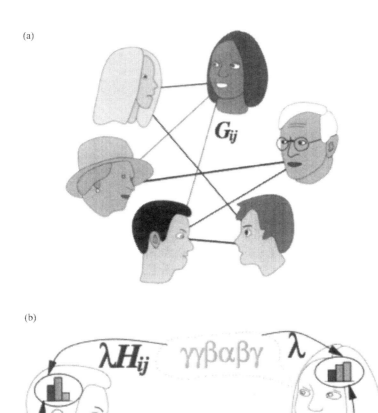

(b)

Figure 1 (a) The speech community; the pair of speakers i, j interacts with frequency G_{ij}. (b) Schematic of an interaction. A speaker uses the stored frequency distribution (shown as a histogram) of variant frequencies to produce tokens of a linguistic variable (whose variants are denoted by α, β, and γ). As described in the text, both speakers listen to both sequences of tokens produced: the arrows indicate the retention of uttered tokens in the stores, and the labels indicate the weight ascribed to the tokens as they are introduced to the store.

a speaker notionally dips into this bag and selects a ball at random and uses its color to decide which variant to utter.

After the interaction, both speakers update their stores, feeding back in the frequencies with which variants were actually produced in the interaction both by themselves and the interlocutor; see Figure 1b. In the "bag of balls" picture, the mathematical rules prescribed in the work of Baxter et al. (2006) correspond to discarding a fraction λ of the balls in the bag and replacing them in such a way that the number of balls of a given color introduced to the bag is proportional to the number of tokens of the corresponding variant that were produced in the interaction. The parameter λ is thus a measure of how rapidly a speaker forgets utterances. The number of balls originating from speaker j's utterances that land in speaker i's bag is further proportional to a factor H_{ij}, which we call the *weight* that speaker i ascribes to speaker j's utterances, relative to her own. If H_{ij} is large, that implies speaker i gives a correspondingly large weight to speaker j's utterances. Variation in H_{ij} thus models weighted interactor selection. Because λ and H_{ij} are rather abstract parameters, they may be difficult (or impossible) to measure in practice. In the following sections we discuss our approach to handling this difficulty.

More detailed definitions of the model can be found in Baxter et al. (2006), Baxter, Blythe, and McKane (2008), and Baxter, Blythe, Croft, and McKane (2009). Its most important properties are that the stochastic nature of the token production means that variant frequencies fluctuate over time and that because no new variants are created, these fluctuations may eventually cause extinction of variants, ultimately leaving a single variant remaining. The single-variant state represents fixation of that variant. Thus, in this form, the USM serves to describe the propagation of an innovation present at some frequency in the initial population of utterances.

Neutral Interactor Selection

We have introduced the term "neutral interactor selection" to describe the case in which no weighting is applied to variants based on the identity of their users *other than* what arises naturally through variation in the frequency with which different speakers interact with one another. In particular, this prevents the notion of a convention being associated with a specific community, or possessing a particular social value, from affecting the frequency that a speaker uses a particular variant.

Trudgill (1986, 2004) has hypothesized that these types of social biases in language use were absent in certain cases in which a new dialect was formed by dialect mixture; that is, new dialect formation is the result of neutral interactor selection. An example for which a great deal of empirical data is available is the emergence of the New Zealand English dialect (Gordon et al., 2004). In the most simplistic terms, the picture is that speakers from various parts of Great Britain and Ireland settled in New Zealand in the mid-19th century, bringing their own regional dialect with them. The first generation of speakers born in New Zealand was characterized by variability—both between and within individual speakers—in the linguistic variants used. The second generation saw convergence onto a single (relatively) homogeneous dialect; that is, roughly speaking, across a range of variables, one variant went to fixation. The timescale for this process is remarkably short: two generations, or approximately 40–50 years, in a community numbering on the order of 100,000 speakers (Gordon et al., 2004; see also Baxter et al., 2009).

The key observation made by Trudgill (2004) is that for almost all variables, the variant that went to fixation was the one that initially was in the majority. This provides evidence that social valuation of variants is not playing a role in the fixation process, because otherwise one might expect variants used by socially important speakers to be the ones to fix.

What further insight does the USM lend to this process of new dialect formation? In terms of the model, we take the absence of social forces to imply that the weights H_{ij} should all be set to the same constant for all pairs of interacting speakers. Otherwise, some speakers would be accorded greater influence than others. To get a feel for the nature of the model's predictions, we plot the evolution of the system for a single run of a computer simulation of the model in Figure 2.

In this simulation, a community of 40 speakers, all of whom interact with each other, was prepared in a state in which half of them were categorical users of a variant α and the other half were categorical users of an alternative variant β. Plotted as a function of time is the usage frequency of the α variant for a speaker from each of the two groups. In the background are fine-grained time series, which reveal fluctuations in usage frequencies on very short timescales. The heavier, foreground plots are running averages and therewith reveal the typical behavior of the model. Three phases can be identified from this latter data. Initially, both speakers begin to use both variants as a consequence of contact between the two sets of speakers. In the second phase, this variability is maintained (albeit with fluctuations) until, in the third phase, both speakers (and, indeed, the entire community) uses α exclusively.

Qualitatively similar behavior is seen in larger communities, and when the network of interactions connecting speakers is varied (subject to keeping

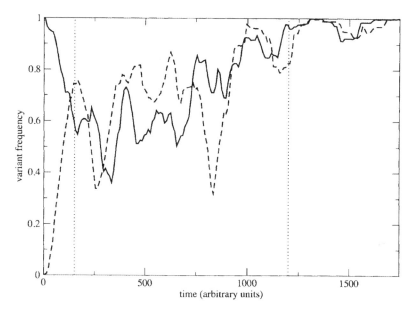

Figure 2 Simulation of the fate of a variant that fixes in a community of $N = 40$ speakers. Initially half of the speakers use the variant categorically; the remainder uses a variant that goes extinct. The heavy solid line shows how the frequency with which a speaker from the first subgroup uses the ultimately successful variant evolves over time. Likewise, the heavy broken line shows the usage frequency of that variant for a speaker who initially does not use it (and, therefore, rises from zero). Both heavy curves are running averages of underlying rapidly fluctuating data, shown in light gray. Vertical dotted lines delineate three phases: an early phase where usage frequencies converge; an intermediate phase where both speakers are variable in their usage; and a final phase where the unsuccessful variant is eliminated.

all of the H_{ij} weights equal). Again, there is an initial phase where usage of both variants spreads rapidly across the entire community, even if initially these usages are geographically dispersed. After this phase, speakers exhibit variability, a feature that was observed in the first native generation of New Zealand English speakers (Gordon et al., 2004). In the above simple case, it is perhaps obvious that there is a 50% chance that variant α goes to fixation, as initially half the population used it. We have found that, on any network, the neutral weighting implies that the fixation probability of a variant is equal to its initial frequency. Therefore, variants initially in the majority are more likely to fix, as observed by Trudgill (2004). The stochastic nature of the model means that minority variants may also fix, and as we have argued elsewhere (Baxter et al., 2009), the observed outcome (two minority variants going to fixation) is consistent with predictions of the USM with only neutral interactor selection operating.

What this model does not account for is the rapid convergence onto the use of a single conventional variant across the entire community. The origin of this discrepancy lies in the second phase of the process, during which competing variants are used variably. As there is, by assumption, nothing to choose between these variants, nor the speakers who happen to use them, the variant frequencies fluctuate in both directions until such time that, by chance, one of them has gone extinct. In a large population, more tokens of a given variant are uttered than in a small one; therefore, the time taken for a variant to go extinct by chance increases with the size of the community, and it is this fact that leads to the model predicting a convergence time for New Zealand English being much longer than the observed 40–50 years (Baxter et al., 2009).

More precisely, the USM in general predicts that on average fixation will occur after I/λ^2 interactions, where I is a number that depends on the community size, interaction frequencies and strengths, and the initial frequency of the successful variant. It is here that we have to interpret the meaning of parameters like λ and H_{ij}. Our strategy is to return to the "bag of balls" picture described earlier and relate the time a ball (token) remains in the bag (store) to the parameter λ. We find (Baxter et al., 2009) that, as a fraction of a speaker's lifetime (which we take to be 50 years), this lifetime is given by the formula

$$t_{mem} = \frac{-\ln \varepsilon}{\sqrt{GI(T^*/T)}}, \tag{1}$$

which takes into account that a speaker participates only in a fraction G of interactions, T^* tokens of a variable are uttered in a speaker's lifetime (T per interaction), and that once the probability of a token still being in the store has fallen below the value ε, it is deemed forgotten (we generally take ε to be 1%). Research on infants (Rovee-Collier, 1995) suggests that t_{mem} should be at least 2 days (and for adults, longer). The way to interpret this formula is to realize that any factor that exposes a speaker to greater variation (use of two or more variants) demands greater forgetfulness on the part of the speaker, so that a variant can go extinct by chance. These factors include interacting more frequently (larger G), slower rate of fixation (larger I), and more tokens of a variable being produced (larger T^*/T).

In the work of Baxter et al. (2009) it is shown that under the assumption of neutral interactor selection, $I > 0.46N^2T$ for *any* social network structure for a surviving variant whose initial frequency is 75%. This surprising network-independent result comes back to the fact that whereas the use of multiple variants can spread quickly through the community, fixation of a single one requires all speakers to coordinate by chance. Using $N = 100,000$ speakers, a suitable value for New Zealand at the onset of the new dialect formation process, the average value of $G = 2/N$ and $\varepsilon = 1\%$, we find the memory time exceeds the 2-day threshold for any variable that a speaker encounters less than about 800 times in her lifetime. Because the lowest token rate among the New Zealand variables analyzed by Gordon et al. (2004) was estimated as being at least 70 *per hour* (Baxter et al., 2009), we conclude that a model invoking only neutral interactor selection, which, in turn, is implied by Trudgill's (2004) theory, does not explain the rapid formation of the New Zealand English dialect. This motivates the study of stronger selection mechanisms (i.e., those that model social forces).

Weighted Interactor Selection

The next strongest selection mechanism, weighted interactor selection, admits greater weighting of a token at the time that it is produced (through social factors such as prestige, covert prestige, etc.) but does not permit that value to be conferred to the variant itself (and, e.g., being favored at times when the prestigious speaker is not the one producing the variant). In the USM, these effects are operationalized through the parameter H_{ij}.

This model can be used for sociolinguistic theories that differentiate *innovators* or *leaders* from followers or later adopters (Labov, 2001; Milroy & Milroy, 1985). Here, we will try out specific scenarios to see if weighted interactor selection alone can, in principle, reduce fixation times and explain the rapid convergence of the New Zealand English dialect or whether replicator selection is necessary.

We illustrate with a simple extension to the model of the previous section. We assign a fraction f of the N speakers to a *prestige* group but assume that regardless of what group a speaker is in, she participates in the same fraction of interactions and assigns the same weight to tokens produced by members of her own group. Where prestige enters is that members of the nonprestige group boost the weight H_{ij} by a factor $p > 1$ when interacting with a member of the prestige group. For mathematical convenience, we also assume a reciprocal $1/p$ weighting (a "stigma") ascribed to nonprestige utterances by prestige hearers.

Following the procedure of Baxter et al. (2009; see also Baxter et al., 2008), we find for this model the factor I appearing in formula 1 satisfies the relation

$$I > 0.46 N^2 T \frac{[fp^2 + (1 - f)]^2}{fp^4 + (1 - f)}, \tag{2}$$

again for a variant initially used with a frequency of 75% and for any network structure. What is interesting about this formula is that if the prestige factor is very large, fixation times are reduced (relative to the neutral interactor selection result) by the factor f; that is, if a small group enjoys high prestige, fixation times can be dramatically reduced, and hence it may become possible that the memory time given by formula 1 exceeds the 2-day threshold, and we are no longer required to reject the model.

For the lowest frequency variables relevant to the New Zealand English study ($T^* = 100,000$ and $1,000,000$) and the values of N and G used earlier ($N = 100,000$, $G = 2/N$), we plot in Figure 3 the range of values of f and p that correspond to a memory time of more than 2 days. For higher frequency variables (larger T^*) this region is much smaller. What is perhaps unexpected is a threshold on the size of the prestige group, which, if exceeded, implies a fixation time that leads to a memory time of less than 2 days regardless of how prestigious the prestige group is; that is, in order for prestige to speed up the process of language change, there needs to be a sufficiently large nonprestige group to be affected by it. This speed-up has been reported in a number of different models (Baxter et al., 2008; Blythe, 2007; Sood, Antal, & Redner, 2008; Sood & Redner, 2005). The common thread is that, as here, these models exhibit *heterogeneity* (i.e., large variation in network density, prestige, or other characteristics across the community). It might be worthwhile to determine empirically the extent to which this heterogeneity exists in reality.

We conclude this section by considering whether the simple prestige model here might explain the rapid convergence of the New Zealand English dialect. First, we notice from Figure 3 that a prestige factor p larger than about 4.25 is needed. The probability that a variant used by a member of the prestige group goes to fixation is p^2 larger than that for a variant used by a nonprestige speaker. If this prestige group can be identified with a set of immigrants from a particular region, all using a specific variant, that variant would be about 18 times more likely to succeed than one used with the same frequency by nonprestige speakers. This runs contrary to the observation that the majority variant typically fixed, not one that might be associated with a prestige group (Trudgill, 2004).

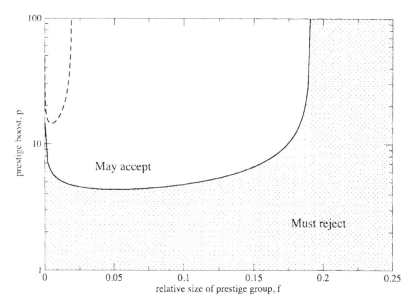

Figure 3 Application of the 2-day memory-window criterion to the simple model of prestige discussed in this section. With a token frequency $T^* = 100,000$, fixation of a variant within a single 50-year lifetime demands a token memory lifetime of less than 2 days for combinations of the size of the prestige group f (as a fraction of the whole community) and the prestige boost factor p within the shaded region. For these combinations, we argue that the model must be rejected as a potential explanation for rapid new-dialect formation. The dashed line shows the boundary of this region for the larger token frequency $T^* = 1,000,000$.

On the other hand, if prestige in the emergent New Zealand society became associated with speakers *independently* of which historical British or Irish variant(s) they happened to be using, all available variants are distributed among the prestige speakers. Then the fixation probability of a variant is once again equal to its initial frequency, as it was for neutral interactor selection, and hence compatible with the majority rule reported by Trudgill (2004). Meanwhile, the prestige-induced speed-up remains intact, as the prestige speakers still get to affect nonprestige speakers disproportionately.

There are, however, a couple of difficulties with this explanation for new-dialect formation. First, the bound in expression 2 applies when the interaction weight H_{ij} between speakers from the same group is very large. If this is decreased, I increases, and a correspondingly larger prestige value is needed to counteract this. Without relevant empirical data or a theoretical argument to constrain these weights, it becomes hard to decide whether an explana-tion motivated by a model is tenable. Furthermore, it appears that models of weighted interactor selection that are similar in spirit but differ in subtle techni-cal ways can lead to greatly extended fixation times due to *local leader* effects (Schneider-Mizell & Sander, 2009). In this context, a local leader is an individ-ual whose behavior is weakly affected by—but strongly affects—other members of a group. If contact between groups is mediated by nonleaders, adoption of one group's variant by another is inhibited due to the local leaders paying scant attention to individual group members. This, in turn, can be traced to the key property of weighted interactor selection: that biases like prestige are tied to speakers and do not travel with the variants they produce. Clearly, progress on three fronts—theory, empirical data gathering, and model analysis—is neces-sary to determine whether weighted interactor selection alone can account for instances of language change.

Discussion and Conclusion

In this work our aim has been to develop an understanding of the role that the speech community plays in evolutionary language dynamics. Our main tool has been a mathematical model, the USM. This model follows the usage-based approach: Speakers track the frequencies with which variants are used by members of their community and they base their own production frequencies by aggregating this information over many successive interactions. In this model, tokens that have more recently been heard have a stronger weight than those heard long in the past.

Using this model, we have investigated the consequences that different types of selection identified earlier have on the course of language change. Our methodology is to examine progressively stronger selection mechanisms and to ask whether these are sufficient to explain observed changes. Here, we have concentrated on the question of new-dialect formation, using data from New Zealand English.

A neutral evolution model, with no selection operating, accounts for the frequency effect (that the majority variant is most likely to spread). Neutral interactor selection reflects solely the effects of network structure on language change. Neutral interactor selection accounts for the high degree of variabil-ity at the first stage of new-dialect formation but not the speed at which a homogeneous new dialect is formed. The findings for weighted interactor se-lection, using a model with a subset of leaders (the prestige group) whose language use is selected by the remaining members of the community, are less clear-cut. A variant initially used by a prestige group may be adopted by the wider community, and rapidly too; however, it requires a strong disparity between both the size of the prestige and nonprestige groups and the weights associated with their utterances. The observation that apparently minor changes to the interactor weights can have profound effects on fixation times suggests that one cannot be too confident about a model whose parameters are (currently at least) rather unconstrained.

The conflict of demands for rapid convergence and neutrality within the initial population of variants points us toward a mechanism for language change based around replicator selection—that is, a fitness value that becomes attached to the ultimately successful variants. If this fitness is applied according to variant frequencies at some early time, the selected variants can then easily be brought to fixation in the available time (this is a classical fitness model from population genetics; see, e.g., Ewens, 2004). One possibility is if the prestige initially associated with certain individuals is then transferred to variants they use frequently. We believe this is an interesting proposition for future research.

Revised version accepted 15 June 2009

References

Baxter, G., Blythe, R. A., Croft, W., & McKane, A. J. (2006). Utterance selection model of language change. *Physical Review E, 73*, 046118.

Baxter, G., Blythe, R. A., Croft, W., & McKane, A. J. (2009). Modeling language change: An evaluation of Trudgill's theory of the emergence of New Zealand English. *Language Variation and Change, 21*, 257–296.

Baxter, G., Blythe, R. A., & McKane, A. J. (2008). Fixation and consensus times on a network: A unified approach. *Physical Review Letters, 101*, 258701.

Blythe, R. A. (2007). The propagation of a cultural or biological trait by neutral genetic drift in a subdivided population. *Theoretical Population Biology, 71*, 454–472.

Bybee, J. L. (2001). *Phonology and language use.* Cambridge: Cambridge University Press.

Bybee, J. L. (2007). *Frequency of use and the organization of language.* Oxford: Oxford University Press.

Castellano, C., Fortunato, S., & Loreto, V. (2007). Statistical physics of social dynamics. *Reviews of Modern Physics, 81*, 591–646.

Clifford, P., & Sudbury, A. (1973). A model for spatial conflict. *Biometrika, 60*, 581–588.

Croft, W. (2000). *Explaining language change: An evolutionary approach.* Harlow, UK: Longman.

Croft, W. (2009). Toward a social cognitive linguistics. In V. Evans & S. Pourcel (Eds.), *New directions in cognitive linguistics* (pp. 395–420). Amsterdam: Benjamins.

Croft, W. (2010). The origins of grammaticalization in the verbalization of experience. *Linguistics, 48*.

Crow, J. F., & Kimura, M. (1970). *Introduction to population genetics theory*. New York: Harper and Row.

Dawkins, R. (1989). *The selfish gene* (New ed.). New York: Oxford University Press.

Delli Gatti, D., Gaffeo, E., Gallegati, M., Giulioni, G., Kirman, A., Palestrini, A. et al. (2007). Complex dynamics and empirical evidence. *Information Sciences, 177*, 1204–1221.

Ellis, N. C., & Larsen-Freeman, D. (2006). Language emergence: Implications for applied linguistics. *Applied Linguistics, 27*, 559–589.

Ewens, W. J. (2004). *Mathematical population genetics: 1. Theoretical introduction.* (2nd ed.). New York: Springer.

Gordon, E., Campbell, L., Hay, J., MacLagan, M., Sudbury, A., & Trudgill, P. (2004). *New Zealand English: Its origins and evolution*. Cambridge: Cambridge University Press.

Helbing, D., Johansson A., & Al-Abideen, H. Z. (2007). The dynamics of crowd disasters: An empirical study. *Physical Review E, 75*, 046109.

Hull, D. L. (1988). *Science as a process: An evolutionary account of the social and conceptual development of science.* Chicago: University of Chicago Press.

Hull, D. L. (2001). *Science and selection: Essays on biological evolution and the philosophy of science.* Cambridge: Cambridge University Press.

Ke, J., & Holland, J. H. (2006). Language origin from an emergentist perspective. *Applied Linguistics, 27*, 691–716.

Knospe, W., Santen, L., Schadschneider, A., & Schreckenberg, M. (2004). Empirical test for cellular automaton models of traffic flow. *Physical Review E, 70*, 016115.

Labov, W. (2001). *Principles of linguistic change. II. Social factors.* Oxford: Basil Blackwell.

Langacker, R. W. (1988). A usage-based model. In B. Rudzka-Ostyn (Ed.), *Topics in cognitive linguistics* (pp. 127–161). Amsterdam: Benjamins.

Milroy, J., & Milroy, L. (1985). Linguistic change, social network and speaker innovation. *Journal of Linguistics, 21*, 339–384.

Rovee-Collier, C. (1995). Time windows in cognitive development. *Developmental Psychology, 31*, 147–165.

Schneider-Mizell, C. M., & Sander, L. (2009). A generalized voter model on complex networks. *Journal of Statistical Physics, 136*, 59–71. Retrieved from http://arxiv.org/abs/0804.1269

Smith, K., Kirby, S., & Brighton, H. (2003). Iterated learning: A framework for the evolution of language. *Artificial Life, 9*, 371–386.

Sood, V., & Redner, S. (2005). Voter model on heterogeneous graphs. *Physical Review Letters, 94*, 178701.

Sood, V., Antal, T., & Redner, S. (2008). Voter models on heterogeneous networks. *Physical Review E, 77*, 041121.

Steels, L. (2000). Language as a complex adaptive system. In M. Schoenauer et al. (Eds.), *Parallel problem solving from nature PPSN VI* (Lecture Notes in Computer Science Vol. 1917, pp. 17 26). Berlin: Springer.

Trudgill, P. (1986). *Dialects in contact*. Oxford: Basil Blackwell.

Trudgill, P. (2004). *New-dialect formation: The inevitability of colonial Englishes*. Edinburgh: Edinburgh University Press.

Language Learning   ISSN 0023-8333

Linking Rule Acquisition in Novel Phrasal Constructions

Jeremy K. Boyd

Princeton University

Erin A. Gottschalk

Princeton University

Adele E. Goldberg

Princeton University

All natural languages rely on sentence-level form-meaning associations (i.e., linking rules) to encode propositional content about who did what to whom. Although these associations are recognized as foundational in many different theoretical frameworks (Goldberg, 1995, 2006; Lidz, Gleitman, & Gleitman, 2003; Pinker, 1984, 1989) and are—at least in principle—learnable (Allen, 1997; Morris, Cottrell, & Elman, 2000), very little empirical work has been done to establish that human participants are able to acquire them from the input. In the present work, we provided adult participants with 3 min worth of exposure to a novel syntactic construction and then tested to see what was learned. Experiment 1 established that participants are able to accurately deploy newly acquired linking rules in a forced-choice comprehension task, and that constructional knowledge largely persists over a 1-week period. In Experiment 2, participants were exposed to the linking rules immanent in one of two novel constructions and were asked to describe novel events using their exposure construction. The data indicate that participants were successful in using their exposure construction's linking rules in production, and that performance was equally good regardless of the specifics of the target linking pattern. These results indicate that linking rules can be learned relatively easily by adults, which, in turn, suggests that children may also be capable of learning them directly from the input.

Correspondence concerning this article should be addressed to Jeremy K. Boyd or Adele E. Goldberg, Department of Psychology, Green Hall, Princeton University, Princeton, NJ 08544. Internet: jkboyd@princeton.edu or adele@princeton.edu

Introduction

Grammar allows speakers to encode and decode semantic relationships in sentences—to identify who did what to whom—in a number of ways. For a transitive event in which an agent acts on a patient, for example, English links the agent to the subject position of an active sentence and links the patient to the object. Likewise, in Latin, the same agent-patient relationship is signaled through the use of nominative case marking on the agent and accusative case marking on the patient. The grammatical knowledge that underlies these sorts of syntax-semantics mappings goes by various names: linking rules (Pinker, 1984, 1989), mapping principles (Lidz, Gleitman, & Gleitman, 2003), or argument structure constructions (Goldberg, 1995, 2006). And, although there is widespread agreement that mapping knowledge is deployed in online sentence production (Ferreira & Slevc, 2007; Levelt, 1989) and comprehension (McRae, Spivey-Knowlton, & Tanenhaus, 1998), there is substantial disagreement concerning its origins.

According to *nativist* mapping theories, syntax-semantics associations exist as part of an inborn linguistic endowment known as Universal Grammar (UG; Baker, 1988; Lidz et al., 2003; Pinker, 1984, 1989); that is, speakers' linguistic competence includes knowledge of linking rules because they are *born* with knowledge of linking rules. In contrast, *constructionist* theories propose that mapping generalizations are *learned* from the input, with learning constrained by pragmatics, categorization principles, attentional biases, and other domain-general factors (Casenhiser & Goldberg, 2005; Goldberg, 2004; Morris, Cottrell, & Elman, 2000; Perfors, Kemp, Tenenbaum, & Wonnacott, 2007; Tomasello, 2003). Both of these approaches agree that syntax-semantics mappings are subject to constraints and biases. They disagree, however, concerning the locus of these constraints—whether they are innate and specific to language or whether they emerge from domain-general cognitive processes.

Nativist mapping theories are attractive in that they provide a straightforward way to account for certain crosslinguistic tendencies in argument realization. For example, prominent semantic arguments (e.g., agents) tend to be expressed in prominent syntactic positions (e.g., subject position). Moreover, nativist mapping approaches have played a large role in the literature on semantic and syntactic bootstrapping. Both of these theories assume preexisting mapping knowledge that children use to guide grammatical and word learning (Landau & Gleitman, 1985; Pinker, 1984, 1989). In Pinker's work, for instance, learners bootstrap into the grammar by associating semantic categories like agent and patient with syntactic categories like subject and object. These associations are specified in innate linking rules, which are predicted to have a uniform effect across all normally developing children learning any of the world's languages. Unfortunately, however, Pinker provides no evidence to indicate that an innate mapping account should be preferred to an account in which mappings are constrained by domain-general factors (e.g., Goldberg, 2004, 2006). Instead, the hypothesis that linking rules are innately specified in UG is treated as an assumption that is required to get grammar learning off the ground.

Naigles, Gleitman, and Gleitman (1993) called this sort of postulate the "weakest link" in semantic and syntactic bootstrapping proposals and write that because

> some of these correspondence [linking] rules vary cross-linguistically . . . it is not possible to say that the learner is provided with all of them by nature—as part of the language faculty . . . . Clearly the topic of how correspondence [linking] rules develop cries out for investigation, and has not been resolved or even addressed by us. (pp. 136–137)

Along the same lines, Bowerman (1990) offers a critique of nativist mapping theories in which she notes that because the syntax-semantics associations that are present in many of the world's constructions violate putative innate linking rules, nativist theories must posit a learning mechanism to acquire noncanonical linkings. Because the learning mechanism would compete against a UG bias that favors the innate linking patterns, this predicts that noncanonical constructions should be acquired later by children. As Bowerman noted, however, naturalistic corpus data fail to support this prediction.

Although this sort of finding tends to suggest that nativist mapping theories are less than empirically adequate, it is not the case that learning theories are able to offer a perfectly convincing story about the development of mapping generalizations either. The emphasis from constructionists has been on the conservative nature of children's early learning, with demonstrations focusing on children's failure to generalize beyond the input until they have been exposed to a vast amount of data at age 3.5 or beyond (Akhtar & Tomasello, 1997; Braine, 1976; Ingram & Thompson, 1996; Lieven, Pine, & Baldwin, 1997; for reviews, see Tomasello, 2000, 2003). The implication of this work is that constructions must be learned, because they are acquired so late and in such a piecemeal fashion.

Likewise, a number of computational models have demonstrated that constructions and the mapping generalizations that they specify are, *in principle*, learnable from the input without the need for specifically linguistic constraints

(Allen, 1997; Morris et al., 2000). However, although these models suggest that children can learn mapping generalizations—as does the data on children's early conservative behavior—they do not conclusively prove that this is the case. Such a conclusion would be bolstered by studies that demonstrate actual construction learning in a controlled experimental setting. There has, however, been precious little work along these lines, and the studies that have addressed this issue have not definitively demonstrated that participants learn to associate specific syntactic positions with specific semantic arguments.

The current work builds on a series of earlier studies in the area of novel construction learning (Casenhiser & Goldberg, 2005; Goldberg, Casenhiser, & Sethuraman, 2004; Goldberg, Casenhiser, & White, 2007). In these experiments, adults and 6-year-olds were exposed to a phrasal construction that paired a novel *form* with a novel *meaning* (cf. studies in which only the form is novel: Akhtar, 1999; Ambridge, Theakston, Lieven, & Tomasello, 2006; Wonnacott, Newport, & Tanenhaus, 2008). In a subsequent forced-choice comprehension task, both groups proved able to distinguish new instances of the novel construction from known construction types. Learning was very fast—participants received only 3 min of exposure, which is reminiscent of fast mapping in word learning (Carey & Bartlett, 1978)—and, interestingly, acquisition was facilitated when participants were exposed to a low-variance input sample centered around a particular novel verb. This effect has been observed in nonlinguistic learning (Elio & Anderson, 1984; Posner, Goldsmith, & Welton, 1967), is consistent with an underlying general-purpose learning mechanism (Borovsky & Elman, 2006; Perfors et al., 2007), and is potentially quite useful in language development, as many constructions are represented by a handful of high-frequency exemplars in the input, which presumably form a low-variance nucleus that seeds category development (Ellis & Ferreira-Junior, 2009; Goldberg et al., 2004; Zipf, 1935).

One important limitation of this earlier work was that it did not explore whether learners acquired mapping knowledge that links specific semantic arguments to specific syntactic positions: The results are consistent with participants having learned the novel construction as a global gestalt, without having attached any particular significance to the semantic roles being played by its different nominals. The current work addresses this shortcoming in two experiments with adult learners. The experiments rely on a new comprehension measure (Experiment 1) and a production task (Experiment 2) to assess whether the specifics of constructional linking rules have been acquired. They additionally explore three other issues: whether novel constructions—like natural language constructions—are stored in long-term memory (Experiment 1); whether the learning process is biased such that some constructions are easier to learn than others (Experiment 2); and whether novel constructions count as real language (Experiments 1 and 2).

Experiment 1

The primary goal of Experiment 1 was to investigate whether syntax-semantics mappings can be learned when participants are given brief exposure to a novel syntactic construction. After exposure, participants were asked to listen to brand new exemplars of the construction and choose which of two movies depicted its meaning. Crucially, the movies demonstrated reversible actions, and so specific mapping knowledge was required for above-chance performance.

A secondary goal of Experiment 1 was to determine whether the knowledge that participants obtain from exposure to a novel construction can be maintained over time. If the constructional knowledge that is acquired is short-lived, then this would seem to go against a category-based learning account (e.g., Goldberg et al., 2007), because memory traces of experience with constructional exemplars need to be stored to form the basis of an abstract constructional category. In order to determine whether memory for novel constructions is maintained over time, we tested participants' comprehension immediately following exposure, and at a 1-week lag.

Participants
Thirty-two undergraduate native speakers of English were recruited from the Princeton University Department of Psychology subject pool and took part in Experiment 1 in exchange for course credit. Each participant was randomly assigned to either an experimental condition or a control condition.

Novel Construction
The construction that participants in the experimental condition were exposed to describes events in which objects appear at a location, and takes the form $NP_1 NP_2 V$, where NP_1 is the appearing object (the *theme*), NP_2 is the location at which NP_1 appears (the *locative*), and V is a nonce verb that describes a manner of appearance. The sentence *The bird the flower moopos*, for example, signifies an event in which a bird (the theme) magically fades into view on top of a flower (the locative).

All instantiations of the novel construction that were used in the present experiment paired two English definite NPs (e.g., *the bird* and *the flower*) with a verb ending in –*o* (e.g., *moopo*). Previous work using this paradigm has indicated that constructional acquisition is facilitated when learners are given morphological cues to construction meaning on the verb (Casenhiser & Goldberg, 2005). Note, however, that whereas the –*o* suffix may help participants identify the sentences that they hear as belonging to the class of constructions signifying appearance, it carries no information about which NP is the theme and which is the locative. In order to learn about these features of the novel construction, participants must instead attend to word order cues.

Twenty-eight exemplars of the novel construction were generated for use in Experiment 1. Participants were familiarized with 16 of these in an initial *exposure* block. In the following *test* block, their comprehension ability was tested on 12 new exemplars of the construction. Crucially, there was no lexical overlap between the constructional exemplars in the two blocks—that is, an entirely new set of nouns and verbs was used in the test block items. This means that in order for participants to do well at test, they could not rely on lexically specific details of the novel construction, but instead had to depend on its more abstract features.

Exposure

Participants in the experimental condition were exposed to the novel construction in the context of 16 short, computer-animated movies. Each movie began by showing a construction's locative argument at the center of the screen. The participant then heard a present tense exemplar of the novel construction (e.g., *The bird the flower moopos*). Following this, the construction's theme argument magically appeared at the location. The movie then ended with a final past tense exemplar of the construction (e.g., *The bird the flower moopoed*). Figure 1 provides a storyboard for an exposure movie. All exposure movies were approximately 12 s in duration.

Previous work on the learning of both novel and attested constructions has shown that acquisition is facilitated when the overall similarity of the constructional exemplars used during exposure is increased (i.e., when variance in the input sample is decreased; Casenhiser & Goldberg, 2005; Goldberg et al., 2004, 2007; Maguire, Hirsh-Pasek, Golinkoff, & Brandone, 2008). In order to take advantage of this feature of the learning mechanism in the present experiment, the overall similarity of the items in the exposure block was increased in the following way. Five different novel verbs (*moopo*, *feigo*, *suuto*, *vako*, and *keybo*) were used in the constructions that occurred in exposure movies, but their token frequencies were skewed so that *moopo* was used in half of the exposure movies (i.e., eight) and the remaining four verbs were evenly divided among

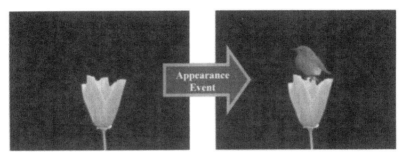

"The bird the flower moopos."   "The bird the flower moopoed."

Figure 1 In the exposure block, participants viewed short movies in which present and past tense exemplars of the novel construction were paired with on-screen appearance events (e.g., a bird magically fading into view on top of a flower, as in the before-and-after frames shown here).

the remaining eight exposure movies. This type of input is ecologically valid, as tokens of argument structure constructions are typically overrepresented by examples involving a particular verb (Ellis & Ferreira-Junior, 2009; Goldberg, 2006; Goldberg et al., 2004; Zipf, 1935).

Each verb in the exposure movies was associated with a distinct manner of appearance. The different manners all had a magical quality, in that there was never an obvious causal agent associated with the appearance act. *Moopo*, for example, described appearance events in which the theme argument faded into view, whereas *keybo* described events in which the theme appeared from behind a cloud of sparkles.

A control condition was included in Experiment 1 to verify that good performance at test in the experimental condition was due to learning that occurred as a result of exposure to the novel construction. The control condition featured the same movies used in the experimental condition, but with the novel construction replaced by voiceovers in which the theme and locative arguments were named, in turn, by nouns. Each control participant viewed half of the 16 exposure movies paired with theme-locative utterances (e.g., *bird . . . flower*) and the other half paired with locative-theme utterances (e.g., *flower . . . bird*). This ensured that the control condition's voiceovers were related to what was shown in the movies, but that there was no consistent mapping pattern available to be learned. The order of argument presentation was additionally counterbalanced across participants so that, for example, the movie shown in Figure 1 occurred with *bird . . . flower* for half of the control participants and with *flower . . . bird* for the other half.

Testing

Test trials contained three elements: a voiceover consisting of a new sentence that had not been heard during exposure, and two movies played simultaneously side-by-side—a target movie and a distractor. The target movie depicted the event described by the voiceover sentence, and the distractor movie depicted an alternative event. For each test trial, participants were instructed to listen to the voiceover sentence and then point to the movie that matched it. Test movies looped indefinitely, and participants were instructed to watch them as many times as necessary before responding. Correct responses were points to the target movie; incorrect responses were points to the distractor movie.

The test block contained three different trial types: appearance, transitive, and mapping. In *appearance* trials, the voiceover was an exemplar of the novel construction (e.g., *The frog the apple zoopos*). This sentence occurred with a target movie depicting an appearance event (e.g., a frog appearing on an apple) and a distractor movie depicting a transitive event (e.g., a frog pushing an apple). *Transitive* trials were structurally identical to appearance trials, except that now the voiceover featured a transitive sentence with a novel verb (e.g., *The dog zats the chair*). The target movie showed a transitive event (e.g., a dog pushing a chair), and the distractor movie showed an appearance event (e.g., a dog appearing on a chair). Transitive trials served as a control to ensure that good performance on appearance trials did not occur because participants had a general preference for appearance movies. Figure 2 gives examples of appearance and transitive trials.

Although above-chance performance on both appearance and transitive trials would indicate that participants who received brief exposure to the novel construction are able to distinguish it, formally and semantically, from a known construction type, this would not guarantee that mappings from specific syntactic positions to specific semantic arguments (i.e., linking rules) had been learned. In order to get at this question, Experiment 1 also featured *mapping* trials. These had the same tripartite structure as transitive and appearance trials, but utilized reversible events that made above-chance performance impossible in the absence of linking rules. Figure 3 shows an example mapping trial.

Over the course of the test block, each participant saw six appearance trials, six mapping trials, and six transitive trials, with nine target movies appearing on the left and nine appearing on the right. For both appearance and mapping trials, the exemplars of the novel construction that participants heard contained no nouns or verbs that had been seen during the exposure block. This ensured that correct responding could only occur on the basis of constructional

"The frog the apple moopos."

"The dog zats the chair."

Figure 2 In appearance trials (top panel), participants heard the novel construction and viewed simultaneously displayed movies showing an appearance target (e.g., a frog magically appearing on an apple, left) and a transitive distractor (e.g., a frog pushing an apple, right). In transitive trials (bottom panel), participants heard a transitive construction and viewed simultaneously displayed movies showing a transitive target (e.g., a dog pushing a chair, right) and an appearance distractor (e.g., a dog magically appearing on a chair, left).

representations that abstracted over the item-specific details of the exposure exemplars.

Procedure

Participants were tested individually. At the beginning of the exposure block, each participant was instructed to pay attention to the exposure movies. They then viewed all 16 movies in different random orders.

At the beginning of the test block, participants were instructed to listen to the voiceover sentences in the test trials and to point to the onscreen movie that depicted the event described in the sentence. They were additionally encouraged to view each test trial as many times as necessary before responding (i.e., before pointing to one movie or the other).

Figure 3 In mapping trials, participants heard the novel construction and viewed simultaneously displayed movies showing reversible appearance events. Given the sentence *The hamster the lizard maytos*, for example, participants would choose between a movie in which a hamster magically appeared on top of a lizard (the target, left) and a movie in which a lizard magically appeared on top of a hamster (the distracter, right).

The 18 test trials were divided into two halves, with each half balanced in terms of the number of appearance, transitive, and mapping trials it contained. Each half started with a set of randomly interleaved transitive and appearance trials (three of each) and ended with three randomly ordered mapping trials. For each test item, the half in which it appeared was counterbalanced across participants. Participants in the control condition were administered both halves back-to-back, immediately after the exposure block. For experimental participants however, one half was administered immediately after exposure and the other was administered after a 1-week interval. Test instructions were repeated before testing in the 1-week session.

Results

We performed two analyses over the data. The first aimed to determine whether exposure to the novel construction in the experimental condition led to better performance at test relative to controls. Because participants in the experimental group were tested at two lags—immediately after exposure and at a 1-week delay—whereas participants in the control group were tested at the immediate lag only, we excluded all of the experimental group's 1-week data from the comparison between the two groups. This eliminated test lag as a potential confound. Mean percent correct scores were calculated on a participant-by-participant basis from the remaining data, and are summarized by condition and trial type in Table 1.

The Table 1 means were submitted to a 2 × 3 ANOVA with condition (control vs. experimental) as a between-participants variable and trial type

Table 1 Mean percent correct by condition and trial type

	Condition	
Trial type	Control	Experimental
Transitive	83.33	87.50
Appearance	45.83	81.25
Mapping	42.71	75.00

(transitive vs. appearance vs. mapping) as a within-participants variable. The results show a main effect of condition, $F(1, 30) = 15.87$, $p < .001$, demonstrating that experimental participants did learn on the basis of brief exposure. There was, additionally, a main effect of trial type, $F(2, 60) = 6.43$, $p < .01$, and a marginal interaction of condition and trial type, $F(2, 60) = 2.37$, $p = .10$, suggesting that the effect of condition may not have been equivalent across the different types of test trials. To investigate this possibility, a series of two-tailed Welch t tests—which correct for unequal group variances by adjusting the degrees of freedom—was conducted. As expected, participants in the control and experimental groups performed similarly when tested on the already familiar transitive construction, $t(29.52) = -0.52$, $p = .61$, but the experimental group outperformed controls on both appearance trials, $t(29.97) = -3.31$, $p < .01$, and mapping trials, $t(29.06) = -2.40$, $p = .02$. This pattern of results is depicted graphically in Figure 4. Equivalent performance on transitive trials presumably reflects similar levels of experience with the transitive construction. The experimental group's significantly better performance on appearance and mapping trials, however, suggests a positive effect of exposure to the novel construction (i.e., learning).

We additionally evaluated each of the cells in the design relative to chance. The six means specified in Table 1 were compared to a hypothesized mean of 50% using a series of two-tailed t tests. The results show that transitive trials were statistically above chance in both the control group, $t(15) = 6.32$, $p < .0001$, and the experimental group, $t(15) = 6.26$, $p < .0001$. In contrast, controls were at chance on both types of trials that required knowledge of the novel construction [appearance: $t(15) = -0.54$, $p = .60$; mapping: $t(15) = -0.85$, $p = .41$], whereas experimental participants were above chance on the same trials [appearance: $t(15) = 4.20$, $p < .001$; mapping: $t(15) = 2.42$, $p = .02$]. Together with the paired t test results reported here, this outcome demonstrates learning in the experimental condition that is sufficient to distinguish the experimental group both from controls, and from chance.

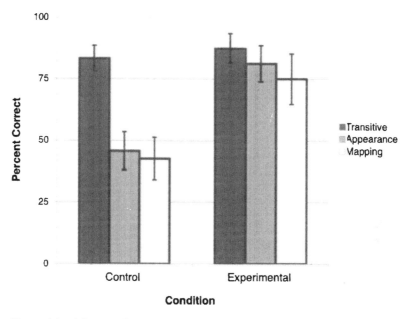

Figure 4 Participant performance on transitive, appearance, and mapping trials in the control and experimental conditions. Error bars show the standard error of the mean.

Our second analysis of the Experiment 1 data aimed to evaluate whether participants' knowledge of the novel construction persisted significantly beyond exposure. To answer this question, we calculated mean percent correct scores for each of the experimental participants according to trial type and test lag. A summary of the relevant means is given in Table 2.

Participants were submitted to a 2 × 3 ANOVA, with test lag (immediate vs. 1 week) and trial type (transitive vs. appearance vs. mapping) as within-participants factors. The results show a main effect of trial type,

Table 2 Mean percent correct by test lag and trial type

Trial type	Test lag	
	Immediate	1-Week
Transitive	87.50	97.92
Appearance	81.25	87.50
Mapping	75.00	66.67

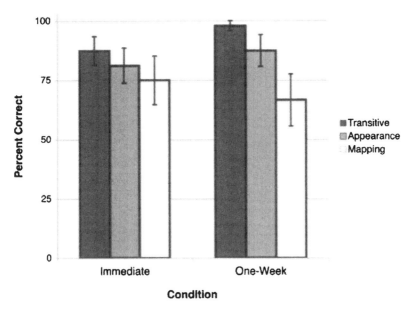

Figure 5 Participant performance on transitive, appearance, and mapping trials immediately after exposure and at a 1-week delay. Error bars show the standard error of the mean.

$F(2, 30) = 3.44$, $p = .045$, with participants performing best on transitive trials, then appearance trials, then mapping trials, and a null effect of test lag, $F(1, 15) = 0.15$, $p = 0.71$, suggesting that there was no overall decrement in performance from immediate testing to testing 1 week later. Additionally, there was a null interaction of test lag and trial type, $F(2, 30) = 1.29$, $p = 0.29$, which is consistent with the notion that there was no decrement in performance from the immediate to 1-week lags, even when considering the different trial types individually. Figure 5 summarizes these results.

Although the null effect of test lag combined with the null interaction suggests that constructional knowledge did not decay over the 1-week period, even when broken down by trial type, we felt that it was important to evaluate performance in each of the cells of the design according to chance. To this end, the Table 2 means were compared to a hypothesized mean of 50% using a series of two-tailed t tests. As noted previously, this analysis showed above-chance performance on all trial types when testing was conducted immediately after exposure. When testing was conduced at a 1-week lag, however, transitive and appearance trials were still above chance [transitive: $t(15) = 23$,

$p < .0001$; appearance: $t(15) = 5.58$, $p < .0001$], but mapping performance was not statistically above chance, $t(15) = 1.52$, $p = .15$. This suggests that the specifics of syntax-semantics mappings may in fact decay if not reinforced.

Experiment 1 Discussion

The experimental group in Experiment 1 performed reliably better than the control group on exactly those trials that tested knowledge of the novel construction. This outcome replicates the finding from previous studies that even brief exposure to a novel construction can have a facilitatory effect (Casenhiser & Goldberg, 2005; Goldberg et al., 2004). It significantly extends this line of work, however, by documenting above-chance performance on mapping trials—a trial type that had not been used in previous work. Crucially, these trials required participants to associate an exemplar of the novel construction to one of two reversible appearance events. That participants were able to correctly do so at above-chance levels is most straightforwardly explained by their ability to rapidly acquire linking rules that map the first NP of the novel construction to its theme argument, and the second NP to its locative argument. The present study thus provides the first demonstration that the linking rules associated with a novel construction can be quickly and accurately learned from the input.

The present results additionally bear on the question of how long-lasting the knowledge acquired through brief exposure to a novel construction is. We find that the *general* association of $NP_1 NP_2 V$ forms with appearance events is robust after 1 week, both when compared to performance at the immediate lag and when compared to chance. At the same time, although direct comparison between mapping trial performance at the immediate and 1-week lags showed no significant difference, we found that only performance at the immediate lag was statistically above chance. Note that specific constructional knowledge in the form of linking rules is presumably more difficult to learn than the general association between $NP_1 NP_2 V$ forms and appearance events. Linking rules are not mastered immediately in naturalistic first language learning (Tomasello, 2000), and they are likely difficult to learn robustly in the present experiment, in which exposure to the novel construction was, by design, quite limited. Having to acquire more detailed knowledge over a very brief time period may have led to incomplete learning or to the acquisition of complete representations that were less entrenched and, therefore, not as stable over time. These less robust representations may have been sufficient to support above-chance performance on mapping trials at the immediate lag but not at the 1-week lag. Further testing is required to determine what kinds of exposure conditions are necessary to support the development of linking rules that are more persistent over time.

Experiment 2

The question of whether linking rules are learned can also be addressed using a production measure. In Experiment 2, participants were given brief exposure to one of two novel appearance constructions and were then asked to describe entirely new appearance events using their exposure construction. If participants are able to quickly associate specific semantic arguments with specific syntactic positions, then they should produce their exposure construction's two arguments in a fixed, nonrandom order that mirrors the input that they received. Such behavior would constitute important corroborating evidence in favor of the argument that linking rules can be quickly learned.

Experiment 2 additionally provides data bearing on *flexibility* in the acquisition of linking rules, in that the two novel constructions that participants were exposed to had identical meanings but different linking patterns. If participants perform similarly on both constructions at test, then this would suggest that the learning mechanism is able to flexibly acquire different sorts of linking rules in a very short time. Alternatively, if one construction outperforms the other, then this may be evidence that some sort of bias is operative in linking rule development.

Finally, the presence of good production abilities in Experiment 2 would place on much firmer footing the argument that novel constructions count as real language, and that the type of learning that participants are undertaking in novel construction learning paradigms is specifically linguistic. If Experiment 2's participants can use a novel construction to describe new events, then this—along with the comprehension data from Experiment 1—would demonstrate that novel constructions are functionally equivalent to natural language constructions.

Participants
Seventy-two adult native speakers of English were recruited from the Princeton University Department of Psychology subject pool and participated in Experiment 2 in exchange for course credit. They were randomly assigned in equal numbers to control, theme-locative-verb, or locative-theme-verb conditions.

Novel Constructions
Experiment 2 utilized two novel constructions. In the theme-locative-verb (TLV) condition, participants received brief exposure to the same $NP_1 NP_2 V$

construction used in Experiment 1, in which NP_1 mapped to the construction's theme argument and NP_2 mapped to its locative argument. In the locative-theme-verb (LTV) condition, participants received exposure to roughly the same construction, but with the linking pattern reversed so that NP_1 now mapped to the locative argument and NP_2 mapped to the theme.

The experiment made use of eight exemplars of the TLV construction and eight exemplars of the LTV construction, which were created by reversing the order of the two NPs in the TLV exemplars.

Exposure Movies

The exposure movies used in Experiment 2 followed the same format shown in Figure 1—a present tense exemplar of a novel construction, followed by an onscreen appearance event, followed by the same exemplar in the past tense. The Experiment 2 movies, however, differed from those used in Experiment 1 in that they were live-action (not computer animated) and were fewer in number. In Experiment 1, participants had 16 exposure trials and saw different movies on each trial. Experiment 2 also had 16 trials, but now each participant saw eight different movies shown twice each in random order. These changes did not result in noticeably different learning outcomes and were implemented solely in order to make the results of Experiment 2 more directly comparable with the results of other studies using the same paradigm (e.g., Casenhiser & Goldberg, 2005; Goldberg et al., 2004).

Additionally, the same frequency structure from Experiment 1 was adopted in Experiment 2: Half of the constructional tokens seen during exposure featured the nonce verb *moopo*, whereas the remaining tokens were evenly divided among four other verbs (*feigo*, *suuto*, *vako*, and *keybo*).

Control participants in Experiment 2 watched the same movies that participants in the TLV and LTV conditions did, but with noun-noun voiceovers that consisted of a theme argument followed by a locative argument in half of the trials, and the opposite order in the other half. As in Experiment 1, this ensured that no consistent linking patterns were extractable from the input in the control condition.

Production Trials

Immediately after the exposure block, participants took part in a production block in which they were shown a series of novel appearance events in the context of magic tricks performed by the experimenter, and were asked to describe the tricks using the "same kinds of sentences" heard during exposure. For each trick, the experimenter first introduced the items used in the trick—a theme item and a locative item. The theme item was then hidden—out of the participant's view—inside the locative item. Finally, the experimenter uttered *Abracadabra!*, and the theme item "magically" appeared from (or in) the locative item.

Three different tricks were used in the experiment, always in the same order: a handkerchief appeared from a cloth bag, a quarter appeared in a wooden box, and then a lollipop appeared from a different bag. The order in which the items used in each trick were introduced was counterbalanced across participants as a means of eliminating possible effects of introduction order.

Procedure

Participants were tested individually and took part in an exposure block followed by a production block. The exposure block began with instructions to pay attention to the exposure movies; participants then viewed 16 exposure movies in different random orders. Total exposure time was roughly 3 min.

For the production block, participants were instructed to provide descriptions for the magic tricks noted above using the "same kinds of sentences" seen during exposure. Participant utterances were audio-recorded for later coding and analysis.

Analysis and Results

For utterances produced by participants in the TLV and LTV conditions, our primary interest was in whether the linking rules associated with each construction had been learned. To this end, we coded the relative order in which the two NP arguments were produced. Utterances that consisted of a theme argument followed by a locative argument followed by a verb were coded as theme-before-locative (TL). Similarly, utterances that consisted of a locative argument followed by a theme argument followed by a verb were coded as locative-before-theme (LT). For a minority of utterances, participants either failed to produce both arguments, incorrectly realized arguments as PPs, or produced transitive SVO orders. All of these utterance types were coded as other (O).

The control group provides a baseline measure of participants' syntax-semantics mapping tendencies. Reliable deviations from this baseline in the TLV and LTV groups would indicate that significant learning of linking patterns had occurred. Because exposure in the control condition consisted of hearing the exposure movies described by noninformative noun-noun utterances, we treated all noun-noun combinations produced at test as potentially following the example set during exposure. Noun-noun combinations consisting of a theme followed by a locative were coded as TL. Noun-noun combinations consisting

Table 3 Frequency distribution of participants by condition and response type

	Response type		
Condition	Theme-before-locative (TL)	Locative-before-theme (LT)	Other (O)
TLV	20	3	1
LTV	3	12	9
Control	11	9	4

of a locative followed by a theme were coded as LT. Utterances that followed the noun-noun pattern but failed to mention both the theme and the locative arguments shown in a magic trick were coded as O. Likewise, all utterances that failed to follow the noun-noun pattern were coded as O. For the most part, these consisted either of normal English descriptions of the magic tricks (e.g., "The lollipop came out of the bag") or of descriptions that failed to indicate a preferred argument order (e.g., "Handkerchief bag . . . bag handkerchief").

To enable the use of nonparametric statistics, we then categorized all participants as either TL-responders, LT-responders, or O-responders based on the type of utterance produced on the majority of their test trials (i.e., on at least two out of their three trials). If, for example, a participant described the first magic trick that they saw with an LT utterance and the second and third magic tricks with TL utterances, they were coded as a TL-responder. This method of categorization was sufficient to classify 71 of the 72 participants in Experiment 2. The single remaining participant who produced one TL utterance, one LT utterance, and one O utterance was classified as an O-responder. The result of this categorization process was a frequency distribution of participants, organized according to condition and response type, as in Table 3.

In the analyses that follow, we employed Pearson's chi-squared test and Fisher's exact test to determine what kinds of patterns are discernable in the Table 3 data. The chi-squared test was used whenever all of the expected values in a contingency table analysis were at least 5. For all other cases, we relied on Fisher's exact test.

O-Responders

Before assessing whether participants in the TLV and LTV conditions were able to, with minimal input, learn the linking rules associated with their respective constructions, we first excluded O-responders from consideration. This was motivated by the possibility that O-responders may have based their utterances on an incorrect message-level interpretation of events. Transitive and intransitive productions, for instance, may reflect transitive and intransitive interpretations of the magic tricks shown at test, rather than the intended appearance interpretation (although see the General Discussion section for more discussion on transitive interpretations). This sort of analysis—the exclusion of data points that fail to follow intended utterance patterns—is relatively common in production experiments (e.g., Bock, 1986; Bock & Loebell, 1990).

Post hoc analysis of the distribution of O-responders by condition showed that there were significantly more O-responders in the LTV than TLV condition, Fisher's exact test, two-tailed $p = .01$. The significance of this outcome is discussed in the Experiment 2 Discussion section.

Learning
We found that the distributions of TL and LT responders in the TLV and LTV conditions were reliably different, $\chi^2(1) = 17.04$, $p < .0001$, with more TL-responders in the TLV condition and more LT-responders in the LTV condition. This reflects the fact that participants tended to follow the argument order exemplified by the construction to which they were exposed. To determine whether it was statistically more likely than chance to have mostly TL-responders in the TLV condition and mostly LT-responders in the LTV condition, the distributions of TL-responders and LT-responders in these conditions were compared against the baseline provided by control participants. The results show that there were statistically more TL-responders in the TLV condition than the control condition (TLV: 87%; control: 55%), $\chi^2(1) = 5.43$, $p = .02$. Likewise, there were more LT-responders in the LTV condition than in the control condition (LTV: 80%; control: 45%), $\chi^2(1) = 4.38$, $p = .04$.

These results indicate that the order in which nominal arguments were produced *with* minimal exposure to stable linking patterns was different than the order in which they were produced *without* exposure to stable linking patterns. Participants very quickly adopted the linking rules featured in their exposure construction and produced utterances that were congruent with these rules at test. Further, when considering only TL and LT productions, it made no difference which linking pattern served as a learning template: Equivalent increases above baseline were evident in both conditions and the distributions of responders who followed the target order for their condition were statistically identical, Fisher's exact test, two-tailed $p = .66$.

Experiment 2 Discussion
The outcome of Experiment 2 reinforces the finding in Experiment 1 that linking rules can be learned from the input. Given brief exposure to a novel

construction, participants viewed completely new appearance events in the form of magic tricks performed by the experimenter and were able to correctly map specific semantic arguments to specific syntactic constituents. This result holds additional significance in that it was obtained using a production measure. Combined with the comprehension results from Experiment 1, this suggests that the novel constructions that participants were exposed to are functionally equivalent to natural language constructions: Both novel and known construction types are used to map back and forth from semantic to syntactic representations. This strengthens the argument that the representations being learned in these experiments have a specifically linguistic character. We return to this point in more detail in the General Discussion section.

The present results are also difficult for some nativist mapping theories to accommodate. The ease with which the TLV and LTV linking patterns were acquired goes against at least one well-known nativist mapping proposal. Pinker (1989) claimed that locatives are universally mapped to oblique arguments. This generalization is approximately true in English, which encodes most obliques as PPs, not NPs.[1] However, the fact that participants in Experiment 2 readily encoded locatives as NPs indicates that they had no qualms about violating both Pinker's putative universal *and* the dominant encoding method used in English. Their behavior is thus fully consistent with an attempt to learn from and replicate regularities present in the input.

At the same time, however, the data suggest that there may have been a learning bias. Post hoc analysis revealed that the distribution of TL-responders to LT-responders in the control condition was not different than 50-50, $\chi^2(1) = 0.10, p = .75$. Whereas this outcome fails to suggest a bias toward one type of linking pattern over another, we also determined that there were significantly more O-responders in the LTV condition than the TLV condition (see Table 3 and the O-Responders subsection), intimating that some participants who were exposed to the LTV pattern resisted learning or producing it.

The possible bias in favor of TL orders is reminiscent of a possible agent-before-patient bias found in Wonnacott et al. (2008). In that study, adult native speakers of English who were trained to map novel forms to transitive events showed better production and comprehension performance when the form was consistent with an agent-before-patient argument order. Both this result and the TL preference in Experiment 2 can be interpreted in a number of ways. Proponents of innate mapping theories might, for example, claim that they show the operation of innate linking rules that specify the mapping of themes and agents to more prominent syntactic positions than locatives and patients. Although there is nothing in the present data to rule out this possibility, there are at least two alternative explanations that also merit consideration.

First, a bias in favor of TL and agent-before-patient orders could be the result of transfer from English, as both biases involve the unmarked (more frequent) word order. For example, although the LT order does exist in English (e.g., *On the mat sat the cat*), the TL order is much more frequent (*The cat sat on the mat*). Both our results and Wonnacott et al.'s (2008) are thus consistent with a possible preference to utilize the dominant mapping patterns found in participants' first language. This hypothesis predicts that biases that favor TL or agent-before-patient orders should be attenuated in languages that prefer alternative orders. Similarly, biases that are due to interference from English should be diminished in children who are still in the process of acquiring English (see, for example, Akhtar, 1999).

Alternatively, an underlying preference to produce *cognitively accessible* material first may account for the TL and agent-before-patient biases, particularly insofar as these orders tend to dominate crosslinguistically. The appearance events used in the present experiments and the transitive events used by Wonnacott et al. (2008) have certain characteristics in common. Both event types feature one participant that is inherently more active than another: the theme argument in appearance events and the agent argument in transitive events. It may thus be that the smaller number of O-responders in the TLV condition of Experiment 2, and the preference for agent-before-patient orders in Wonnacott et al. (2008) both result from a tendency to name the most active and accessible event participant first. This interpretation is consistent with results from the language production literature, which indicate a preference to produce accessible material earlier (Bock & Irwin, 1980; Ferreira & Dell, 2000).

General Discussion

We take the converging evidence from comprehension and production as a compelling indication that linking rules can be learned with very little exposure. Given an exemplar of a novel construction that has zero lexical overlap with exposure items (i.e., no shared nouns or verbs), participants are able to correctly map it to a target event, even in the presence of a distracter that differs only with respect to the linking pattern that is exemplified (Experiment 1). Similarly, given a completely novel appearance event, participants are able to correctly describe it using whatever linking pattern was present in their input (Experiment 2). The present results further suggest that the syntax-semantics mapping knowledge that participants acquire is quite robust: Even small amounts of exposure were enough (a) to build representations that persisted significantly beyond the exposure event, and (b) to support production.

The production outcome is additionally significant because it strongly suggests that participants treated the constructions that they were exposed to as true linguistic objects. A number of studies have demonstrated that novel word and multiword expressions take on many of the processing characteristics associated with known linguistic expressions as speakers gain experience with them (Leach & Samuel, 2007; Wonnacott et al., 2008). Additionally, although the present experiments were not designed to address processing concerns, it is clear that our participants were able use the constructions that they learned to fulfill the two primary linguistic functions: comprehension (Experiment 1) and production (Experiment 2). It thus seems reasonable to conclude that although the constructions that we utilized were indeed new, they are nonetheless linguistic.

A possible alternative interpretation of the present results might claim that learning was fast in both experiments because the target construction was not truly novel, since English allows two NPs to appear before the verb in topicalized transitives, as in *Bagels, I cooked*. On this view, *The bird the flower moopos* would be interpreted such that the flower is an agent that somehow *causes* the bird to appear, whereas the bird is a patient that has been moved from postverbal object position to the front of the sentence, as in *The bird, the flower produces* (Lidz & Williams, 2009). If this were the case, then the quick constructional learning reported here and elsewhere (Casenhiser & Goldberg, 2005; Goldberg et al., 2004) might be considered less surprising, because participants would only need to learn to associate a particular meaning (caused appearance) with an already familiar topicalized transitive construction.

Although this account fails to explain why learning was also fast in Experiment 2's LTV condition, we were interested in finding out more about the interpretations that participants assigned to their exposure construction. To this end, we included a debriefing session immediately following Experiment 2's production block, and explicitly asked 21 of the 48 TLV and LTV participants what they thought the construction that they had been exposed to meant. Their answers were coded according to whether they imputed a semantically transitive relationship between the two NP arguments, or whether the relationship was consistent with the intended meaning involving a theme and a locative in a nontransitive relationship. The results show that 18 of the 21 participants surveyed (i.e., 86%) clearly interpreted the relationship as intended, not as semantically transitive. They described the novel constructions as referring to events in which an argument "somehow arrived" at a location, "magically appeared" at

a location, or "came onto" a location. In contrast, only 2 out of the 21 participants surveyed (i.e., 9.5%) interpreted the novel constructions transitively, and
neither of these appeared to assign the agent role to the second NP, contra Lidz
& Williams (2009). One final participant failed to provide a description of the
construction's meaning, and instead noted only that the sentences that she had
heard were odd in that they contained novel verbs. Because individuals in the
21-person sample overwhelmingly interpreted the construction that they were
exposed to in the intended manner, $\chi^2(1) = 12.8$, $p < .0001$, we chose not
debrief the remaining 27 participants.

Conclusion

The present results suggest multiple avenues for future research. First and
foremost, additional testing is needed to determine whether young children
learn novel constructions with the same apparent ease and aptitude displayed
by adults. Although fast construction learning by children might suggest that
multiword phrasal patterns—like words themselves—can be learned quickly
during first language acquisition (Carey & Bartlett, 1978), it may also be the
case that novel constructions are learned on an item-by-item basis and only
achieve abstract status over time. Evidence in favor of this last hypothesis
comes from a recent study that applied Experiment 1's methods to 5-year-olds
and showed that—relative to an adult control group—the representations that
were acquired were more strongly tied to specific constructional exemplars that
had been seen in the past, and were less than fully abstract (Boyd & Goldberg,
2009). More research, however, is clearly needed in this area to elucidate the
factors that account for this pattern of results.

Finally, our findings intimate that there may indeed be biases that affect
learning, making some syntax-semantics mapping patterns more difficult to
acquire than others. The data fail to mediate, however, between nativist proposals, which treat biases as the result of innate, domain-specific representations,
and constructionist models, which argue that biases are the result of pragmatics
and domain-general constraints on learning and processing. Be that as it may,
to the extent that robust correlations exist between the input that learners are
exposed to and the representations that they develop, the present data sit well
with constructionist models, which allot a prominent role to learning. Regardless, however, of the theory that is used to interpret them, these results serve as
a foundational step toward exploring the processes by which speakers acquire
mappings between syntactic devices such as word order, and semantics.

Revised version accepted 19 May 2009

Note

1 There are a few lexical items that encode goal arguments as NPs in English (e.g., *approach* and *reach*), but it is much more commonplace for locations to be expressed as PPs.

References

Akhtar, N. (1999). Acquiring basic word order: Evidence for data-driven learning of syntactic structure. *Journal of Child Language, 26*, 339–356.

Akhtar, N., & Tomasello, M. (1997). Young children's productivity with word order and verb morphology. *Developmental Psychology, 33*(6), 952–965.

Allen, J. (1997). Probabilistic constraints in acquisition. In A. Sorace, C. Heycock, & R. Shillcock (Ed.), *Proceedings of the GALA '97 conference on language acquisition* (pp. 300–305). Edinburgh: University of Edinburgh Human Communications Research Center.

Ambridge, B., Theakston, A., Lieven, E., & Tomasello, M. (2006). The distributed learning effect for children's acquisition of an abstract syntactic construction. *Cognitive Development, 21*(2), 174–193.

Baker, M. (1988). *Incorporation: A theory of grammatical function changing.* Chicago: Chicago University Press.

Bock, J. K. (1986). Syntactic persistence in language production. *Cognitive Psychology, 18*, 355–387.

Bock, J. K., & Irwin, D. E. (1980). Syntactic effects of information availability in sentence production. *Journal of Verbal Learning and Verbal Behavior, 19*(4), 467–484.

Bock, K., & Loebell, H. (1990). Framing sentences. *Cognition, 35*, 1–39.

Borovsky, A., & Elman, J. (2006). Language input and semantic categories: A relation between cognition and early word learning. *Journal of Child Language, 33*, 759–790.

Bowerman, M. (1990). Mapping thematic roles onto syntactic functions: Are children helped by innate linking rules? *Linguistics, 28*, 1253–1289.

Boyd, J. K., & Goldberg, A. E. (2009, January). *Generalizing novel phrasal constructions.* Poster presented at the Annual Meeting of the Linguistic Society of America, San Francisco.

Braine, M. D. S. (1976). Children's first word combinations. *Monographs of the Society for Research in Child Development, 41*(1), 1–104.

Carey, S., & Bartlett, E. (1978). Acquiring a single new word. *Papers and Reports on Child Language Development, 15*, 17–29.

Casenhiser, D., & Goldberg, A. E. (2005). Fast mapping between a phrasal form and meaning. *Developmental Science, 8*(6), 500–508.

Elio, R., & Anderson, J. R. (1984). The effects of information order and learning mode on schema abstraction. *Memory and Cognition, 12*, 20–30.

Ellis, N. C., & Ferreira-Junior, F. (2009). Construction learning as a function of frequency, frequency distribution, and function. *Modern Language Journal, 93*, 370–385.

Ferreira, V. S., & Dell, G. S. (2000). Effect of ambiguity and lexical availability on syntactic and lexical production. *Cognitive Psychology, 40*, 296–340.

Ferreira, V. S., & Sleve, L. R. (2007). Grammatical encoding. In G. M. Gaskell (Ed.), *The Oxford handbook of psycholinguistics* (pp. 453–470). Oxford: Oxford University Press.

Goldberg, A. E. (1995). *Constructions: A construction grammar approach to argument structure*. Chicago: Chicago University Press.

Goldberg, A. E. (2004). But do we need Universal Grammar? Comment on Lidz et al. (2003). *Cognition, 94*, 77–84.

Goldberg, A. E. (2006). *Constructions at work: The nature of generalization in language*. Oxford: Oxford University Press.

Goldberg, A. E., Casenhiser, D. M., & Sethuraman, N. (2004). Learning argument structure generalizations. *Cognitive Linguistics, 15*(3), 289–316.

Goldberg, A.E., Casenhiser, D., & White, T. (2007). Constructions as categories of language. *New Ideas in Psychology, 25*(2), 70–86.

Ingram, D., & Thompson, W. (1996). Early syntactic acquisition in German: Evidence for the Modal Hypothesis. *Language, 72*(1), 97–120.

Landau, B., & Gleitman, L. R. (1985). *Language and experience: Evidence from the blind child*. Cambridge, MA: Harvard University Press.

Leach, L., & Samuel, A. G. (2007). Lexical configuration and lexical engagement: When adults learn new words. *Cognitive Psychology, 55*, 306–353.

Levelt, W. J. M. (1989). *Speaking: From intention to articulation*. Cambridge, MA: MIT Press.

Lidz, J., Gleitman, H., & Gleitman, L. (2003). Understanding how input matters: Verb learning and the footprint of Universal Grammar. *Cognition, 87*, 151–178.

Lidz, J., & Williams, A. (2009). Constructions on holiday. *Cognitive Linguistics, 20*(1), 177–189.

Lieven, E. V. M., Pine, J. M., & Baldwin, G. (1997). Lexically-based learning and early grammatical development. *Journal of Child Language, 24*, 187–219.

Maguire, M. J., Hirsh-Pasek, K., Golinkoff, R. M., & Brandone, A. C. (2008). Focusing on the relation: Fewer exemplars facilitate children's initial verb learning and extension. *Developmental Science, 11*(4), 628–634.

McRae, K., Spivey-Knowlton, M. J., & Tanenhaus, M. K. (1998). Modeling the influence of thematic fit (and other constraints) in on-line sentence comprehension. *Journal of Memory and Language, 38*(3), 283–312.

Morris, W. C., Cottrell, G. W., & Elman, J. (2000). A connectionist simulation of the empirical acquisition of grammatical relations. In S. Wermter & R. Sun (Ed.), *Hybrid neural systems* (pp. 175–193). Berlin: Springer-Verlag.

Naigles, L. G., Gleitman, H., & Gleitman, L. R. (1993). Children acquire word meaning components from syntactic evidence. In E. Dromi (Ed.), *Language and cognition: A developmental perspective* (pp. 104–140). Norwood, NJ: Ablex Publishing.

Perfors, A., Kemp, C., Tenenbaum, J., & Wonnacott, E. (2007). Learning inductive constraints: The acquisition of verb argument constructions. In *Proceedings of the twenty-ninth annual conference of the Cognitive Science Society* (p. 1836). Mahwah, NJ: Lawrence Erlbaum.

Pinker, S. (1984). *Language learnability and language development*. Cambridge, MA: Harvard University Press.

Pinker, S. (1989). *Learnability and cognition: The acquisition of verb-argument structure*. Cambridge, MA: Harvard University Press.

Posner, M. I., Goldsmith, R., & Welton, K. E. J. (1967). Perceived distance and the classification of distorted patterns. *Journal of Experimental Psychology: General, 73*, 28–38.

Tomasello, M. (2000). Do young children have adult syntactic competence? *Cognition, 74*, 209–253.

Tomasello, M. (2003). *Constructing a language: A usage-based theory of language acquisition*. Boston: Harvard University Press.

Wonnacott, E., Newport, E. L., & Tanenhaus, M. K. (2008). Acquiring and processing verb argument structure: Distributional learning in a miniature language. *Cognitive Psychology, 56*, 165–209.

Zipf, G. K. (1935). *The psycho-biology of language*. Boston: Houghton Mifflin.

Language Learning   ISSN 0023-8333

Constructing a Second Language: Analyses and Computational Simulations of the Emergence of Linguistic Constructions From Usage

Nick C. Ellis

University of Michigan

with

Diane Larsen-Freeman

University of Michigan

This article presents an analysis of interactions in the usage, structure, cognition, coadaptation of conversational partners, and emergence of linguistic constructions. It focuses on second language development of English verb-argument constructions (VACs: VL, verb locative; VOL, verb object locative; VOO, ditransitive) with particular reference to the following: (a) Construction learning as concept learning following the general cognitive and associative processes of the induction of categories from experience of exemplars in usage obtained through coadapted micro-discursive interaction with conversation partners; (b) the empirical analysis of usage by means of corpus linguistic descriptions of native and nonnative speech and of longitudinal emergence in the interlanguage of second language learners; (c) the effects of the frequency and Zipfian type/token frequency distribution of exemplars within the Verb and other islands of the construction archipelago (e.g., [Subj V Obj Obl$_{path/loc}$]), by their prototypicality, their generic coverage, and their contingency of form-meaning-use mapping, and (d) computational (emergent connectionist) models of these various factors as they play out in the emergence of constructions as generalized linguistic schema.

We thank our colleagues in this research: Steffi Wulff, Fernando Ferreira-Junior, and Ute Römer.

Correspondence concerning this article should be addressed to Nick C. Ellis or Diane Larsen-Freeman, University of Michigan, 500 E. Washington Street, Ann Arbor, MI 48104. Internet: ncellis@umich.edu or dianelf@umich.edu

The Emergence of Linguistic Constructions From Usage

Language has come to represent the world as we know it; it is grounded in our perceptual experience. Language is used to organize, process, and convey information from one person to another, from one embodied mind to another. Language is also used to establish and maintain social relationships and to enact functions. Language and its use are mutually inextricable; they determine each other.

Learning language involves determining structure from usage and this, like learning about all other aspects of the world, involves the full scope of cognition: the remembering of utterances and episodes, the categorization of experience, the determination of patterns among and between stimuli, the generalization of conceptual schema and prototypes from exemplars, and the use of cognitive models, metaphors, analogies, and images in thinking. At the same time, there is an all-important social dimension to the process. There is nothing that so well characterizes human social action as language. It is in the coadaptation in the micro-discursive encounters between conversation partners that learners experience relevant and accessible exemplars from which they will learn. Cognition, consciousness, experience, embodiment, brain, self, human interaction, society, culture, and history—in other words, phenomena at different levels of scale and time (Larsen-Freeman & Cameron, 2008)—are all inextricably intertwined in rich, complex, and dynamic ways in language, its use, and its learning. So we require perspectives on dynamic interactions at all levels, perspectives provided by general approaches such as Emergentism (Ellis, 1998; Ellis & Larsen Freeman, 2006a, 2006b; Elman, et al., 1996; MacWhinney, 1999), Chaos/Complexity Theory (Holland, 1992, 1998; Larsen-Freeman, 1997, 2002b; Larsen-Freeman & Cameron, 2008), and Dynamic Systems Theory (de Bot, Lowie, & Verspoor, 2007; Ellis, 2007, 2008a; Port & Van Gelder, 1995; Spivey, 2006; Thelen & Smith, 1994; van Geert, 1991) as they apply to usage-based theories of language (Barlow & Kemmer, 2000; Bod, Hay, & Jannedy, 2003; Bybee, 2005; Bybee & Hopper, 2001; Croft & Cruise, 2004) and first language acquisition (Goldberg, 1995, 2003, 2006; Tomasello, 1998, 2003) and second language acquisition (Ellis, 2002, 2005; Larsen-Freeman, 2003; Larsen-Freeman & Long, 1991; Robinson & Ellis, 2008).

This article applies these approaches to investigate linguistic constructions, their cognition, and their development. We focus on the second language development of English verb-argument constructions (VACs: VL verb locative; VOL, verb object locative; VOO, ditransitive) with particular reference to the following:

1. construction learning as concept learning following the general cognitive and associative processes of the induction of categories from experience of exemplars in conversational interaction;
2. the empirical analysis of usage by means of corpus linguistic descriptions of English native-speaker and nonnative speaker speech over time;
3. the islands (Tomasello, 1992) comprising each construction and the effects of frequency and type/token frequency distribution of their constituent exemplars, their prototypicality, and their contingency of form-meaning-use mapping;
4. computational (connectionist) models of these various factors as they play out in the emergence of constructions as generalized linguistic schema.

In addition to the general approaches we have just enumerated, our theoretical framework is also informed by cognitive linguistics, particularly constructionist perspectives (e.g., Bates & MacWhinney, 1987; Goldberg, 1995, 2003, 2006; Lakoff, 1987; Langacker, 1987; Ninio, 2006; Robinson & Ellis, 2008; Tomasello, 2003), corpus linguistics (Biber, Conrad, & Reppen, 1998; Sinclair, 1991, 2004), and psychological theories of cognitive and associative learning as they relate to the induction of psycholinguistic categories from social interaction (Ellis, 1998, 2002, 2003, 2006a, 2006b, 2006c). The basic tenets are as follows: Language is intrinsically symbolic. It is constituted by a structured network of constructions as conventionalized form-meaning-use combinations used for communicative purposes. As speakers communicate, they coadapt their language use on a particular occasion. From such repeated encounters, stable language-using patterns (Larsen-Freeman & Cameron, 2008) emerge. The patterns are eventually broken down and their form-meaning-use is extended in novel ways. Usage leads to these becoming entrenched in the speaker's mind and for them to be taken up by members of the speech community.

Constructions are of different levels of complexity and abstraction; they can comprise concrete and particular items (as in words and idioms), more abstract classes of items (as in word classes and abstract grammatical constructions), or complex combinations of concrete and abstract items (as mixed constructions). The acquisition of constructions is input-driven and depends on the learner's experience of these form-meaning-use combinations in interactions with others. They develop following the same cognitive principles as the learning of other categories, schemata, and prototypes (Cohen & Lefebvre, 2005; Murphy, 2003). Creative linguistic usage emerges from the collaboration of the memories of all of the utterances in a learner's entire history of language use and the frequency-biased abstraction of regularities within them (Ellis, 2002).

Cognitive linguistics, corpus linguistics, and psycholinguistics are alike in their realizations that we cannot separate grammar from lexis, form from function, form from meaning, meaning from context, nor structure from usage.

Constructions specify the morphological, syntactic, and lexical form of language and the associated semantic, pragmatic, and discourse functions (Figure 1). Any utterance is comprised of a number of constructions that are nested. Thus, the expression *Today he walks to town* is constituted of lexical constructions such as *today*, *he*, *walks*, and so forth, morphological constructions such as the verb inflection *s* signaling third-person singular present tense, abstract grammatical constructions such as Subj, VP, and Prepositional Phrases, the intransitive motion Verb-Locative (VL: [Subj V $Obl_{path/loc}$]) verb-argument construction (VAC), and so forth. The function of each of these forms contributes in communicating the speaker's intention.

Psychological analyses of the learning of constructions as form-meaning-use combinations is informed by the literature on the associative learning of cue-outcome contingencies for which the usual determinants include the following: factors relating to the form such as frequency and salience (Ellis, 2002; Larsen-Freeman, 1976); factors relating to the meaning such as significance in the comprehension of the overall utterance, prototypicality, ambiguity, generality, redundancy, and surprise value; factors relating to use such as the social value of particular forms or their value in discourse construction (Celce-Murcia & Larsen-Freeman, 1999; Larsen-Freeman, 2002a, 2003); factors relating to the contingency of form and meaning and use; and factors relating to learner attention, such as automaticity, transfer, and blocking (Ellis, 2002, 2003, 2006b, 2008b). These various factors conspire in the acquisition and use of any linguistic construction.

Whereas some constructions, like *walk*, are concrete, imageable, and specific in their interpretation, others are more abstract and schematic. For example, the caused motion construction, (e.g., X causes Y to move $Z_{path/loc}$ [Subj V Obj $Obl_{path/loc}$]) exists independently of particular verbs; hence "Tom sneezed the paper napkin across the table": is intelligible despite "sneeze" being usually intransitive (Goldberg, 1995). How might verb-centered constructions develop these abstract properties? Semantic bootstrapping accounts suggest that they inherit their schematic meaning from the conspiracy of the particular types of verb that appear in their verb island (Pinker, 1989). The verb is a better predictor of sentence meaning than any other word in the sentence and plays a central role in determining the syntactic structure of a sentence (Tomasello, 1992). There is a close relationship between the types of verbs that typically appear within constructions (in this case, *put, move, push*, etc.); hence, their meaning

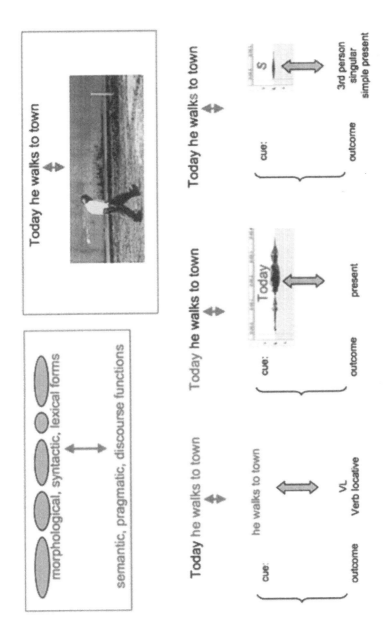

Figure 1 Constructions as form-function mappings. Any utterance comprises multiple nested constructions. Some aspects of form are more salient than others; the amount of energy in *today* far exceeds that in *s*.

as a whole is inducible from the lexical items experienced within them. Ninio (1999) argued that in child language acquisition, individual "pathbreaking" semantically prototypic verbs form the seeds of verb-centered argument-structure patterns, with generalizations of the verb-centered instances emerging gradually as the verb-centered categories themselves are analyzed into more abstract argument structure constructions.

Learning grammatical constructions thus involves the distributional analysis of the language stream and the contingent analysis of perceptual activity following general psychological principles of category learning. Categories have graded structures, with some members being better exemplars than others. The prototype is the best example, the benchmark against which surrounding "poorer," more borderline instances are categorized. The greater the token frequency of an exemplar, the more it contributes to defining the category and the greater the likelihood it will be considered the prototype.

Frequency promotes learning, and psycholinguistics demonstrates that language learners are exquisitely sensitive to input frequencies of patterns at all levels (Ellis, 2002). In the learning of categories from exemplars, acquisition is optimized by the introduction of an initial, low-variance sample centered on prototypical exemplars (Elio & Anderson, 1981, 1984; Posner & Keele, 1968, 1970), which allows learners to get a "fix" on what will account for most of the category members. Then the bounds of the category can later be defined by experience of the full breadth of exemplars. Goldberg, Casenhiser, and Sethuraman (2004) demonstrated that in samples of child language acquisition, for each VAC there is a strong tendency for one single verb to occur with very high frequency in comparison to other verbs used, a profile that closely mirrors that of the mothers' speech to these children. Dale and Spivey (2006) also showed how the child and his or her caregiver produce sequences of words or syntactic phrases during a conversation that match those being heard, a process they call "syntactic coordination." Interesting from our point of view is that the researchers found a Zipf-like distribution in the patterns that were shared with each child and caregiver pair. In other words, there are highly frequent sequences of word classes guiding the recurrent patterns in conversation (Larsen-Freeman & Cameron, 2008). Additionally, in second language acquisition, there is evidence of coadaptation of conversation partners ("foreigner talk discourse"; Larsen Freeman & Long, 1991) and with teachers and students in classrooms, with the result that learners receive an optimal sample of language from which to learn. In natural language, too, Zipf's law (Zipf, 1935) describes how the highest frequency words disproportionately account for the most linguistic tokens. Goldberg et al. (2004) showed that Zipf's law applied within VACs, too, and they argued that this promotes acquisition: tokens of one particular verb account for the lion's share of instances of each particular argument frame, and this pathbreaking verb is also the one with the prototypical meaning from which that construction is derived:

- The Verb Object Locative (VOL) [Subj V Obj Obl$_{path/loc}$] construction was exemplified in children's speech by *put* 31% of the time, *get* 16% of the time, *take* 10% of the time, and *do/pick* 6% of the time, a profile mirroring that of the mothers' speech to these children (with *put* appearing 38% of the time in this construction that was otherwise exemplified by 43 different verbs).
- The Verb Locative (VL) [Subj V Obl$_{path/loc}$] construction was used in children's speech with *go* 51% of the time, matching the mothers' 39%.
- The ditransitive (VOO) [Subj V Obj$_1$ Obj$_2$] was filled by *give* between 53% and 29% of the time in five different children, with mothers' speech filling the verb slot in this frame by *give* 20% of the time.

Consider language as it passes, utterance by utterance, as illustrated in Figure 2. Learners with a history of exposure to this profile of natural language

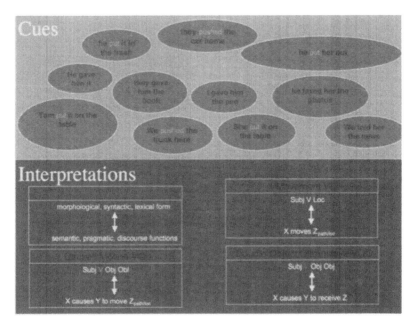

Figure 2 Verb island occupancy as cues to VAC membership.

might thus successfully categorize the different utterances as examples of different VAC categories on the basis of the occupants of the verb islands.

However, if the verbs were the only cues that were available, then VACs could have no abstract meaning above that of the verb itself. For "Tom sneezed the paper napkin across the table" to make sense despite the intransitivity of *sneeze*, the hearer has to make use of additional information from the syntactic frame. In considering how children learn lexical semantics, Gleitman (1990) argued that they made use of clues from syntactic distributional information—nounlike things follow determiners, prepositions most often prepose a noun phrase in English, and so forth. The two alternatives of *semantic* and *syntactic bootstrapping* are by no means mutually exclusive; indeed, they reinforce and complement each other.

In the identification of the caused motion construction (X causes Y to move $Z_{path/loc}$ [Subj V Obj Obl$_{path/loc}$]), the whole frame as an archipelago of islands is important. The Subj island helps to identify the beginning bounds of the parse. More frequent, more generic, and more prototypical occupants will be more easily identified. Pronouns, particularly those that refer to animate entities, will more readily activate the schema (Childers & Tomasello, 2001; Wilson, 2003). As illustrated in Figure 3, the Obj island, too, will be more readily identified when occupied by more frequent, more generic, and more prototypical lexical items (pronouns like *it*, required by discourse constraints, rather than nouns such as *napkin*). So, too, the locative will be activated more readily if opened by a prepositional island populated by a high-frequency, prototypical exemplar such as *on* or *in* (Tomasello, 2003, p. 153). Activation of the VAC schema arises from the conspiracy of all of these features, and arguments about Zipfian type/token distributions and prototypicality of membership extend to all of the islands of the construction.

Thus, frequency of usage defines construction categories. However, there is one additional qualification to be borne in mind. Some lexical types are very specific in the VACs that they occupy; the vast majority of their tokens occur in just one VAC and so they are very reliable and distinctive cues to it. Other lexical types are more widely spread over a range of constructions, and this promiscuity means that they are not faithful cues. *Put* occurs almost exclusively in VOL; it is defining in the acquisition of this VAC and a distinctive and reliable cue in its subsequent recognition. *Turn*, however, occurs both in VL and VOL and is less distinctive in distinguishing between these two. Similarly, *send* is attracted to both the VOO and VOL constructions and so is a less discriminating cue for these categories. Consider the other islands too. It is clear that however useful they are at defining the beginning region of interest in the VAC parse,

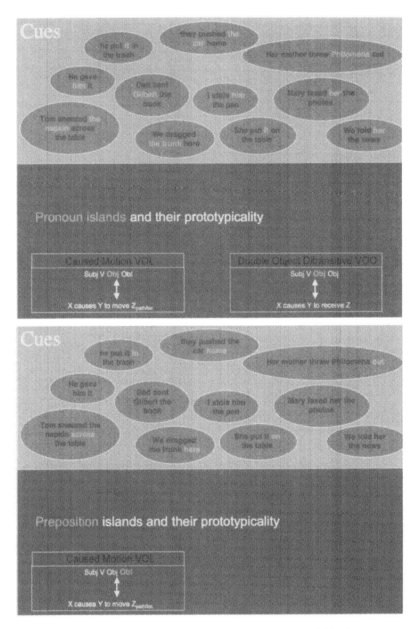

Figure 3 Other syntactic islands and their occupants as cues to VAC identity.

subject pronouns freely occupy any VAC with hardly any discrimination except that concerning animacy of agent. Prepositions are substantially selective for locatives, but as a class, they do not distinguish between the transitive and intransitive VACs, and so on.

The associative learning literature has long recognized that although frequency is important, so, too, is contingency of mapping. Consider how, in the learning of the category of birds, although eyes and wings are equally frequently experienced features in the exemplars, it is wings that are distinctive in differentiating birds from other animals. Wings are important features to learning the category because they are reliably associated with class membership; eyes are neither. Raw frequency of occurrence is less important than the contingency between cue and interpretation. Contingency, or reliability of form-function mapping, is a driving force of all associative learning (Rescorla, 1968). It, and its associated aspects of predictive value, information gain, and statistical association, is therefore central in psycholinguistic theories of language acquisition too (Ellis, 2006b, 2006c, 2008b; Gries & Wulff, 2005; MacWhinney, 1987; Wulff, Ellis, Römer, Bardovi-Harlig, & LeBlanc, 2009).

Taken together, these considerations of language acquisition as the associative learning of schematic constructions from experience of exemplars in usage, adjusted for comprehension/learning, generate a number of hypotheses concerning VAC acquisition:

H1. The frequency distribution for the types occupying the verb island of each VAC will be Zipfian.

H2. The first verbs to emerge in each VAC will be those which appear more frequently in that construction in the input.

H3. The pathbreaking verb for each VAC will be much more frequent than the other members.

H4. The first verbs to emerge in each VAC will be prototypical of that construction's interpretation.

H5. The first verbs to emerge in each construction will be those which are more distinctively associated with that construction in the input.

We also assume similar contributions relating to H1–H5 from the other islands in each VAC, although perhaps to a lesser degree. Ellis and Ferreira-Junior (2009a, 2009b) tested these hypotheses using corpus data of English. Their methods and findings are reported in depth in those articles. What we do here is summarize the findings in order to lay the foundations for emergentist simulations designed to understand the interactions of these factors in development.

The Naturalistic Acquisition of English VACs

Methods

Ellis and Ferreira-Junior (2009a) analyzed the speech of second language learners of English VACs in the European Science Foundation (ESF) corpus (http://www.mpi.nl/world/tg/lapp/esf/esf.html; Dietrich, Klein, & Noyau, 1995; Feldweg, 1991; Perdue, 1993), which collected the spontaneous and elicited second language of adult immigrants recorded longitudinally in interviews every 4–6 weeks for approximately 30 months. They focused on seven English as a second language (ESL) learners living in Britain whose native languages were Italian ($n = 4$) or Punjabi ($n = 3$). Data from 234 sessions were gathered and transcribed for these ESL learners and their native-speaker (NS) conversation partners from a range of activities.

They performed semiautomated searches through the transcriptions to identify the VACs of interest and to tag them as VL, VOL, or VOO following the operationalizations described in the work of Goldberg, Casenhiser & Sethuraman (2004); for example:

a) you come out of my house. [come] [VL]
b) Charlie say # shopkeeper give me one cigar [give] [VOO]
c) no put it in front # thats it # yeah [put] [VOL]

For the NS conversation partners, they identified 14,574 verb tokens (232 types), of which 900 tokens were identified to occur in VL (33 types), 303 in VOL (33 types), and 139 in VOO constructions (12 types). For the ESL learners, they identified 10,448 verb tokens (234 types), of which 436 tokens were found in VL (39 types), 224 in VOL (24 types), and 36 in VOO constructions (9 types).

Hypotheses and Findings

H1. The frequency distributions for the types occupying the verb island of each VAC are Zipfian

The frequency distributions of the verb types in the VL, VOL, and VOO constructions produced by the interviewers and the learners are shown in Figure 4. For the NS interviewers, *go* constituted 42% of the total tokens of VL, *put* constituted 35% of VOL use, and *give* constituted 53% of VOO. After this leading exemplar, subsequent verb types decline rapidly in frequency. For the ESL learners, again, for each construction there was one exemplar that accounted for the lion's share of total productions of that construction: *go* constituted 53% of VL, *put* constituted 68% of VOL, and *give*

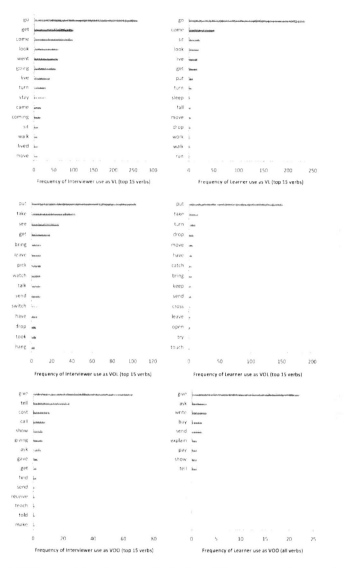

Figure 4 Zipfian type-token frequency distributions of the verbs populating the interviewers' and learners' VL, VOL, and VOO constructions. Note the similar rankings of verbs across interviewers and learners in each VAC.

constituted 64% of VOO. Plots of these frequency distributions as log verb frequency against log verb rank produced straight-line functions explaining in excess of 95% of the variance, thus confirming that Zipf's law is a good description of the frequency distributions with the frequency of any verb being inversely proportional to its rank in the frequency table for that construction, the relationship following a power function.

H2. The verbs to emerge first in each VAC are those which appear more frequently in that construction in the input

The order of emergence of verb types in the learner constructions followed the frequencies in the interviewer data. Correlational analyses across all 80 verb types that featured in any of the NS and/or NNS constructions confirmed this. For the VL construction, frequency of lemma use by learner correlated with that by NS interviewer, $r(78) = 0.97$, $p < .001$. The same analysis for VOL resulted in $r(78) = 0.89$, $p < .001$, and for VOO it resulted in $r(78) = 0.93$, $p < .001$.

H3. The pathbreaking verb for each VAC is much more frequent than the other members

Go was the first-learned verb for VL, put for VOL, and give for VOO. The Zipfian frequency profiles (Figure 4) for the types/tokens confirm H3. The emergent curves (Figures 5–7, left-hand panels; right-hand shows results from simulations to be described in the last part of the article) showed in each case that the verb to first emerge seeded the construction and predominated in its cumulative usage but thereafter the construction grew in membership as verbs similar in meaning to the pathbreaker joined one at a time.

H4. The first-learned verbs in each VAC are prototypical of that construction's interpretation

In order to determine the degree to which different verbs matched the prototypical semantics of the three VACs, Ellis and Ferreira-Junior (2009b) had native English speakers rate the verbs for the degree to which they matched a VL schema (the movement of someone or something to a new place or in a new direction), a VOL schema (someone causes the movement of something to a new place or in a new direction), or a VOO schema (someone causes someone to receive something). They then assessed the association between verb-acquisition order and prototypicality so measured.

For the VL construction the most used verb, go, was rated as 7.4 out of 9 in terms of the degree to which it matched the prototypical schematic meaning.

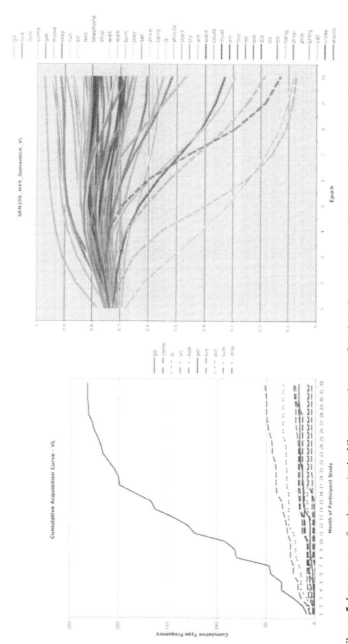

Figure 5 Learner use of verb types in the VL construction as a function of study month (left panel) alongside activation of the VL pattern by different verb types as a function of epoch of training in Simulation 1 (right panel).

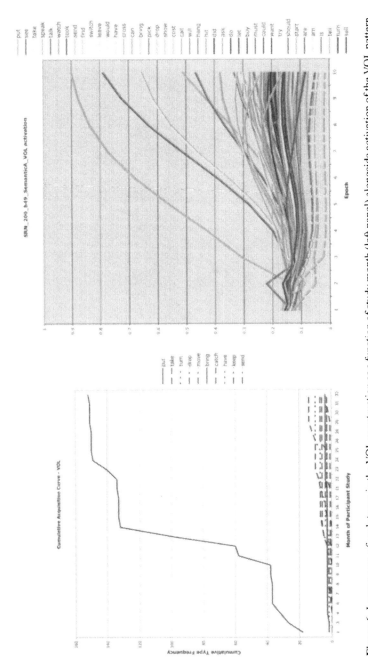

Figure 6 Learner use of verb types in the VOL construction as a function of study month (left panel) alongside activation of the VOL pattern by different verb types as a function of epoch of training in Simulation 1 (right panel).

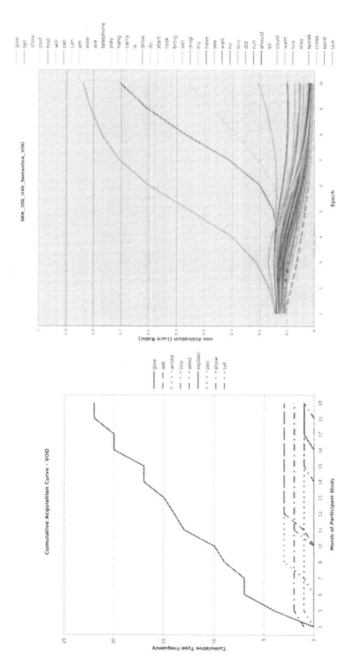

Figure 7 Learner use of verb types in the VOO construction as a function of study month (left panel) alongside activation of the VOO pattern by different verb types as a function of epoch of training in Simulation 1 (right panel).

The correlation between prototypicality of verb meaning and log frequency of learner use was VL $\rho(78) = 0.44$, $p < .001$. They had expected a higher correlation than this but realized that 10 other verbs surpassed *go* in this rating (*walk* [9.0], *move* [8.8], *run* [8.8], *travel* [8.8], *come* [8.4], *drive* [8.2], *arrive* [8.0], *jump* [8.0], *return* [8.0], and *fall* [7.8]. These match the schemata very well, but their additional specific action semantics limit the generality of their use. What is special about *go* is that it is prototypical and generic—thus widely applicable. The same pattern held for the other constructions. For VOL, the most used verb *put* was rated 8.0 in terms of how well it described the construction schema. For the VOO construction, the most used verb *give* was rated 9.0 in terms of how well it described the VOO schema.

In sum, these data demonstrate that learner VAC development is seeded by the highest frequency, prototypical, and generic exemplar across learners and VACs. These are the exemplars that are provided in NS-nonnative speaker interaction. The use of such exemplars presumably facilitates comprehension in the micro-discursive moment and perhaps their subsequent emergence and ultimate acquisition.

Ellis and Ferreira-Junior (2006a) extended these analyses, first to include the dimension of contingency/distinctiveness of form-meaning association and, second, to investigate the contribution of the other islands in the VAC archipelago.

H5. The first verbs to emerge in each construction are those which are more distinctively associated with that construction in the input

To assess the association strength between the verbs and the VACs in which they occur, they used collexeme strength (the log to the base 10 of the *p*-value of the Fisher-Yates exact test), a measure of contingency from collostructional analysis (Gries & Stefanowitsch, 2004; Stefanowitsch & Gries, 2003).

As already described under H2, learner usage was strongly associated with frequency in the NS speech (over the 80 verbs, VL, $r = .97$; VOL, $r = .89$; VOO, $r = .93$). Their analyses under H5 showed that, if anything, learner uptake was predicted even more so by collexeme strength in the NS speech (over the 80 verbs, VL, $r = .96$; VOL, $r = .97$; VOO, $r = .97$).

H6. The frequency distribution for the types occupying each of the islands of each VAC is Zipfian

Ellis and Ferreira-Junior (2009b) determined the frequency distributions of the types occupying each (nonverb) island in the VL (Subj, Prep, Locative), VOL (Subj, Obj, Prep, Locative), and VOO (Subj, Obj_1, Obj_2) constructions produced by the interviewers and the learners. For each construction, the frequency distribution for each island was Zipfian. In each case, for NS and NNS both, the lead exemplars took the lion's share of instances in that island, and the distribution was a power function as indexed by the log frequency versus log type rank regression being linear.

117. The first types to emerge in each VAC island are those which appear more frequently in that construction island in the input

There was a clear correspondence between the types used in each island by the NNSs and the types that occupy them in the NS speech. The interviewers filled the Subj island of VL with the following top eight types, in decreasing order: *you, to* [verb in infinitive phrase], implied *you* [imperative], *I, he, they, we, us*. The corresponding list for the learners was as follows: implied *you* [imperative], *I, you, he, they, to* [verb in infinitive phrase], *she, we*. A similar profile was found for the Subj island for VOL: NS (*you*, implied *you* [imperative], *to, I, they, he, we, she*); NNS (implied *you* [imperative], *I, you, to* [verb in infinitive phrase], *he, the, bag, they*); and for VOO, top four NSs (*I, you*, implied *you* [imperative], *to* [verb in infinitive phrase]), NNS (*they, I, she*, implied *you* [imperative]). Although a potentially infinite range of nouns could occupy the Subj islands in these different constructions, in NS and learner alike, they were populated by far by a few high-frequency generic forms, the pronouns, both to honor discourse constraints and perhaps as a consequence of NSers making adjustments to facilitate comprehension.

The top eight occupants of the Prep island were in NS VLs (*to, in, at, there, from, into, out, back*) and in NNS VLs (*to, in, out, on, down, there, inside, up*). Similar profiles occurred for the Prep island of VOL: NS (*in, on, there, off, out, up, from, to*); NNS (*in, on, there, the table, up, from, the bag, down*). Although a wide range of directions or places could occupy the postverbal island in these two constructions, in NSs and learners alike, it was occupied by far by a few high-frequency generic prepositions.

Finally, we look at the Obj islands of VOO. For Obj_1, the interviewers' top five occupants were (*you, me, him, her, it*) and the NNS learners' top three were (*me, you, him*). For Obj_2, the NS top eight were (*AMOUNTMONEY* [like 20 pounds, 3 pounds, etc.], *the names, a bit, money, a book, a picture, something, the test*) and the NNS top eight were (*money, a letter, hund, something, the money, a bill, a cheque, a lot*).

The general pattern, then, for each island of each VAC, is that there was high correspondence between the top types used in each island by the learners and the types that occupy them in NS input typical of their experience. Although we do not claim that NSs make conscious choices to facilitate acquisition by NSSs, we do believe that there is coadaptation between interlocutors that facilitates comprehension and, therefore, potentially scaffolds acquisition.

H8. The first pathbreaking type for each VAC island is more frequent than the other members

The qualitative patterns summarized under H7 demonstrates that, unlike for the verbs that center the semantics of each VAC, there was no single pathbreaker that initially takes over each of the other islands of the VAC exclusively. Nevertheless, for each construction, there was a high overlap between NS and NNS use of the top 5–10 occupant types, which together make up the predominance of its inhabitation.

H9. The first-learned types in each VAC island are prototypical of that island's contribution to the construction's interpretation

The 5–10 major occupant types for each island described under H7 do indeed seem to be prototypical in role. Although a very wide range of nouns could occupy the Subj islands in the VL, VOL, and VOO constructions, in NS and NNS speech alike, these were occupied by the most frequent, prototypical and generic forms for this slot: pronouns such as *I, you, it, we*, and so forth. The Prep islands in VL and VOL were clearly identified with high frequency prototypical generic prepositions such as *in, on, there, to*, and *off*. Likewise, the Objs in VOO are stereotypic in their interpretations and there is a broad overlap between NS and NNS use: Because of their informational status, people, deictically present (as pronouns), routinely give people (as pronouns) money, letters, bills, or books.

H10. The first types to emerge in each VAC island are those more distinctively associated with that construction island in the input

Their analyses showed that certain subjects were more significantly associated with certain VACs (i.e., *it* and *I* for VOO and implied *you* in the imperative for VOL). Nevertheless, comparison of the data under H5 showed that verbs are generally much more distinctively associated with these VACs than Subjs in terms of collexeme strength. Thus, although the occupants of Subj do follow a Zipfian distribution led by pronouns and thus could indeed signal the beginning of a VAC parse, they tend not to be associated with any particular VAC. Prepositions were much more like the verbs in their selectivity; *to, back, in*, and *out* were distinctively associated with VL, *on, off*, and *up* were strongly selective of VOL, and all of these prepositions were repulsed by VOO. For the Obj_1 islands, any Obj_1 repulsed VL, *it, money, them* and *that* were very significantly distinctive of VOL, and the object pronouns *you, me, him* and *her* were distinctive recipients in VOO.

Together, these analyses demonstrated that although the verb island is most distinctive, the constituency of the other islands is by no means negligible in determining VAC identity. In particular, VL and VOL are highly selective in terms of their Prep occupancy, and Obj_1 types clearly select among VOO, VOL, and VL.

Interim Conclusions

These findings demonstrate a range of influences in the emergence of linguistic constructions. For each VAC island there is the following:

1. the frequency and frequency distribution of the form types;
2. the frequency, the frequency distribution, the prototypicality and generality of the semantic types, their importance in interpreting the overall construction;
3. the reliabilities of the mapping between items 1 and 2;
4. the degree to which the different elements in the VAC sequence (such as Subj V Obj Obl) are mutually informative and form predictable chunks.

There are many factors involved, and so far, all we have done is to look at each, hypothesis by hypothesis, variable by variable, one at a time. However, they interact. What we really want is a model of usage and its effects on acquisition. We can measure these factors individually. However, such counts are vague indicators of how the demands of human interaction affect the content and ongoing coadaptation of discourse, how this is perceived and interpreted, how usage episodes are assimilated into the learner's system, and how the system reacts accordingly. We need a model of learning, development, and emergence. Learning is dynamic; it takes place during processing, as Hebb (1949), Craik and Lockhart (1972), Elman et al. (1996), and Bybee and Hopper (2001) have variously emphasized from their neural, cognitive, connectionist, and linguistic perspectives, and the units of learning are thus the units of language processing episodes. Before learners can use constructions productively, they have to encounter useful exemplars and analyze them, to identify their linguistic form and to map it to meaning and use. Each construction has its form, its meaning, its use, and its contingency of mapping among them. Our analyses here have shown that the input that learners get is biased so that they frequently experience forms that are distinctively associated with prototypical functions or construals. People's actions in the world, their categorization of the world, and their talk about these actions and classifications occur in broadly parallel relative frequencies. We believe that these parallels make constructions learnable, but we need a method for pursuing these ideas.

Connectionist (Emergent) Simulations of Acquisition

Although decontexualized, computer simulation allows the investigation of the dynamic interactions of these factors in language learning, processing, and use. In the remainder of this article we present two different connectionist architectures for the simulation of the emergence of the VACs described here.

Architecture 1

We use serial connectionist models. Simple recurrent networks (SRNs) have a proven utility in simulating language learning: allowing the identification of word boundaries from sequences of phonemes, word classes from sequences of words in small language samples, and phrase structure and lexical semantics from large usage corpora (Borovsky & Elman, 2006; Christiansen & Chater, 2001; Elman, 1990, 1998, 2004; Redington & Chater, 1998).

In SRNs the input to the network is the current item (letter, phoneme, word, phrase, or whatever) in a language stream, and the output represents the network's best guess as to the next item. The difference between the predicted state and the correct subsequent state (the target output) is used by the learning algorithm to adjust the weights in the network at every time step. In this way, the network improves its accuracy with experience. A common architecture involves an input layer (a layer of processing units that receive inputs from sources external to the network itself, whose units code the set of items in the language and whose activity identifies which item is currently being experienced), an output layer (which codes the language in the same way and which sends signals outside the network itself), and a hidden layer (whose units communicate between the inputs and outputs and whose activity represents the internal state of the model). A context layer is a special subset of inputs that receives no external input but which feeds the result of the previous processing back into the internal representations. Thus, at time 2, the hidden layer processes both the input of time 2 and, from the context layer, its own prior state of processing at time 1, and so on, recursively. It is by this means that SRNs capture the sequential nature of temporal inputs.

Elman (1990) trained a network of 31 input nodes, 31 output nodes, and hidden and context vectors of 150 units, each with sequences of words following a simple grammar. A 27,534-word sequence formed the training set and the network had to learn to predict the next word in the sequence. At the end of training, Elman cluster-analyzed the representations that the model had formed across its hidden unit activations for each word + context vector. The resultant dendrogram demonstrated that the network had discovered several major categories of words: large categories of verbs and nouns, smaller categories of inanimate or animate nouns, smaller still categories of human and nonhuman animals, and so forth. This graded, soft, and implicit category structure had emerged from the language input without any semantics or real-world grounding.

Our network architecture is shown in Figure 8. There is a 15 × 14 = 210-unit input layer, which is used to code the most frequent words in the NS

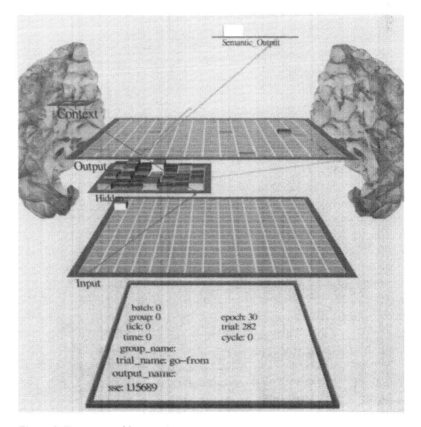

Figure 8 Emergent architecture 1.

constructions. These words and their codings are shown in the Appendix. Input units have activity 0 or 1. In Figure 8, input unit 166 is active; in our coding, this represents the word "go" There are 49 hidden units (HUs) and a context layer (iconified in the diagram for simplicity) of the same dimensions. There is a 15 × 14 = 210-unit output layer that codes the most frequent words in the NS constructions in the same way as the input. There is additionally a three-unit Semantic output layer whose units code the semantics associated with these utterances (1 for VL, 2 for VOL, 3 for VOO). Figure 8 shows the network in a trained state, in which, on experiencing "go," the model is predicting that corresponding VL semantics are likely and that several words could probably follow, including "to," "from," "left," and so forth (shown by raised columns on the corresponding output units).

Simulations were run using the "Emergent" software environment (Aisa, Mingus, & O'Reilly, 2008a, 2008b). The models were feedforward and learned by backpropagation of error. The learning rate was 0.1, no momentum was used, and training was carried out in epochs of 5,980 sweeps (one sweep corresponding to presentation of one word). The epoch sequence was constructed as follows: 1,341 NS Interviewer constructions (900 VL, 302 VOL, and 139 VOO) in the analysis of the ESF data were randomly sorted and then coded into input-output word pairs; for example, the construction "I gave you the money" became ###-I, I-give, give-you, you-the, the-money (### = start of construction marker, verbs were lemmatized). The codes followed the system shown in the Appendix; for example, *go* as a string of 210 zeros (aligned to the input units) with the exception of unit 166 with value 1, ### as a 1 followed by 209 zeros, and so forth. Low-frequency words, which do not appear in the Appendix, are coded with a 1 on unit 201, indicating "word not known."

The model is initialized with random weights. Imagine an epoch where the first construction, by random sort, is "I gave you the money," a VOO construction. Trial 1 shows the input "###" and the model makes some outputs according to its random weights. It is then shown on the output units that the next word is *I* with corresponding VL semantic activity. Its internal state is copied to the context units. It adjusts its weights by backprop to better approximate this outcome in the future, exploiting the connections through its hidden units. On the next trial, the model experiences "I" in the updated context and it makes some prediction according to its current weights. It is then shown on the output units that the next word is "go" with corresponding VL semantic activity, and so on.

The model as a whole was trained over 10 such epochs. At the end of each, it was tested by giving it, without feedback, the 200 words shown in the Appendix, one by one, and for each, its predictions of the corresponding semantics were recorded along with the internal state of activation across the hidden units. We also tested it for its generalized responses to the test patterns "you go to the shop," "put it in there," and "you give me money" in all variants where each word is substituted in turn by a wug pattern (that becomes a "not known" code).

Results

The amount of activation for the different verbs after each of the 10 epochs of training is shown for the VL, VOL, and VOO units in the right-hand panels of Figures 5–7.

In the simulation data in Figure 5 it is clear that the model learns early on that VL is the most probable (default) construction with a baseline activation of around 0.75. The verb that seeds this construction is *go*, followed somewhat later by *come*. Comparison of the learner data and simulation data shows a very similar development profile. The rank order correlation between the VL verb emergence order in the learners and VL activation for those verbs in the simulations at epoch 10 was $\rho = 0.77$.

In Figure 6, for learner and model alike, *put* is the verb which leads the development of VOL. Again, there are similar profiles across the learners and simulations. The rank order correlation between VOL verb emergence in the learners, and verb VOL activation in the simulations at epoch 10 was $\rho = 0.78$.

In Figure 7, there is a clear pacemaker for the VOO construction in simulation and learner alike, *give*. The rank order correlation between learner VOO verb emergence order, and verb VOO activation in the simulations at epoch 10 was $\rho = 0.81$.

Thus, an SRN exposed to NS usage acquires these VACs using the verbs at their center as the primary cues to construction category. The development of the different constructions and the different verbs in each demonstrate that model and learner alike are sensitive to the frequency and frequency distribution of the verbs, of the semantic types, and of the reliabilities of mapping between them.

What of the other cues? Figure 9 shows that the simulation, like the learners, comes to learn that some prepositions are more reliable cues to particular VACs than others (*to, at,* and *into* for VL, *on, up, under* and *over* for VOL, all such prepositions inhibit VOO activation; subject pronouns *they, you* and *he* for VL, inanimate object pronouns *it, them, these* for VOL, animate object pronouns *me, him* for VOO).

Finally, all of these test activations as reported here for the simulations were for individual words, out of context. Yet the driving force of these investigations

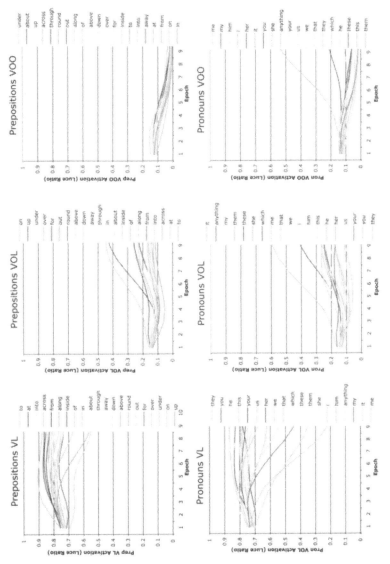

Figure 9 Activation of the VL, VOL, and VOO patterns by different Prepositions and Pronouns in Simulation 1.

was to understand their conspiracy as cue follows cue, and these different features interact dynamically in the activation of abstract VAC schemata. Can the model identify these in the absence of specific word information, in the same way that we know that "Tom wugged the paper napkin across the table" is a VOL? Figure 10 shows VL activation as the prototypical sentence "you go to the shop" is successively experienced, and as possible alternative permutations where one word is replaced by a wug pattern (i.e., an unknown word) and the same for VOL activation with "put it in there" and VOO activation with "you give me money." In each case, it can be seen that activation is cumulative over words, that each construction is successfully activated even when individual component words are wugged, and that the greatest decrement is when the cues from the verb are absent; these are abstract schema, but they have been built from collaborative experience of individual verb islands.

These simulations show how simple general learning mechanisms, exposed to the coadapted language usage typical of NSs as they speak with NNSs, learn abstract verb argument constructions in the same order of emergence as NNSs and using the same cues. The factors that we measured in the first part of this article conspire in the emergence of these constructions from usage.

Architecture 2 (No Semantics)

One response to initial presentations of the results of these simulations is that we give too much to these models by including a semantic layer. Perhaps this information serves as TRICS (The Representations it Crucially Supposes) that cryptoembody rules within the connectionist network so that no real learning is necessary (Lachter & Bever, 1988). We find this a difficult criticism to credit, as any alternative would deny any processes of Semantic Bootstrapping. Language without meaningful reference is no language at all, and anything of any complexity would not be learnable. Nevertheless, it is an interesting exercise to see just what structure is learnable by processes of Syntactic Bootstrapping alone. For that reason we ran the same simulations with the same architecture except for the elimination of the semantic layer. The model was trained with the same input patterns but simply had to predict the next word.

In the absence of semantic output units, there is no explicit way of directly testing its accuracy of categorization of the patterns. However, we can investigate the patterning of its internal states on the hidden units as it experiences different words. We ran this model for 100 epochs, testing the HU activations on experiencing the 200 different test words out of context without feedback after every 10 epochs. Figure 11 shows the dendrograms from a cluster analysis of these patterns for the key verbs of interest. It can be seen, as in the

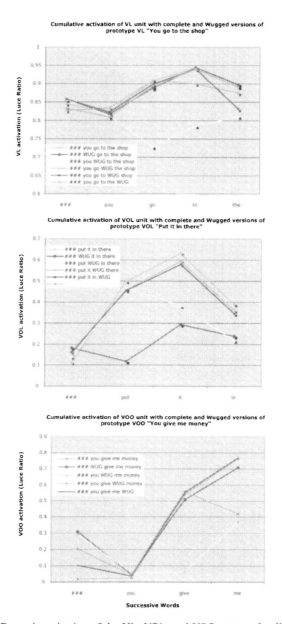

Figure 10 Dynamic activation of the VL, VOL, and VOO patterns by different prototypical sequences with each word wugged in turn after 10 epochs of training of Simulation 1.

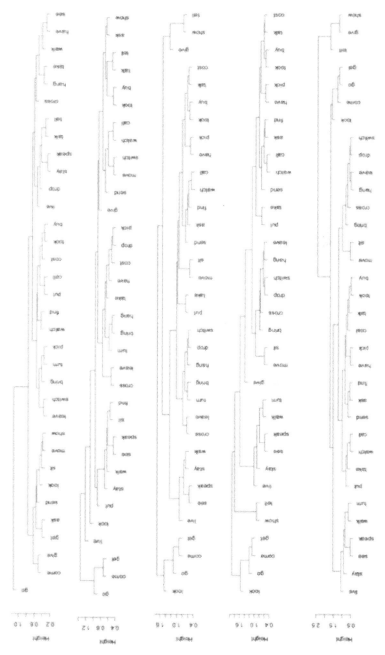

Figure 11 Dendrogram of hidden unit representations from Simulation 2 after 10, 30, 50, 70, and 90 epochs of training when tested.

demonstrations of Elman (1990) and Borovsky & Elman (2006), that structure is emergent. At Epoch 10, *go* is categorized separately from the other verbs; by epoch 30, it is joined by *come* and *get*, and by epoch 50, there is a clear cluster of verbs that we could label VL: *go, come, look, get*. At epoch 30, a nascent VOO category is forming over on the right, including *give, buy, tell, ask*, and *show*. After epoch 50, *give, show*, and *tell*, the prototypical VOO verbs, are in a clear category of their own. *Put* and *take* separate out by epoch 50 and move with other VOL patterns thereafter. Syntagmatic patterning alone is sufficient to allow the model to learn these different categories, albeit more slowly than when semantic information is also available.

Conclusions and Future

Our findings provide empirical support for the hypothesis that the emergence of linguistic constructions can be understood according to psychological principles of category learning and the social principle of coadaptation. Learning is sensitive to input frequency, reliabilities of form-meaning-use mapping, and prototypicality and generality of function. However, there is more to it than that. The structure of language reflects these principles too. It is doubtful that these parallels are accidental—more likely they emerge through usage. A consequence, we believe, is that in natural language, the type-token frequency distributions of construction islands, their prototypicality and generality of function in these roles, and their reliability of mappings between these, together, conspire to optimize learning.

We intend in future simulations to try to tease out the different roles of these factors. In the same way that Simulation 2 denies the role of semantics, so in future models we will investigate the emergence of these constructions in the absence of each factor in turn: What is the effect of providing the model with a flat type-token frequency profile rather that an Zipfian one? What is the effect of making all exemplars equal members of a semantic category rather than populating a radial structure with exemplars varying in prototypicality, etc.? These simulations parallel cognitive neuroscientific connectionist investigations, where the effects of lesioning different parts of the model architecture are investigated, but here we are lesioning simulated language itself rather than brain structure.

Like the other authors of articles in this issue, we believe that the functions of language in human communication have resulted in the evolution through usage of a system that optimally maps human sociocognition onto communicatively effective language form. The result is a system that is readily acquired. We are only at the beginnings of understanding the dynamic emergence of this complex system, but we are sure, at least, that this is the appropriate approach.

Revised version accepted 1 June 2009

References

Aisa, B., Mingus, B., & O'Reilly, R. C. (May 2008a). [Computer Software]. Emergent. Retrieved from http://grey.colorado.edu/emergent/index.php/Main_Page/

Aisa, B., Mingus, B., & O'Reilly, R. C. (2008b). The emergent neural modeling system. *Neural Networks, 21,* 1146–1152.

Barlow, M., & Kemmer, S. (Eds.). (2000). *Usage based models of language.* Stanford, CA: CSLI Publications.

Bates, E., & MacWhinney, B. (1987). Competition, variation, and language learning. In B. MacWhinney (Ed.), *Mechanisms of language acquisition* (pp. 157–193). Hillsdale, NJ: Lawrence Erlbaum.

Biber, D., Conrad, S., & Reppen, R. (1998). *Corpus linguistics: Investigating language structure and use.* New York: Cambridge University Press.

Bod, R., Hay, J., & Jannedy, S. (Eds.). (2003). *Probabilistic linguistics.* Cambridge, MA: MIT Press.

Borovsky, A., & Elman, J. L. (2006). Language input and semantic categories: A relation between cognition and early word learning. *Journal of Child Language, 33,* 759–790.

Bybee, J. (2005, January). *From usage to grammar: The mind's response to repetition.* Paper presented at the Linguistic Society of America, Oakland, CA.

Bybee, J., & Hopper, P. (Eds.). (2001). *Frequency and the emergence of linguistic structure.* Amsterdam: Benjamins.

Celce-Murcia, M., & Larsen-Freeman, D. (1999). *The grammar book: An ESL/EFL teacher's course* (2nd ed.). Boston: Heinle/Cengage.

Childers, J. B., & Tomasello, M. (2001). The role of pronouns in young children's acquisition of the English transitive construction. *Developmental Psychology, 37,* 739–748.

Christiansen, M. H., & Chater, N. (Eds.). (2001). *Connectionist psycholinguistics.* Westport, CT: Ablex.

Cohen, H., & Lefebvre, C. (Eds.). (2005). *Handbook of categorization in cognitive science.* Mahwah, NJ: Elsevier.

Craik, F. I. M., & Lockhart, R. S. (1972). Levels of processing: A framework for memory research. *Journal of Verbal Learning and Verbal Behavior, 11,* 671–684.

Croft, W., & Cruise, A. (2004). *Cognitive linguistics.* Cambridge: Cambridge University Press.

Dale, R., & Spivey, M. (2006). Unraveling the dyad: Using recurrence analysis to explore patterns of syntactic coordination between children and caregivers in conversation. *Language Learning, 56,* 391–430.

de Bot, K., Lowie, W., & Verspoor, M. (2007). A dynamic systems theory to second language acquisition. *Bilingualism: Language and Cognition, 10*, 7–21.

Dietrich, R., Klein, W., & Noyau, C. (Eds.). (1995). *The acquisition of temporality in a second language.* Amsterdam: Benjamins.

Elio, R., & Anderson, J. R. (1981). The effects of category generalizations and instance similarity on schema abstraction. *Journal of Experimental Psychology: Human Learning & Memory, 7*(6), 397–417.

Elio, R., & Anderson, J. R. (1984). The effects of information order and learning mode on schema abstraction. *Memory & Cognition, 12*(1), 20–30.

Ellis, N. C. (1998). Emergentism, connectionism and language learning. *Language Learning, 48*(4), 631–664.

Ellis, N. C. (2002). Frequency effects in language processing. A review with implications for theories of implicit and explicit language acquisition. *Studies in Second Language Acquisition, 24*(2), 143–188.

Ellis, N. C. (2003). Constructions, chunking, and connectionism: The emergence of second language structure. In C. Doughty & M. H. Long (Eds.), *Handbook of second language acquisition* (pp. 33–68). Oxford: Blackwell.

Ellis, N. C. (2005). At the interface: Dynamic interactions of explicit and implicit language knowledge. *Studies in Second Language Acquisition, 27*, 305–352.

Ellis, N. C. (2006a). Cognitive perspectives on SLA: The Associative Cognitive CREED. *AILA Review, 19*, 100–121.

Ellis, N. C. (2006b). Language acquisition as rational contingency learning. *Applied Linguistics, 27*(1), 1–24.

Ellis, N. C. (2006c). Selective attention and transfer phenomena in SLA: Contingency, cue competition, salience, interference, overshadowing, blocking, and perceptual learning. *Applied Linguistics, 27*(2), 1–31.

Ellis, N. C. (2007). Dynamic Systems and SLA: The wood and the trees. *Bilingualism: Language & Cognition, 10*, 23–25.

Ellis, N. C. (2008a). The dynamics of language use, language change, and first and second language acquisition. *Modern Language Journal, 41*(3), 232–249.

Ellis, N. C. (2008b). Usage-based and form-focused language acquisition: The associative learning of constructions, learned-attention, and the limited L2 endstate. In P. Robinson & N. C. Ellis (Eds.), *Handbook of cognitive linguistics and second language acquisition* (pp. 372–405). London: Routledge.

Ellis, N. C., & Ferreira-Junior, F. (2009a). Constructions and their acquisition: Islands and the distinctiveness of their occupancy. *Annual Review of Cognitive Linguistics, 7*, 188–221.

Ellis, N. C., & Ferreira-Junior, F. (2009b). Construction Learning as a function of Frequency, Frequency Distribution, and Function *Modern Language Journal, 93*, 370–386.

Ellis, N. C., & Larsen-Freeman, D. (Eds.). (2006a). Language emergence: Implications for Applied Linguistics [Special issue]. *Applied Linguistics, 27*(4).

Ellis, N. C., & Larsen-Freeman, D. (2006b). Introduction. *Applied Linguistics, 27*(4), 558–589.

Elman, J. L. (1990). Finding structure in time. *Cognitive Science, 14,* 179–211.

Elman, J. L. (1998). Generalization, simple recurrent networks, and the emergence of structure. In M. A. Gernsbacher & S. J. Derry (Eds.), *Proceedings of the twentieth annual conference of the Cognitive Science Society.* Mahwah, NJ: Lawrence Erlbaum.

Elman, J. L. (2004). An alternative view of the mental lexicon. *Trends in Cognitive Science, 8,* 301–306.

Elman, J. L., Bates, E. A., Johnson, M. H., Karmiloff-Smith, A., Parisi, D., & Plunkett, K. (1996). *Rethinking innateness: A connectionist perspective on development.* Cambridge, MA: MIT Press.

Feldweg, H. (1991). *The European Science Foundation Second Language Database.* Nijmegen: Max-Planck-Institute for Psycholinguistics.

Gleitman, L. (1990). The structural source of verb meaning. *Language Acquisition, 1,* 3–55.

Goldberg, A. E. (1995). *Constructions: A construction grammar approach to argument structure.* Chicago: University of Chicago Press.

Goldberg, A. E. (2003). Constructions: A new theoretical approach to language. *Trends in Cognitive Science, 7,* 219–224.

Goldberg, A. E. (2006). *Constructions at work: The nature of generalization in language.* Oxford: Oxford University Press.

Goldberg, A. E., Casenhiser, D. M., & Sethuraman, N. (2004). Learning argument structure generalizations. *Cognitive Linguistics, 15,* 289–316.

Gries, S. T., & Stefanowitsch, A. (2004). Extending collostructional analysis: A corpus-based perspective on "alternations." *International Journal of Corpus Linguistics, 9,* 97–129.

Gries, S. T., & Wulff, S. (2005). Do foreign language learners also have constructions? Evidence from priming, sorting, and corpora. *Annual Review of Cognitive Linguistics, 3,* 182–200.

Hebb, D. O. (1949). *The organization of behaviour.* New York: Wiley.

Holland, J. H. (1992). *Hidden order: How adaption builds complexity.* Reading, MA: Addison-Wesley.

Holland, J. H. (1998). *Emergence: From chaos to order.* Oxford: Oxford University Press.

Lachter, J., & Bever, T. (1988). The relation between linguistic structure and associative theories of language learning: A constructive critique of some connectionist learning models. *Cognition, 28,* 195–247.

Lakoff, G. (1987). *Women, fire, and dangerous things: What categories reveal about the mind.* Chicago: University of Chicago Press.

Langacker, R. W. (1987). *Foundations of cognitive grammar: Vol. 1. Theoretical prerequisites.* Stanford, CA: Stanford University Press.

Larsen-Freeman, D. (1976). An explanation for the morpheme acquisition order of second language learners. *Language Learning, 26*, 125–134.

Larsen-Freeman, D. (1997). Chaos/complexity science and second language acquisition. *Applied Linguistics, 18*, 141–165.

Larsen-Freeman, D. (2002a). The grammar of choice. In E. Hinkel & S. Fotos (Eds.), *New perspectives on grammar teaching* (pp. 105–120). Mahwah, NJ: Lawrence Erlbaum.

Larsen-Freeman, D. (2002b). Language acquisition and language use from a chaos/complexity theory perspective. In C. Kramsch (Ed.), *Language acquisition and language socialization* (pp. 33–46). London: Continuum.

Larsen-Freeman, D. (2003). *Teaching language: From grammar to grammaring.* Boston: Heinle & Heinle.

Larsen-Freeman, D., & Cameron, L. (2008). *Complex systems and applied linguistics.* Oxford: Oxford University Press.

Larsen-Freeman, D., & Long, M. (1991). *An introduction to second language acquisition research.* New York: Longman.

MacWhinney, B. (1987). The Competition model. In B. MacWhinney (Ed.), *Mechanisms of language acquisition* (pp. 249–308). Hillsdale, NJ: Lawrence Erlbaum.

MacWhinney, B. (Ed.). (1999). *The emergence of language.* Hillsdale, NJ: Lawrence Erlbaum.

Murphy, G. L. (2003). *The big book of concepts.* Boston: MIT Press.

Ninio, A. (1999). Pathbreaking verbs in syntactic development and the question of prototypical transitivity. *Journal of Child Language, 26*, 619–653.

Ninio, A. (2006). *Language and the learning curve: A new theory of syntactic development.* Oxford: Oxford University Press.

Perdue, C. (Ed.). (1993). *Adult language acquisition: Crosslinguistic perspectives.* Cambridge: Cambridge University Press.

Pinker, S. (1989). *Learnability and cognition: The acquisition of argument structure.* Cambridge, MA: Bradford Books.

Port, R. F., & Van Gelder, T. (1995). *Mind as motion: Explorations in the dynamics of cognition.* Boston: MIT Press.

Posner, M. I., & Keele, S. W. (1968). On the genesis of abstract ideas. *Journal of Experimental Psychology, 77*, 353–363.

Posner, M. I., & Keele, S. W. (1970). Retention of abstract ideas. *Journal of Experimental Psychology, 83*, 304–308.

Redington, M., & Chater, N. (1998). Connectionist and statistical approaches to language acquisition: A distributional perspective. *Language and Cognitive Processes, 13*, 129–192.

Rescorla, R. A. (1968). Probability of shock in the presence and absence of CS in fear conditioning. *Journal of Comparative and Physiological Psychology, 66*, 1–5.

Robinson, P., & Ellis, N. C. (Eds.). (2008). *A handbook of cognitive linguistics and second language acquisition*. London: Routledge.

Sinclair, J. (1991). *Corpus, concordance, collocation*. Oxford: Oxford University Press.

Sinclair, J. (2004). *Trust the text: Language, corpus and discourse*. London: Routledge.

Spivey, M. (2006). *The continuity of mind*. Oxford: Oxford University Press.

Stefanowitsch, A., & Gries, S. T. (2003). Collostructions: Investigating the interaction between words and constructions. *International Journal of Corpus Linguistics, 8*, 209–243.

Thelen, E., & Smith, L. B. (1994). *A dynamic systems approach to the development of cognition and action*. Cambridge MA: MIT Press.

Tomasello, M. (1992). *First verbs: A case study of early grammatical development*. New York: Cambridge University Press.

Tomasello, M. (2003). *Constructing a language*. Boston: Harvard University Press.

Tomasello, M. (Ed.). (1998). *The new psychology of language: Cognitive and functional approaches to language structure*. Mahwah, NJ: Lawrence Erlbaum.

van Geert, P. (1991). A dynamic systems model of cognitive and language growth. *Psychological Review, 98*, 3–53.

Wilson, S. (2003). Lexically specific constructions in the acquisition of inflection in English. *Journal of Child Language, 30*, 75–115.

Wulff. S., Ellis, N. C., Römer, U., Bardovi-Harlig, K., & LeBlanc, C. (2009). The acquisition of tense-aspect: Converging evidence from corpora, cognition, and learner constructions. *Modern Language Journal, 93*, 354–370.

Zipf, G. K. (1935). *The psycho-biology of language: An introduction to dynamic philology*. Cambridge, MA: MIT Press.

Appendix

The 200 Most Frequent Words From the Interviewers' Constructions and Their Code Numbers Mapping Them to Input and Output Units

1	###	35	bit	69	money	103	along
2	all	36	book	70	names	104	at
3	any	37	box	71	people	105	away
4	english	38	brochures	72	person	106	down
5	next	39	building	73	phone	107	for
6	some	40	buses	74	picture	108	from
7	again	41	business	75	place	109	in
8	anywhere	42	cafe	76	police	110	inside
9	around	43	car	77	prison	111	into
10	back	44	cars	78	questions	112	of
11	here	45	centre	79	road	113	on
12	left	46	chance	80	room	114	out
13	not	47	child	81	school	115	over
14	off	48	children	82	shop	116	round
15	outside	49	city	83	something	117	through
16	right	50	clothes	84	station	118	to
17	straight	51	coat	85	string	119	under
18	then	52	country	86	table	120	up
19	there	53	course	87	television	121	anything
20	upstairs	54	cup	88	test	122	he
21	a	55	directions	89	thing	123	her
22	an	56	doctor	90	things	124	him
23	the	57	door	91	top	125	i
24	and	58	end	92	town	126	it
25	one	59	friend	93	travel	127	me
26	account	60	ground	94	water	128	my
27	action	61	home	95	way	129	she
28	air	62	hospital	96	wife	130	that
29	amountmoney	63	house	97	window	131	them
30	anybody	64	letter	98	woman	132	these
31	arms	65	map	99	work	133	they
32	ashtray	66	media	100	about	134	this
33	bag	67	microphone	101	above	135	us
34	bin	68	middle	102	across	136	we

137	which	153	wait	169	move	185	switch
138	you	154	want	170	sit	186	take
139	your	155	can	171	stay	187	talk
140	carry	156	will	172	walk	188	took
141	did	157	am	173	turn	189	watch
142	drive	158	are	174	get	190	send
143	hit	159	is	175	bring	191	ask
144	let	160	do	176	cross	192	buy
145	lets	161	could	177	drop	193	call
146	play	162	must	178	hang	194	cost
147	run	163	should	179	have	195	find
148	sell	164	would	180	leave	196	give
149	start	165	come	181	pick	197	show
150	stop	166	go	182	put	198	tell
151	telephone	167	live	183	see	199	where
152	try	168	look	184	speak	200	who

Language Learning   ISSN 0023-8333

A Usage-Based Approach to Recursion
in Sentence Processing

Morten H. Christiansen

Cornell University

Maryellen C. MacDonald

University of Wisconsin-Madison

Most current approaches to linguistic structure suggest that language is recursive, that recursion is a fundamental property of grammar, and that independent performance constraints limit recursive abilities that would otherwise be infinite. This article presents a usage-based perspective on recursive sentence processing, in which recursion is construed as an acquired skill and in which limitations on the processing of recursive constructions stem from interactions between linguistic experience and intrinsic constraints on learning and processing. A connectionist model embodying this alternative theory is outlined, along with simulation results showing that the model is capable of constituent-like generalizations and that it can fit human data regarding the differential processing difficulty associated with center-embeddings in German and cross-dependencies in Dutch. Novel predictions are furthermore derived from the model and corroborated by the results of four behavioral experiments, suggesting that acquired recursive abilities are intrinsically bounded not only when processing complex recursive constructions, such as center-embedding and cross-dependency, but also during processing of the simpler, right- and left-recursive structures.

Introduction

Ever since Humboldt (1836/1999, researchers have hypothesized that language makes "infinite use of finite means." Yet the study of language had to wait nearly

We thank Jerry Cortrite, Jared Layport, and Mariana Sapera for their assistance in data collection and Brandon Kohrt for help with the stimuli. We are also grateful to Christina, Behme, Shravan Vasishth, and two anonymous reviewers for their comments on an earlier version of this article.

Correspondence concerning this article should be addressed to Morten H. Christiansen, Department of Psychology, Uris Hall, Cornell University, Ithaca, NY 14853. Internet: christiansen@cornell.edu

a century before the technical devices for adequately expressing the unbound-
edness of language became available through the development of recursion
theory in the foundations of mathematics (cf. Chomsky, 1965). Recursion has
subsequently become a fundamental *property* of grammar, permitting a finite
set of rules and principles to process and produce an infinite number of expressions. Thus, recursion has played a central role in the generative approach
to language from its very inception. It now forms the core of the Minimalist
Program (Boeckx, 2006; Chomsky, 1995) and has been suggested to be the
only aspect of the language faculty unique to humans (Hauser, Chomsky, &,
Fitch, 2002).

Although generative grammars sanction infinitely complex recursive constructions, people's ability to deal with such constructions is quite limited. In
standard generative models of language processing, the unbounded recursive
power of the grammar is therefore typically harnessed by postulating *extrinsic* memory limitations (e.g., on stack depth; Church, 1982; Marcus, 1980).
This article presents an alternative, usage-based view of recursive sentence
structure, suggesting that recursion is not an innate property of grammar or
an a priori computational property of the neural systems subserving language.
Instead, we suggest that the ability to process recursive structure is acquired
gradually, in an item-based fashion given experience with specific recursive
constructions. In contrast to generative approaches, constraints on recursive
regularities do not follow from extrinsic limitations on memory or processing;
rather they arise from interactions between linguistic experience and architectural constraints on learning and processing (see also Engelmann & Vasishth,
2009; MacDonald & Christiansen, 2002), *intrinsic* to the system in which the
knowledge of grammatical regularities is embedded. Constraints specific to
particular recursive constructions are acquired as part of the knowledge of the
recursive regularities themselves and therefore form an integrated part of the
representation of those regularities. As we will see next, recursive constructions
come in a variety of forms; but contrary to traditional approaches to recursion,
we suggest that intrinsic constraints play a role not only in providing limitations
on the processing of complex recursive structures, such as center-embedding,
but also in constraining performance on the simpler right- and left-branching
recursive structures—albeit to a lesser degree.

Varieties of Recursive Structure

Natural language is typically thought to involve a variety of recursive constructions.[1] The simplest recursive structures, which also tend to be the most

common in normal speech, are either right-branching as in (1) or left-branching as in (2):

(1) a. John saw the dog that chased the cat.
     b. John saw the dog that chased the cat that bit the mouse.
(2) a. The fat black dog was sleeping.
     b. The big fat black dog was sleeping.

In the above example sentences, (1a) can be seen as incorporating a single level of right-branching recursion in the form of the embedded relative clause *that chased the cat*. Sentence (1b) involves two levels of right-branching recursion because of the two embedded relative clauses *that chased the cat* and *that bit the mouse*. A single level of left-branching recursion is part of (2a) in the form of the adjective *fat* fronting *black dog*. In (2b) two adjectives, *big* and *fat*, iteratively front *black dog*, resulting in a left-branching construction with two levels of recursion. Because right- and left-branching recursion can be captured by iterative processes, we will refer to them together as *iterative* recursion (Christiansen & Chater, 1999).

Chomsky (1956) showed that iterative recursion of infinite depth can be processed by a finite-state device. However, recursion also exists in more complex forms that cannot be processed in its full, unbounded generality by finite-state devices. The best known type of such *complex* recursion is center-embedding as exemplified in (3):

(3) a. The dog that John saw chased the cat.
     b. The cat that the dog that John saw chased bit the mouse.

These sentences provide center-embedded versions of the right-branching recursive constructions in (1). In (3a), the sentence *John saw the dog* is embedded as a relative clause within the main sentence *the dog chased the cat*, generating one level of center-embedded recursion. Two levels of center-embedded recursion can be observed in (3b), in which *John saw the dog* is embedded within *the dog chased the cat*, which, in turn, is embedded within *the cat bit the mouse*.

The processing of center-embedded constructions has been studied extensively in psycholinguistics for more than half a century. These studies have shown, for example, that English sentences with more than one center-embedding [e.g., sentence (3b)] are read with the same intonation as a list of random words (Miller, 1962), cannot easily be memorized (Foss & Cairns, 1970; Miller & Isard, 1964), are difficult to paraphrase (Hakes & Foss, 1970; Larkin & Burns, 1977) and comprehend (Blaubergs & Braine, 1974; Hakes,

Evans, & Brannon, 1976; Hamilton & Deese, 1971; Wang, 1970), and are judged to be ungrammatical (Marks, 1968). These processing limitations are not confined to English. Similar patterns have been found in a variety of languages, ranging from French (Peterfalvi & Locatelli, 1971), German (Bach, Brown, & Marslen-Wilson, 1986), and Spanish (Hoover, 1992) to Hebrew (Schlesinger, 1975), Japanese (Uehara & Bradley, 1996) and Korean (Hagstrom & Rhee, 1997). Indeed, corpus analyses of Danish, English, Finnish, French, German, Latin, and Swedish (Karlsson, 2007) indicate that doubly center-embedded sentences are practically absent from spoken language. Moreover, it has been shown that using sentences with a semantic bias or giving people training can improve performance on such structures, but only to a limited extent (Blaubergs & Braine, 1974; Powell & Peters, 1973; Stolz, 1967).

Symbolic models of sentence processing typically embody a rule-based competence grammar that permits unbounded recursion. This means that the models, unlike humans, can process sentences with multiple center-embeddings. Since Miller and Chomsky (1963), the solution to this mismatch has been to impose extrinsic memory limitations exclusively aimed at capturing the human performance limitations on doubly center-embedded constructions. Examples include limits on stack depth (Church, 1982; Marcus, 1980), limits on the number of allowed sentence nodes (Kimball, 1973) or partially complete sentence nodes in a given sentence (Stabler, 1994), limits on the amount of activation available for storing intermediate processing products as well as executing production rules (Just & Carpenter, 1992), the "self-embedding interference constraint" (Gibson & Thomas, 1996), and an upper limit on sentential memory cost (Gibson, 1998).

No comparable limitations are imposed on the processing of iterative recursive constructions in symbolic models. This may due to the fact that even finite-state devices with bounded memory are able to process right- and left-branching recursive structures of infinite length (Chomsky, 1956). It has been widely assumed that depth of recursion does not affect the acceptability (or processability) of iterative recursive structures in any interesting way (e.g., Chomsky, 1965; Church, 1982; Foss & Cairns, 1970; Gibson, 1998; Reich, 1969; Stabler, 1994). Indeed, many studies of center-embedding in English have used right-branching relative clauses as baseline comparisons and found that performance was better relative to the center-embedded stimuli (e.g., Foss & Cairns, 1970; Marks, 1968; Miller & Isard, 1964). A few studies have reported more detailed data on the effect of depth of recursion in right-branching constructions and found that comprehension also decreases as depth of recursion increases in these structures, although not too the same degree as with center-embedded stimuli (e.g., Bach et al., 1986; Blaubergs & Braine, 1974). However, it is not clear from these results whether the decrease in performance is caused by recursion per se or is merely a byproduct of increased sentence length.

In this article, we investigate four predictions derived from an existing connectionist model of the processing of recursive sentence structure (Christiansen, 1994; Christiansen & Chater, 1994). First, we provide a brief overview of the model and show that it is capable of constituent-based generalizations and that it can fit key human data regarding the processing of complex recursive constructions in the form of center-embedding in German and cross-dependencies in Dutch. The second half of the article describes four online grammaticality judgment experiments testing novel predictions, derived from the model, using a word-by-word self-paced reading task. Experiments 1 and 2 tested two predictions concerning iterative recursion, and Experiments 3 and 4 tested predictions concerning the acceptability of doubly center-embedded sentences using, respectively, semantically biased stimuli from a previous study (Gibson & Thomas, 1999) and semantically neutral stimuli.

A Connectionist Model of Recursive Sentence Processing

Our usage-based approach to recursion builds on a previously developed Simple Recurrent Network (SRN; Elman, 1990) model of recursive sentence processing (Christiansen, 1994; Christiansen & Chater, 1994). The SRN, as illustrated in Figure 1, is essentially a standard feed-forward network equipped with an extra layer of so-called context units. The hidden unit activations from the previous time step are copied back to these context units and paired with the

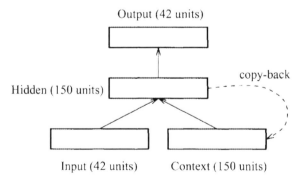

Figure 1 The basic architecture of the SRN used here as well as in Christiansen (1994) and Christiansen and Chater (1994). Arrows with solid lines denote trainable weights, whereas the arrow with the dashed line denotes the copy-back connections.

S	$\rightarrow$	NP VP .
NP	$\rightarrow$	N I N PP I N rel I PossP N I N and NP
VP	$\rightarrow$	V_i I V_t NP I V_o (NP) I V_c $that$ S
rel	$\rightarrow$	who VP I who NP V_{tlo}
PP	$\rightarrow$	prep N_{loc} (PP)
PossP	$\rightarrow$	(PossP) N Poss

Figure 2 The context-free grammar used to generate training stimuli for the connectionist model of recursive sentence processing developed by Christiansen (1994) and Christiansen and Chater (1994).

current input. This means that the current state of the hidden units can influence the processing of subsequent inputs, providing the SRN with an ability to deal with integrated sequences of input presented successively.

The SRN was trained via a word-by-word prediction task on 50,000 sentences (mean length: 6 words; range: 3–15 words) generated by a context-free grammar (see Figure 2) with a 38-word vocabulary.[2] This grammar involved left-branching recursion in the form of prenominal possessive genitives, right-branching recursion in the form of subject relative clauses, sentential complements, prepositional modifications of NPs, and NP conjunctions, as well as complex recursion in the form of center-embedded relative clauses. The grammar also incorporated subject noun/verb agreement and three additional verb argument structures (transitive, optionally transitive, and intransitive). The generation of sentences was further restricted by probabilistic constraints on the complexity and depth of recursion. Following training, the SRN performed well on a variety of recursive sentence structures, demonstrating that the SRN was able to acquire complex grammatical regularities.[3]

Usage-Based Constituents

A key question for connectionist models of language is whether they are able to acquire knowledge of grammatical regularities going beyond simple co-occurrence statistics from the training corpus. Indeed, Hadley (1994) suggested that connectionist models could not afford the kind of generalization abilities necessary to account for human language processing (see Marcus, 1998, for a similar critique). Christiansen and Chater (1994) addressed this challenge using the SRN from Christiansen (1994). In the training corpus, the noun *boy* had been prevented from ever occurring in a NP conjunction (i.e., NPs such as *John and boy* and *boy and John* did not occur). During training, the SRN had therefore only seen singular verbs following *boy*. Nonetheless, the network was able to correctly predict that a plural verb must follow *John and boy* as prescribed by the grammar. Additionally, the network was still able to correctly predict a plural verb when a prepositional phrase was attached to *boy* as in *John and boy from town*. This suggests that the SRN is able to make nonlocal generalizations based on the structural regularities in the training corpus (see Christiansen & Chater, 1994, for further details). If the SRN relied solely on local information, it would not have been able to make correct predictions in either case.

Here, we provide a more stringent test of the SRN's ability to make appropriate constituent-based generalizations, using the four different types of test sentences shown in (4):

(4) a. Mary says that John and **boy** see.   (known word)
     b. Mary says that John and **zog** see.   (novel word)
     c. *Mary says that John and **near** see.   (illegal word)
     d. Mary says that John and **man** see.   (control word)

Sentence (4a) is similar to what was used by Christiansen and Chater (1994) to demonstrate correct generalization for the known word, *boy*, used in a novel position. In (4b), a completely novel word, *zog*, which the SRN had not seen during training (i.e., the corresponding unit was never activated during training) is activated as part of the NP conjunction. As an ungrammatical contrast, (4c) involves the activation of a known word, *near*, used in a novel but illegal position. Finally, (4d) provides a baseline in which a known word, *man*, is used in a position in which it is likely to have occurred during training (although not in this particular sentence).

Figure 3 shows the summed activation for plural verbs for each of the four sentence types in (4). Strikingly, both the known word in a novel position as well as the completely novel word elicited activations of the plural verbs that were just as high as for the control word. In contrast, the SRN did not activate plural verbs after the illegal word, indicating that it is able to distinguish between known words used in novel positions (which are appropriate given its distributionally defined lexical category) versus known words used in an ungrammatical context. Thus, the network demonstrated sophisticated generalization abilities, ignoring local word co-occurrence constraints while appearing to comply with structural information at the constituent level. It is important to note, however, that SRN is unlikely to have acquired constituency in a categorical form (Christiansen & Chater, 2003) but instead have acquired constituents

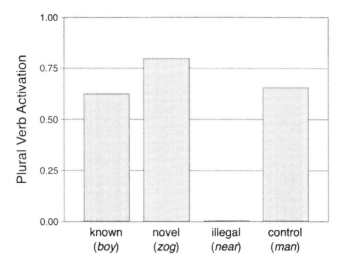

Figure 3 Activation of plural verbs after presentation of the sentence fragment *Mary says that John and N...*, where *N* is either a known word in a known position (*boy*), a novel word (*zog*), a known word in an illegal position (*near*), or a control word that have previously occurred in this position (*man*).

that are more in line with the usage-based notion outlined by Beckner and Bybee (this issue).

Deriving Novel Predictions
Simple Recurrent Networks have been employed successfully to model many aspects of psycholinguistic behavior, ranging from speech segmentation (e.g., Christiansen, Allen, & Seidenberg, 1998; Elman, 1990) and word learning (e.g., Sibley, Kello, Plaut, & Elman, 2008) to syntactic processing (e.g., Christiansen, Dale, & Reali, in press; Elman 1993; Rohde, 2002; see also Ellis & Larsen-Freeman, this issue) and reading (e.g., Plaut, 1999). Moreover, SRNs have also been shown to provide good models of nonlinguistic sequence learning (e.g., Botvinick & Plaut, 2004, 2006; Servan-Schreiber, Cleeremans, & McClelland, 1991). The human-like performance of the SRN can be attributed to an interaction between intrinsic architectural constraints (Christiansen & Chater, 1999) and the statistical properties of its input experience (MacDonald & Christiansen, 2002). By analyzing the internal states of SRNs before and after training with right-branching and center-embedded materials, Christiansen and Chater found that this type of network has a basic architectural bias toward locally bounded dependencies similar to those typically found in iterative

recursion. However, in order for the SRN to process multiple instances of iterative recursion, exposure to specific recursive constructions is required. Such exposure is even more crucial for the processing of center-embeddings because the network in this case also has to overcome its architectural bias toward local dependencies. Hence, the SRN does not have a built-in ability for recursion, but instead it develops its human-like processing of different recursive constructions through exposure to repeated instances of such constructions in the input.

In previous analyses, Christiansen (1994) noted certain limitations on the processing of iterative and complex recursive constructions. In the following, we flesh out these results in detail using the Grammatical Prediction Error (GPE) measure of SRN performance (Christiansen & Chater, 1999; MacDonald & Christiansen, 2002). To evaluate the extent to which a network has learned a grammar after training, performance on a test set of sentences is measured. For each word in the test sentences, a trained network should accurately predict the next possible words in the sentence; that is, it should activate all and only the words that produce grammatical continuations of that sentence. Moreover, it is important from a linguistic perspective not only to determine whether the activated words are grammatical given prior context but also which items are not activated despite being sanctioned by the grammar. Thus, the degree of activation of grammatical continuations should correspond to the probability of those continuations in the training set. The GPE assesses all of these facets of SRN performance, taking correct activations of grammatical continuations, correct suppression of ungrammatical continuations, incorrect activations of ungrammatical continuations, and incorrect suppressions of grammatical continuations into account (see Appendix A for details).

The GPE scores range between 0 and 1, providing a very stringent measure of performance. To obtain a perfect GPE score of 0, the SRN must not only predict all and only the next words prescribed by grammar but also be able to scale those predictions according to the lexical frequencies of the legal items. The GPE for an individual word reflects the difficulty that the SRN experienced for that word given the previous sentential context, and it can be mapped qualitatively onto word reading times, with low GPE values reflecting a prediction for short reading times and high values indicating long predicted reading times (MacDonald & Christiansen, 2002). The mean GPE averaged across a sentence expresses the difficulty that the SRN experienced across the sentence as a whole, and such GPE values have been found to correlate with sentence grammaticality ratings (Christiansen & Chater, 1999), with low mean GPE scores predicting low grammatical complexity ratings and high

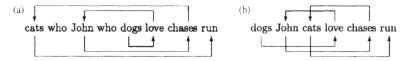

(a) cats who John who dogs love chases run

(b) dogs John cats love chases run

Figure 4 An illustration of the dependencies between subject nouns and verbs (arrows below) and between transitive verbs and their objects (arrows above) in sentences with two center-embeddings (a) and two cross-dependencies (b).

scores indicating a prediction for high complexity ratings. Next, we first use mean sentence GPE scores to fit data from human experiments concerning the processing of complex recursive constructions in German and Dutch, after which we derive novel predictions concerning human grammaticality ratings for both iterative and center-embedded recursive constructions in English and present four experiments testing these predictions.

Center-Embedding Versus Cross-Dependency

Center-embeddings and cross-dependencies have played an important role in the theory of language. Whereas center-embedding relations are nested within each other, cross-dependencies cross over one another (see Figure 4). As noted earlier, center-embeddings can be captured by context-free grammars, but cross-dependencies require a more powerful grammar formalism (Shieber, 1985). Perhaps not surprisingly, cross-dependency constructions are quite rare across the languages of the world, but they do occur in Swiss-German and Dutch. An example of a Dutch sentence with two cross-dependencies is shown in (5), with subscripts indicating dependency relations.

(5)   De mannen$_1$ hebben Hans$_2$ Jeanine$_3$ de paarden helpen$_1$ leren$_2$ voeren$_3$

   Literal: The men have Hans Jeanine the horses help teach feed

   Gloss: The men helped Hans teach Jeanine to feed the horses

Although cross-dependencies have been assumed to be more difficult to process than comparable center-embeddings, Bach et al. (1986) found that sentences with two center-embeddings in German were significantly harder to process than comparable sentences with two cross-dependencies in Dutch.

In order to model the comparative difficulty of processing center-embeddings versus cross-dependencies, we trained an SRN on sentences generated by a new grammar in which the center-embedded constructions were replaced by cross-dependency structures (see Figure 5). The iterative

$$S \rightarrow \text{NP VP .}$$

$$S_{cd} \rightarrow N_1 \ N_2 \ V_{1(tlo)} \ V_{2(i)} \ .$$

$$S_{cd} \rightarrow N_1 \ N_2 \ N \ V_{1(tlo)} \ V_{2(tlo)} \ .$$

$$S_{cd} \rightarrow N_1 \ N_2 \ N_3 \ V_{1(tlo)} \ V_{2(tlo)} \ V_{3(i)} \ .$$

$$S_{cd} \rightarrow N_1 \ N_2 \ N_3 \ N \ V_{1(tlo)} \ V_{2(tlo)} \ V3_{(tlo)} \ .$$

$$\text{NP} \rightarrow \text{N | N PP | N rel | PossP N | N } and \text{ NP}$$

$$\text{VP} \rightarrow V_i \ | \ V_t \ \text{NP} \ | \ V_o \ (\text{NP}) \ | \ V_c \ that \ \text{S}$$

$$\text{rel} \rightarrow who \ \text{VP}$$

$$\text{PP} \rightarrow \text{prep N}_{loc} \ (\text{PP})$$

$$\text{PossP} \rightarrow (\text{PossP}) \ \text{N Poss}$$

Figure 5 The context-sensitive grammar used to generate training stimuli for the connectionist model of recursive sentence processing developed by Christiansen (1994).

recursive constructions, vocabulary, and other grammar properties remained the same as in the original context-free grammar. Thus, only the complex recursive constructions differed across the two grammars. In addition, all training and network parameters were held constant across the two simulations. After training, the cross-dependency SRN achieved a level of general performance comparable to that of the center-embedding SRN (Christiansen, 1994). Here, we focus on the comparison between the processing of the two complex types of recursion at different depths of embedding.

Bach et al. (1986) asked native German speakers to provide comprehensibility ratings of German sentences involving varying depths of recursion in the form of center-embedded constructions and corresponding right-branching paraphrases with the same meaning. Native Dutch speakers were tested using similar Dutch materials but with the center-embedded constructions replaced by cross-dependency constructions. The left-hand side of Figure 6 shows the Bach et al. results, with the ratings for the right-branching paraphrase sentences subtracted from the matching complex recursive test sentences to remove effects of processing difficulty due to length. The SRN results—the mean sentence GPE scores averaged over 10 novel sentences—are displayed on the right-hand side of Figure 6. For both humans and SRNs, there is no difference in processing difficulty for the two types of complex recursion at one level of embedding. However, for doubly embedded constructions, center-embedded structures

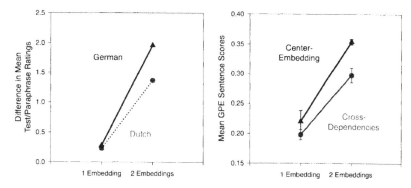

Figure 6 Human performance (from Bach et al., 1986) on center-embedded constructions in German and cross-dependency constructions in Dutch with one or two levels of embedding (left panel). SRN performance on similar complex recursive structures (right panel).

(in German) are harder to process than comparable cross-dependencies (in Dutch). These simulation results thus demonstrate that the SRNs exhibit the same kind of qualitative processing difficulties as humans do on the two types of complex recursive constructions (see also Christiansen & Chater, 1999). Crucially, the networks were able to match human performance without needing complex external memory devices (such as a stack of stacks; Joshi, 1990). Next, we go beyond fitting existing data to explore novel predictions made by the center-embedding SRN for the processing of recursive constructions in English.

Experiment 1: Processing Multiple Right-Branching Prepositional Phrases

In most models of sentence processing, multiple levels of iterative recursion are represented by having the exact same structure occurring several times (e.g., multiple instances of a PP). In contrast, the SRN learns to represent each level of recursion slightly differently from the previous one (Elman, 1991). This leads to increased processing difficulty as the level of recursion grows because the network has to keep track of each level of recursion separately, suggesting that depth of recursion in iterative constructions should affect processing difficulty beyond a mere length effect. Based on Christiansen's (1994) original analyses, we derived specific predictions for sentences involving zero, one, or two levels of right-branching recursion in the form of PP modifications of an NP[4] as shown in (6):

(6) a. The nurse with the vase says that the flowers by the window resemble roses. (1 PP)

   b. The nurse says that the flowers in the vase by the window resemble roses. (2 PPs)

   c. The blooming flowers in the vase on the table by the window resemble roses. (3 PPs)

Predictions were derived from the SRNs for these three types of sentences and tested with human participants using a variation of the "stop making sense" sentence-judgment paradigm (Boland, 1997; Boland, Tanenhaus, & Garnsey, 1990; Boland, Tanenhaus, Garnsey, & Carlson, 1995), with a focus on grammatical acceptability rather than semantic sensibility. Following the presentation of each sentence, participants rated the sentence for grammaticality on a 7-point scale; these ratings were then compared with the SRN predictions.

Method
Participants
Thirty-six undergraduate students from the University of Southern California received course credit for participation in this experiment. All participants in this and subsequent experiments were native speakers of English with normal or corrected-to-normal vision.

Materials
Nine experimental sentences were constructed with 1 PP, 2 PPs, and 3 PPs versions as in (6). All items are from this and subsequent experiments are included in Appendix B. Each sentence version had the same form as (6a)–(6c). The 1 PP sentence type began with a definite NP modified by a single PP (*The nurse with the vase*), followed by a sentential complement verb and a complementizer (*says that*), a definite NP modified by a second single PP (*the flowers by the window*), and a final transitive VP with an indefinite noun (*resemble roses*). The 2 PP sentence type began with the same definite NP as 1 PP stimuli, followed by the same sentential complement verb and complementizer, a definite NP modified by a recursive construction with 2 PPs (*the flowers in the vase by the window*), and the same final transitive VP as 1 PP stimuli. The 3 PP sentence type began with a definite NP including an adjective (*The blooming flowers*), modified by a recursive construction with 3 PPs (*in the vase on the table by the window*), and the same transitive VP as in the other two sentence types. Each sentence was 14 words long and always ended with the same final NP (*the window*) and VP (*resemble roses*).

The three conditions were counterbalanced across three lists. In addition, 9 practice sentences and 42 filler sentences were created to incorporate a variety of recursive constructions of equal complexity to the experimental sentences. Two of the practice sentences were ungrammatical as were nine of the fillers. Twenty-one additional stimulus items were sentences from other experiments and 30 additional fillers mixed multiple levels of different kinds of recursive structures.

Procedure

Participants read sentences on a computer monitor, using a word-by-word center presentation paradigm. Each trial started with a fixation cross at the center of the screen. The first press of the space bar removed the fixation cross and displayed the first word of the sentence, and subsequent presses removed the previous word and displayed the next word. For each word, participants decided whether what they had read so far was a grammatical sentence of English. Participants were instructed that both speed and accuracy were important in the experiment and to base their decisions on their first impression about whether a sentence was grammatical. If the sentence read so far was considered grammatical, the participants would press the space bar—if not, they would press a NO key when the sentence became ungrammatical. The presentation of a sentence ceased when the NO was pressed.

When participants finished a sentence, either by reading it all the way through with the space bar or by reading it part way and then pressing the NO key when it became ungrammatical, the screen was cleared and they would be asked to rate how "good" this sentence was.[5] The participants would respond by pressing a number between 1 and 7 on the keyboard, with 1 indicating that the sentence was "perfectly good English" and 7 indicating that it was "really bad English." Participants were encouraged to use the numbers in between for intermediate judgments. The computer recorded the response of the participant.

Participants were assigned randomly to three counterbalanced lists. Each participant saw a different randomization of experimental and filler items.

SRN Testing

The model was tested on three sets of sentences corresponding to the three types shown in (6). The determiner *the* and the adjective in (6c) (*blooming*) could not be included in test sentences because they were not found in the training grammar. Moreover, the actual lexical items used in the network simulations were different from those in the human experiment because of limitations imposed by the training vocabulary, but the lexical categories remained the same. The three sentence types had the same length as in the experiment, save that (6c) was one word shorter. All sentences involved at least two PPs [although only in (6b) and (6c) were they recursively related]. The crucial factor differentiating the three sentence types is the number of PPs modifying the subject noun (*flowers*) before the final verb (*resemble*). The sentence types were created to include 1, 2, or 3 PPs in this position. In order to ensure that the sentences were equal in length, right-branching sentential complements (*says that . . .*) were used in (6a) and (6b) such that the three sentence types are of the same global syntactic complexity. Mean GPE scores were recorded for 10 novel sentences of each type.

Results and Discussion
SRN Predictions
Although the model found the sentences relatively easy to process, there was a significant effect of depth of recursion on GPE scores, $F(2, 18) = 13.41, p < .0001$, independent of sentence length (see Table 1). Thus, the model predicted an effect of sentence type for human ratings, with 3 PPs (6c) rated substantially worse than 2 PPs (6b), which, in turn, should be rated somewhat worse than 1 PP (6a).

Rejection Data
The PP stimuli were generally grammatically acceptable to our participants, with only 6.48% (21 trials) rejected during the reading/judgment task. Only 4.63% of the 1 PP stimuli and 3.70% of the 2 PP stimuli were rejected, and the difference between the two rejection scores was not significant, $\chi^2(1) < 0.1$. In contrast, 11.11% of the items with 3 PPs were rejected—an increase in rejection rate that was significant compared with the 2 PP condition, $\chi^2(1) = 3.51, p < .05$, but only marginally significant in comparison with the 1 PP condition, $\chi^2(1) = 2.43, p = .0595$. Thus, there was a tendency to perceive the 1 PP and 2 PP stimuli as more grammatical than the counterpart with 3 PPs. Figure 7 shows the cumulative profile of rejections across word position in the sentences, starting at the fourth word. Rejections across the three sentence types were more likely to occur toward the end of a sentence, with two thirds of the rejections occurring during the presentation of the last four words, and with only three sentences rejected before the presentation of the 10th word (i.e., *by* in Figure 7). The rejection profile for the 3 PP stimuli suggests that it is the occurrence of the third PP (*by the window*) that makes these stimuli less acceptable than the 1 PP and 2 PP stimuli.

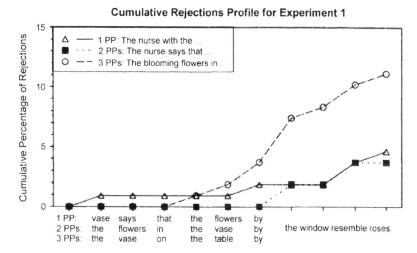

Figure 7 The cumulative percentage of rejections for each PP condition at each word position is shown starting from the fourth word.

Table 1 The processing difficulty of multiple PP modifications of NPs

	SRN predictions		Human results	
No. of PPs	Mean GPE	SD	Mean rating	SD
1 PP	0.153	0.008	2.380	0.976
2 PPs	0.161	0.015	2.704	0.846
3 PPs	0.214	0.042	3.269	0.925

Note. NP = noun phrase; PP = prepositional phrase.

Grammaticality Ratings

The ratings for the three sentence types are shown in Table 1. As predicted by the connectionist model, there was a significant effect of sentence type, $F_1(2, 70) = 10.87, p < .0001; F_2(2, 16) = 12.43, p < .001$, such that the deeper the level of recursion, the worse the sentences were rated. The model also predicted that there should be only a small difference between the ratings for the 1 PP and the 2 PP stimuli but a significant difference between the stimuli with the 2 PPs and 3 PPs. The experiment also bears out this prediction t. The stimuli with the 2 PPs were rated only 13.62% worse than the 1 PP stimuli—a difference that was only marginally significant, $F_1(1, 35) = 2.97, p = .094; F_2(1, 8) = 4.56, p = .065$. The items with 3 PPs elicited the worst ratings, which were 37.36% worse than the 1 PP items and 20.89% worse than the 2 PP items. The rating difference between the sentences with 2 PPs and 3 PPs was significant, $F_1(1, 35) = 5.74, p < .005; F_2(1, 8) = 10.90, p < .02)$.

The human ratings thus confirmed the predictions from the connectionist model: Increasing the depth of right-branching recursion has a negative effect on processing difficulty that cannot be attributed to a mere length effect. As predicted by the model, the deeper the level of recursion across the three types of stimuli, the worse the sentences were rated by the participants. This result is not predicted by most other current models of sentence processing, in which right-branching recursion does not cause processing difficulties beyond potential length effects (although see Lewis & Vasishth, 2005).

Experiment 2: Processing Multiple Left-Branching Possessive Genitives

In addition to the effect of multiple instances of right-branching iterative recursion on processing as confirmed by Experiment 1, Christiansen (1994) also observed that the depth of recursion effect in left-branching structures varied in its severity depending on the sentential position in which such recursion occurs. When processing left-branching recursive structures involving multiple prenominal genitives, the SRN learns that it is not crucial to keep track of what occurs before the final noun. This tendency is efficient early in the sentence but creates a problem with recursion toward the end of sentence because the network becomes somewhat uncertain where it is in the sentence. We tested this observation in the context of multiple possessive genitives occurring in either subject (7a) or object (7b) positions in transitive constructions:

(7) a. Jane's dad's colleague's parrot followed the baby all afternoon. (Subject)
    b. The baby followed Jane's dad's colleague's parrot all afternoon. (Object)

Method
SRN Testing
The model was tested as in Experiment 1 on two sets of 10 novel sentences corresponding the two types of sentences in (7).

Participants
Thirty-four undergraduate students from the University of Southern California received course credit for participation in this experiment.

Materials
We constructed 10 experimental items with the same format as (7). As in (7a), the Subject stimuli started with three prenominal genitives, of which the first

always contained a proper name (*Jane's dad's colleague's*), followed by the subject noun (*parrot*), a transitive verb (*followed*), a simple object NP (*the baby*), and a duration adverbial (*all afternoon*). The Object stimuli reversed the order of the two NPs, placing the multiple prenominal genitives in the object position and the simple NP in the subject position, as illustrated by (7b). The conditions were counterbalanced across two lists, each containing five sentences of each type. Additionally, there were 9 practice items (including one ungrammatical), 29 filler items (of which 9 were ungrammatical), and 20 items from other experiments.

Procedure
Experiment 2 involved the same procedure as Experiment 1.

Results and Discussion
SRN Predictions
Comparisons of mean sentence GPE for the two types of sentence materials predicted that having two levels of recursion in an NP involving left-branching prenominal genitives should be significantly less acceptable in an object position compared to a subject position, $F(1, 9) = 110.33, p < .0001$.

Rejection Data
Although the genitive stimuli seemed generally acceptable, participants rejected twice as many sentences (13.24%) as in Experiment 1. The rejection profiles for the two sentence types are illustrated in Figure 8, showing that the rejections are closely associated with the occurrence of the multiple prenominal genitives. However, there was no overall difference in the number of sentences rejected in the Subject (13.53%) and Object (12.94%) conditions, $\chi^2(1) < 1$.

Grammaticality Ratings
As predicted by the SRN model, the results in Table 2 show that multiple prenominal genitives were less acceptable in object position than in subject position, $F_1(1, 33) = 5.76, p < .03; F_2(1, 9) = 3.48, p = .095$. These results suggest that the position of multiple instances of recursion within a sentence affects its acceptability.

Experiment 3: Processing Multiple Semantically Biased Center-Embeddings

In contrast to iterative recursion, complex recursion in the form of center-embedding has often been used as an important source of information about

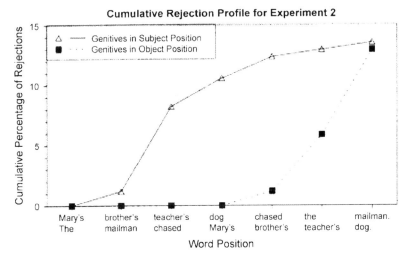

Figure 8 The cumulative percentage of rejections for sentences incorporating multiple prenominal genitives in subject or object positions.

complexity effects in human sentence processing (e.g., Blaubergs & Braine, 1974; Foss & Cairns, 1970; Marks, 1968; Miller, 1962; Miller & Isard, 1964; Stolz, 1967). Of particular interest is a study by Gibson and Thomas (1999) investigating the role of memory limitations in the processing of doubly center-embedded object relative clause constructions. Consistent with the external memory limitation account of Gibson (1998), they found that when deleting the middle VP [*was cleaning every week* in (8a)], the resulting ungrammatical sentence (8b) was rated no worse that the original grammatical version.

(8) a. The apartment that the maid who the service had sent over was cleaning every week was well decorated. (3 VPs)

Table 2 The processing difficulty of multiple possessive genitives

	SRN predictions		Human results	
Genitive position	Mean GPE	*SD*	Mean rating	*SD*
Sub NP	0.222	0.006	3.606	1.715
Obj NP	0.299	0.025	3.965	1.752

Note. Sub NP = subject noun phrase; Obj NP = object noun phrase.

b. *The apartment that the maid who the service had sent over was well decorated. (2 VPs)

In contrast, Christiansen (1994) noted that the SRN tended to expect that doubly center-embedded sentences would end when it had received two verbs, suggesting that (8b) should actually be rated better than (8a). Christiansen and Chater (1999) further demonstrated that this prediction is primarily due to intrinsic architectural limitations on the processing on doubly center-embedded material rather than insufficient experience with these constructions.[6] Gibson and Thomas' results came from offline ratings, whereas in Experiment 3 we use the online method from the previous two experiments and predict that with this more sensitive measure, sentences such as the ungrammatical (8b) will actually be rated better than grammatical sentences like (8a).

Method
SRN Testing
The model was tested as in Experiments 1 and 2 on two sets of 10 novel sentences corresponding to the sentence types in (8).

Participants
Thirty-six undergraduate students from the University of Southern California received course credit for participation in this experiment.

Materials
Six experimental items were selected from the Gibson and Thomas (1999) stimuli, focusing on the key grammatical (3 VP) versus ungrammatical (2 VPs) version of each sentence as in (8). The two conditions were counterbalanced across two lists, three of each type. In addition, there were 9 practice items (including 2 ungrammatical), 30 filler items (of which 9 were ungrammatical), and 27 items from other experiments.

Procedure
Experiment 3 involved the same procedure as Experiments 1 and 2.

Results and Discussion
SRN Predictions
The mean GPE scores across the two types of sentences followed the preliminary findings by Christiansen and Chater (1999): The grammatical 3-VP sentences were rated significantly worse than the ungrammatical 2-VP sentences, $F(1, 9) = 2892.23, p < .0001$.

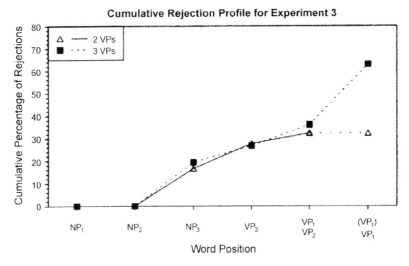

Figure 9 The cumulative percentage of rejections averaged across NP and VP regions in semantically biased center-embedded sentences with 2 VPs or 3 VPs.

Rejection Data

Because the stimuli from Gibson and Thomas (1999) were not equated for length, the number of rejections were averaged for each NP and VP region rather than for each word. The resulting cumulative rejection profile is shown in Figure 9, indicating that significantly more 3 VP sentences were rejected than 2 VP sentences [63% vs. 32.4%; $\chi^2(1) = 20.21, p < .0001$].

Grammaticality Ratings

As predicted by the SRN model (Table 3), the grammatical 3 VP sentences were rated significantly worse than their ungrammatical 2 VP counterparts, $F_1(1, 35) = 15.55, p < .0001; F_2(1, 5) = 6.85, p < .05$. These results suggest

Table 3 The processing difficulty of multiple semantically biased center-embeddings

	SRN predictions		Human results	
No. of VPs	Mean GPE	SD	Mean rating	SD
2 VPs	0.307	0.010	4.778	1.268
3 VPs	0.404	0.005	5.639	1.037

Note. VPs = verb phrases.

humans share the SRN's processing preference for the ungrammatical 2 VP construction over the grammatical 3 VP version (for similar SRN results and additional data for German, see Engelmann & Vasishth, 2009).

Experiment 4: Processing Multiple Semantically Neutral Center-Embeddings

Two potential concerns about the Gibson and Thomas (1999) stimuli used in Experiment 3 are that (a) the results could be an artifact of length because the sentences were not controlled for overall length and (b) the stimuli included semantic biases [e.g., *apartment/decorated*, *service/sent over* in (6b)] that may have increased the plausibility of the 2 VP stimuli. In Experiment 4, we sought to replicate the results from Experiment 3 with semantically neutral stimuli adapted from Stolz (1967), in which adverbs replaced the missing verbs in 2 VP constructions to control for overall length as in (9):

(9) a. The chef who the waiter who the busboy offended appreciated admired the musicians. (3 VPs)
     b. *The chef who the waiter who the busboy offended frequently admired the musicians. (2 VPs)

Method
SRN Testing
The training corpus on which the model was trained did not include semantic constraints (e.g., animacy). Instead, the difference between the center-embedded test items used to make SRN predictions for Experiments 3 and 4 was one of argument structure. The Gibson and Thomas (1999) stimuli in Experiment 3 used optionally transitive verbs, whereas the Experiment 4 stimuli contained transitive verbs. The model was tested as in the previous experiments on two sets of 10 novel sentences matching the structure of the two sentence types in (9).

Participants
Thirty-four undergraduate students from the University of Southern California received course credit for participation in this experiment.

Materials
Ten semantically neutral doubly center-embedded items were adapted from Stolz (1967), each with a 3 VP and 2 VP version as in (9). The conditions were counterbalanced across two lists, each containing five sentences of each

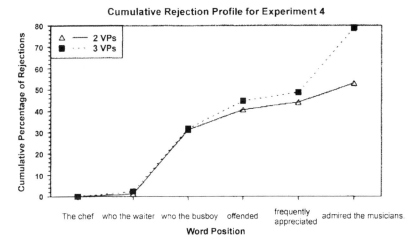

Cumulative Rejection Profile for Experiment 4

Figure 10 The cumulative percentage of rejections averaged across word position in semantically neutral center-embedded sentences with 2 VPs or 3 VPs.

type. Additionally, there were 9 practice items (including one ungrammatical), 29 filler items (of which 9 were ungrammatical), and 20 items from other experiments.

Procedure
Experiment 4 involved the same procedure as Experiments 1–3.

Results and Discussion
SRN Predictions
As in Experiment 3, the mean GPE scores predicted that 3 VP sentences should be rated significantly worse than 2 VP sentences, $F(1, 9) = 43.60, p < .0001$.

Rejection Data
The cumulative rejection profile for the neutral items in the current experiment replicated that for the semantically biased stimuli in the previous experiment (Figure 10): significantly more 3 VP sentences (78.8%) were rejected than the corresponding 2 VP constructions [52.9%; $\chi^2(1) = 25.33, p < .0001$].

Grammaticality Ratings
Again, in line with the SRN predictions (Table 4), the 3 VP sentences were rated significantly worse than their 2 VP counterparts, $F_1(1, 33) = 7.88, p < .01; F_2(1, 9) = 27.46, p < .001$. Thus, the ungrammatical 2 VP constructions

Table 4 The processing difficulty of multiple semantically neutral center-embeddings

	SRN predictions		Human results	
No. of VPs	Mean GPE	SD	Mean rating	SD
2 VPs	0.360	0.015	5.553	1.251
3 VPs	0.395	0.008	6.165	0.672

Note. VPs = verb phrases.

are preferred over the grammatical 3 VP versions even when controlling for overall length and the influence of semantic bias.

General Discussion

We have presented simulation results from a connectionist implementation of our usage-based approach to recursion, indicating that the model has sophisticated constituent-based generalization abilities and is able to fit human data regarding to the differential processing difficulty of center-embedded and cross-dependency constructions. Novel predictions were then derived from the model and confirmed by the results of four grammaticality judgment experiments. Importantly, this model was not developed for the purpose of fitting these data but was, nevertheless, able to predict the patterns of human grammaticality judgments across three different kinds of recursive structure. Indeed, as illustrated by Figure 11, the SRN predictions not only provide a close fit with the human ratings *within* each experiment but also capture the increased complexity evident *across* Experiments 1–4. Importantly, the remarkably good fit between the model and the human data both within and across the experiments were obtained without changing any parameters across the simulations. In contrast, the present pattern of results provides a challenge for most other accounts of human sentence processing that rely on arbitrary, externally specified limitations on memory or processing to explain patterns of human performance.

Like other implemented computational models, the specific instantiation of our usage-based approach to recursive sentence processing presented here is not without limitations. Although the model covers several key types of recursive sentence constructions, its overall coverage of English is limited in both vocabulary size and range of grammatical regularities. Another limiting factor is that the model predicts only the next word in a sentence. Despite mounting evidence highlighting the importance of prediction to learning, in general (Niv & Schoenbaum, 2008), and language processing, in particular (e.g., Federmeier, 2007; Levy, 2008; Hagoort, in press; Pickering & Garrod, 2007), incorporating

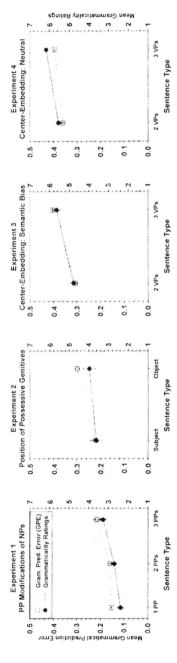

Figure 11 Comparison between SRN predictions of sentence complexity (left *y*-axes: mean GPE) and human ratings (right *y*-axes: mean grammaticality ratings) for four recursive sentence types: (a) multiple PP modifications of NPs (Experiment 1), (b) multiple possessive genitives in subject or object positions (Experiment 2), (c) doubly center-embedded, semantically biased sentences with 2 VPs or 3 VPs (Experiment 3), and (d) doubly center-embedded, semantically neutral sentences with 2 VPs or 3 VPs (Experiment 4).

semantic interpretation of sentences is an important goal for future work along with the scaling up of models to deal with the full complexity of language. Fortunately, there has already been encouraging connectionist work in this direction. For example, SRN models implementing multiple-cue integration have been scaled up to deal with both artificial (Christiansen & Dale, 2001) and full-blown (Reali, Christiansen, & Monaghan, 2003) child-directed speech, the latter even while predicting parts-of-speech information (see Christiansen et al., in press, for a discussion). Other recent work has successfully pushed the boundaries of SRN models of language still further toward increased coverage and semantic interpretation (e.g., Rohde, 2002; Sibley et al., 2008).

Given the characteristics of SRN recursive abilities, our usage-based approach to recursion predicts that substantial individual differences should exist in the processing of specific recursive constructions, not only across development but also across languages. Consistent with this prediction, observational data on preschoolers' language development show that recursive language production emerges gradually over time, structure for structure, rather than wholesale (Dickinson, 1987). In a training study, Roth (1984) further demonstrated that experience with recursive constructions is the key factor in preschoolers' comprehension of recursive structures (and not general cognitive development, including of working memory). In a similar vein, predictions from an SRN model regarding the importance of experience in processing singly embedded subject and object relative clauses (MacDonald & Christiansen, 2002) have been confirmed by a training study with adult participants (Wells et al., 2009). More generally, life experience, in the form of education, has been shown to affect the ability to comprehend complex recursive sentences (Dabrowska, 1997), likely due to differential exposure to language both in terms of the quantity and complexity of the linguistic material. Finally, differences in recursive abilities have also been found across languages. For example, Hoover (1992) showed that doubly center-embedded constructions are more easily processed in Spanish than in English (even when morphological cues were removed in Spanish). Similarly, substantial differences in perceived processing difficulty for the exact same types of recursive structure have been demonstrated across a variety of other languages—including English, German, Japanese, and Persian (Hawkins, 1994)—again highlighting the importance of linguistic experience in explaining recursive processing abilities. Indeed, Evans and Levinson (in press) argue that

> Recursion is not a necessary or defining feature of every language. It is a well-developed feature of some languages, like English or Japanese, rare

but allowed in others (like Bininj Gun-wok), capped at a single level of nesting in others (Kayardild), and in others, like Pirahã, it is completely absent. (p. 28)

In conclusion, we have hypothesized that recursion is not a built-in property of the mechanisms supporting language; rather, as originally suggested by Stolz (1967), the ability to use specific constructions recursively is acquired in an item-based manner. The close fit between our model and the human data provides initial support for this hypothesis (see also Engelmann & Vasishth, 2009). Assuming that future work is able to substantiate the usage-based approach to recursion further, then it would have important theoretical ramifications not only in underscoring the importance of experience in language processing (Wells et al., 2009) but also in suggesting that recursion is unlikely to be key factor in language evolution (Christiansen & Chater, 2008).

Revised version accepted 19 May 2009

Notes

1 Formally, recursion can be defined as follows: If X is a (non-terminal) symbol and α and β are non-empty strings of symbols and terminals, then right-branching recursion occurs when $X \to \alpha\, X$ (i.e., there is a derivation from X to $\alpha\, X$), left-branching recursion when $X \to \beta\, X$, and center-embedding when $X \to \alpha\, X\, \beta$. Recursion can also arise as a consequence of a recursive *set* of rules, none of which need individually be recursive. Thus, rules of the form $X \to \alpha\, Y$ and $Y \to \beta\, X$ together form a recursive rule set because they permit the derivation of a structure, such as $[_X\, \alpha\, [_Y\, \beta\, [_X\, \alpha\, [_Y\, \beta\, [_X \ldots]]]]]$, involving several levels of right-branching recursion. Similarly, recursive rule sets can be used to derive left-branching and center-embedded constructions.

2 Of the 42 input/output units only 38 were used to represent the vocabulary and other lexical material in a localist format. The remaining four units were saved for other purposes, including for the use as novel, untrained words (as discussed below).

3 All simulations were replicated multiple times (including with variations in network architecture and corpus composition) with qualitatively similar results.

4 Although the sentences with multiple PPs have more attachment ambiguities, our materials always resolve any ambiguity with the most frequent interpretation in English, such that each PP attaches to the NP immediately dominating it. There is no good evidence in the literature that ambiguities resolved with their most favored interpretation are any harder to process than unambiguous sentences, and so the presence of more attachment ambiguity in the 3PP condition should not have affected our results.

5　Obtaining the offline grammaticality ratings after continuous online judgments may have negatively affected the ratings of the sentences that were not read to completion. Future work can address this issue by omitting the online judgments and/or collecting reading times instead.

6　When trained on a corpus that contained only doubly center-embedded constructions, there was only little improvement in performance, similar to the limited effects of training in humans (Blaubergs & Braine, 1974; Powell & Peters, 1973; Stolz, 1967). Christiansen and Chater (1999) further established that the SRN's intrinsic constraints on center-embedding are independent of the size of the hidden unit layer.

References

Bach, E., Brown, C., & Marslen-Wilson, W. (1986). Crossed and nested dependencies in German and Dutch: A psycholinguistic study. *Language and Cognitive Processes, 1*, 249–262.

Blaubergs, M. S., & Braine, M. D. S. (1974). Short-term memory limitations on decoding self-embedded sentences. *Journal of Experimental Psychology, 102*, 745–748.

Boeckx, C. (2006). *Linguistic minimalism: Origins, concepts, methods, and aims*. New York: Oxford University Press.

Boland, J. E. (1997). The relationship between syntactic and semantic processes in sentence comprehension. *Language and Cognitive Processes, 12*, 423–484.

Boland, J. E., Tanenhaus, M. K., & Garnsey, S. M. (1990). Evidence for the immediate use of verb control information in sentence processing. *Journal of Memory and Language, 29*, 413–432.

Boland, J. E., Tanenhaus, M. K., Garnsey, S. M., & Carlson, G. N. (1995). Verb argument structure in parsing and interpretation: Evidence from *wh*-questions. *Journal of Memory and Language, 34*, 774–806.

Botvinick, M., & Plaut, D. C. (2004). Doing without schema hierarchies: A recurrent connectionist approach to normal and impaired routine sequential action. *Psychological Review, 111*, 395–429.

Botvinick, M., & Plaut, D.C. (2006). Short-term memory for serial order: A recurrent neural network model. *Psychological Review, 113*, 201–233.

Chomsky, N. (1956). Three models for the description of language. *IRE Transactions on Information Theory, 2*, 113–124.

Chomsky, N. (1965). *Aspects of the theory of syntax*. Cambridge, MA: MIT Press.

Chomsky, N. (1995). *The minimalist program*. Cambridge, MA: MIT Press.

Christiansen, M. H. (1994). *Infinite languages, finite minds: Connectionism, learning and linguistic structure*. Unpublished doctoral dissertation, University of Edinburgh.

Christiansen, M. H.. Allen, J., & Seidenberg, M. S. (1998). Learning to segment speech using multiple cues: A connectionist model. *Language and Cognitive Processes, 13*, 221–268.

Christiansen, M. H., & Chater, N. (1994). Generalization and connectionist language learning. *Mind and Language, 9*, 273–287.

Christiansen, M. H.. & Chater, N. (1999). Toward a connectionist model of recursion in human linguistic performance. *Cognitive Science, 23*, 157–205.

Christiansen, M. H.. & Chater, N. (2003). Constituency and recursion in language. In M. A. Arbib (Ed.), *The handbook of brain theory and neural networks* (2nd ed., pp. 267–271). Cambridge, MA: MIT Press.

Christiansen, M. H.. & Chater, N. (2008). Language as shaped by the brain. *Behavioral and Brain Sciences, 31*, 489–558.

Christiansen, M. H., & Dale, R. (2001). Integrating distributional, prosodic and phonological information in a connectionist model of language acquisition. In J. D. Moore & K. Stenning (Eds.), *Proceedings of the 23rd annual conference of the Cognitive Science Society* (pp. 220–225). Mahwah, NJ: Lawrence Erlbaum.

Christiansen, M. H., Dale, R., & Reali, F. (in press). Connectionist explorations of multiple-cue integration in syntax acquisition. In S.P. Johnson (Ed.), *Neoconstructivism: The new science of cognitive development.* New York: Oxford University Press.

Church, K. (1982). *On memory limitations in natural language processing.* Bloomington: Indiana University Linguistics Club.

Dabrowska, E. (1997). The LAD goes to school: A cautionary tale for nativists. *Linguistics, 35*, 735–766.

Dickinson, S. (1987). Recursion in development: Support for a biological model of language. *Language and Speech, 30*, 239–249.

Elman, J. L. (1990). Finding structure in time. *Cognitive Science, 14*, 179–211.

Elman, J. L. (1991). Distributed representation, simple recurrent networks, and grammatical structure. *Machine Learning, 7*, 195–225.

Elman, J. L. (1993). Learning and development in neural networks: The importance of starting small. *Cognition, 48*, 71–99.

Engelmann, F., & Vasishth, S. (2009). *Processing grammatical and ungrammatical center embeddings in English and German: A computational model.* Unpublished manuscript.

Evans, N., & Levinson, S. (in press). The myth of language universals: Language diversity and its importance for cognitive science. *Behavioral and Brain Sciences.*

Federmeier, K. D. (2007). Thinking ahead: The role and roots of prediction in language comprehension. *Psychophysiology, 44*, 491–505.

Foss, D. J., & Cairns, H. S. (1970). Some effects of memory limitations upon sentence comprehension and recall. *Journal of Verbal Learning and Verbal Behavior, 9*, 541–547.

Gibson, E. (1998). Linguistic complexity: Locality of syntactic dependencies. *Cognition, 68*, 1–76.

Gibson, E., & Thomas, J. (1996). The processing complexity of English center-embedded and self-embedded structures. In C. Schütze (Ed.), *Proceedings of the NELS 26 sentence processing workshop* (pp. 45–71). Cambridge, MA: MIT Press.

Gibson, E., & Thomas, J. (1999). Memory limitations and structural forgetting: The perception of complex ungrammatical sentences as grammatical. *Language and Cognitive Processes, 14*, 225–248.

Hadley, R. F. (1994). Systematicity in connectionist language learning. *Mind and Language, 9*, 247–272.

Hagoort, P. (in press). Reflections on the neurobiology of syntax. In D. Bickerton & E. Szathmáry (Eds.), *Biological foundations and origin of syntax. Strüngmann Forum Reports* (Vol. 3). Cambridge, MA: MIT Press.

Hagstrom, P., & Rhee, R. (1997). The Dependency Locality Theory in Korean. *Journal of Psycholinguistic Research, 26*, 189–206.

Hakes, D. T., Evans, J. S., & Brannon, L. L (1976). Understanding sentences with relative clauses. *Memory and Cognition, 4*, 283–290.

Hakes, D. T., & Foss, D. J. (1970). Decision processes during sentence comprehension: Effects of surface structure reconsidered. *Perception and Psychophysics, 8*, 413–416.

Hamilton, H. W., & Deese, J. (1971). Comprehensibility and subject-verb relations in complex sentences. *Journal of Verbal Learning and Verbal Behavior, 10*, 163–170.

Hauser, M. D., Chomsky, N., & Fitch, W. T. (2002). The faculty of language: What is it, who has it, and how did it evolve? *Science, 298*, 1569–1579.

Hawkins, J. A. (1994). *A performance theory of order and constituency*. Cambridge: Cambridge University Press.

Hoover, M. L. (1992). Sentence processing strategies in Spanish and English. *Journal of Psycholinguistic Research, 21*, 275–299.

Joshi, A. K. (1990). Processing crossed and nested dependencies: An automaton perspective on the psycholinguistic results. *Language and Cognitive Processes, 5*, 1–27.

Just, M. A., & Carpenter, P. A. (1992). A capacity theory of comprehension: Individual differences in working memory. *Psychological Review, 99*, 122–149.

Karlsson, F. (2007). Constraints on multiple center embedding of clauses. *Journal of Linguistics, 43*, 365–392.

Kimball, J. (1973). Seven principles of surface structure parsing in natural language. *Cognition, 2*, 15–47.

Larkin, W., & Burns, D. (1977). Sentence comprehension and memory for embedded structure. *Memory and Cognition, 5*, 17–22.

Levy, R. (2008). Expectation-based syntactic comprehension. *Cognition, 106*, 1126–1177.

Lewis, R. L., & Vasishth, S. (2005). An activation-based model of sentence processing as skilled memory retrieval. *Cognitive Science, 29*, 375–419.

MacDonald, M. C., & Christiansen, M. H. (2002). Reassessing working memory: A comment on Just & Carpenter (1992) and Waters & Caplan (1996). *Psychological Review, 109*, 35–54.

Marcus, G. F. (1998). Rethinking eliminative connectionism. *Cognitive Psychology, 37*, 243–282.

Marcus, M. (1980). *A theory of syntactic recognition for natural language.* Cambridge, MA: MIT Press.

Marks, L. E. (1968). Scaling of grammaticalness of self-embedded English sentences. *Journal of Verbal Learning and Verbal Behavior, 7*, 965–967.

Miller, G. A. (1962). Some psychological studies of grammar. *American Psychologist, 17*, 748–762.

Miller, G. A., & Chomsky, N. (1963). Finitary models of language users. In R. D. Luce, R. R. Bush, & E. Galanter (Eds.), *Handbook of mathematical psychology* (Vol. 2, pp. 419–492). New York: Wiley.

Miller, G. A., & Isard, S. (1964). Free recall of self-embedded English sentences. *Information and Control, 7*, 292–303.

Niv, Y., & Schoenbaum, G. (2008). Dialogues on prediction errors. *Trends in Cognitive Sciences, 12*, 265–272.

Peterfalvi, J. M., & Locatelli, F (1971). L'acceptabilité des phrases [The acceptability of sentences]. *L' Année Psychologique, 71*, 417–427.

Pickering, M. J., & Garrod, S. (2007). Do people use language production to make predictions during comprehension? *Trends in Cognitive Sciences, 11*, 105–110.

Plaut, D. C. (1999). A connectionist approach to word reading and acquired dyslexia: Extension to sequential processing. *Cognitive Science, 23*, 543–568.

Powell, A., & Peters, R. G. (1973) Semantic clues in comprehension of novel sentences. *Psychological Reports, 32*, 1307–1310.

Reali, F., Christiansen, M. H., & Monaghan, P. (2003). Phonological and distributional cues in syntax acquisition: Scaling up the connectionist approach to multiple-cue integration. In R. Alterman & D. Kirsh (Eds.), *Proceedings of the 25th annual conference of the Cognitive Science Society* (pp. 970–975). Mahwah, NJ: Lawrence Erlbaum.

Reich, P. (1969). The finiteness of natural language. *Language, 45*, 831–843.

Rohde, D. L. T. (2002). *A connectionist model of sentence comprehension and production.* Unpublished doctoral dissertation, School of Computer Science, Carnegie Mellon University, Pittsburgh, PA.

Roth, F. P. (1984). Accelerating language learning in young children. *Child Language, 11*, 89–107.

Schlesinger, I. M. (1975). Why a sentence in which a sentence in which a sentence is embedded is embedded is difficult. *Linguistics, 153*, 53–66.

Servan-Schreiber, D., Cleeremans, A., & McClelland, J.L. (1991). Graded state machines: The representation of temporal dependencies in simple recurrent networks. *Machine Learning, 7*, 161–193.

Shieber, S. (1985). Evidence against the context-freeness of natural language. *Linguistics and Philosophy, 8*, 333—343.

Sibley, D. E., Kello, C. T., Plaut, D. C., & Elman, J. L. (2008). Large-scale modeling of wordform learning and representation. *Cognitive Science, 32*, 741–754.

Stabler, E. P. (1994). The finite connectivity of linguistic structure. In C. Clifton, L. Frazier, & K. Rayner (Eds.), *Perspectives on sentence processing* (pp. 303–336). Hillsdale, NJ: Lawrence Erlbaum.

Stolz, W. S. (1967). A study of the ability to decode grammatically novel sentences. *Journal of Verbal Learning and Verbal Behavior, 6*, 867–873.

Uehara, K., & Bradley, D. (1996). The effect of -ga sequences on processing Japanese multiply center-embedded sentences. In *11th Pacific-Asia conference on language, information, and computation* (pp. 187–196). Seoul: Kyung Hee University.

von Humboldt, W. (1999). *On language: On the diversity of human language construction and its influence on the metal development of the human species.* Cambridge: Cambridge University Press. (Original work published 1936)

Wang, M. D. (1970). The role of syntactic complexity as a determiner of comprehensibility. *Journal of Verbal Learning and Verbal Behavior, 9*, 398–404.

Wells, J., Christiansen, M. H., Race, D. S., Acheson, D. J., & MacDonald, M. C. (2009). Experience and sentence processing: Statistical learning and relative clause comprehension. *Cognitive Psychology, 58*, 250–271.

Appendix A
Grammatical Prediction Error

To map SRN predictions onto human performance in our experiments, we use the GPE measure. This SRN performance score has been shown to provide a good model of human behavioral measures, including reading times and grammaticality ratings (Christiansen & Chater, 1999; MacDonald & Christiansen, 2002; Wells et al., 2009). The GPE provides an indication of how well a network is obeying the training grammar when making its predictions. The GPE for predicting a particular word is calculated as:

$$GPE = 1 - \frac{H}{H + F + M}$$

Hits (H) and false positives (F) consist of the accumulated activations of the set of units, G, that are grammatical and the set of incorrectly activated ungrammatical units, U, respectively:

$$H = \sum_{i \in G} u_i \quad F = \sum_{i \in U} u_i$$

Missing activation (M; i.e., false negatives) is calculated as a sum over the (positive) discrepancy, m_i, between the target activation for a grammatical unit, t_i, and the actual activation of that unit, u_i:

$$M = \sum_{i \in G} m_i \qquad m_i = \begin{cases} 0 & \text{if } t_i - u_i \leq 0 \\ t_i - u_i & \text{otherwise} \end{cases} \qquad t_i = \frac{(H + F)f_i}{\sum_{j \in G} f_j}$$

The desired activation, t_i, is computed as a proportion of the total activation determined by the lexical frequency, f_i, of the word that u_i designate and weighted by the sum of the lexical frequencies, f_j, of all the grammatical units. Although not an explicit part of the above equations, correct rejections are also taken into account under the assumption that they correspond to zero activation for units that are ungrammatical given previous context.

Appendix B
Stimulus Materials

Experiment 1: Multiple Right-Branching Prepositional Phrases
The student from the city says that the girl from the forest likes pets.
The student says that the girl from the city near the forest likes pets.
The girl from the school in the city near the forest likes pets.

The nurse with the vase says that the flowers by the window resemble roses.
The nurse says that the flowers in the vase by the window resemble roses.
The flowers in the vase on the table by the window resemble roses.

The boss from the office says that the posters across the hall tell lies.
The boss says that the posters in the office across the hall tell lies.
The posters on the desk in the office across the hall tell lies.

The woman at the mall says that the bank behind the airport helps people.
The woman says that the bank at the mall behind the airport helps people.
The bank on the street at the mall behind the airport helps people.
The expert from the town says that the buildings with the flooding need repair.

The expert says that the buildings from the area with the flooding need repair.
The buildings in the town from the area with the flooding need repair.

The man with the drawing says that the story about the river makes sense.
The man says that the story about the castle by the river makes sense.
The story about the drawing of the castle by the river makes sense.

The ranger on the hill says that the deer outside the village avoids hunters.
The ranger says that the deer on the hill outside the village avoids hunters.
The deer on the hill by the lake outside the village avoids hunters.

The chemist on the stairway says that the paint on the balcony contains lead.
The chemist says that the paint in the bedroom with the balcony contains lead.
The paint on the stairway to the bedroom with the balcony contains lead.

The musician by the keyboard says that the guitar from the concert requires
     tuning.
The musician says that the guitar with the broken amp from the concert requires
     tuning.
The guitar by the keyboard with the broken amp from the concert requires
     tuning.

Experiment 2: Multiple Left-Branching Possessive Genitives
Mary's brother's teacher's dog chased the mailman.
The mailman chased Mary's brother's teacher's dog.

Bill's friend's uncle's cat attacked the hamster.
The hamster attacked Bill's friend's uncle's cat.

Jane's dad's colleague's parrot followed the baby.
The baby followed Jane's dad's colleague's parrot.

Ben's band's singer's girlfriend cheated the promoter.
The promoter cheated Ben's band's singer's girlfriend.

Donald's heir's chauffeur's wife avoided the gardener.
The gardener avoided Donald's heir's chauffeur's wife.

John's mom's neighbor's boy visited the doctor.
The doctor visited John's mom's neighbor's boy.

Ann's fiancé's cousin's husband hired the builder.
The builder hired Ann's fiancé's cousin's husband.

Jim's buddy's sister's trainer liked the team.
The team liked Jim's buddy's sister's trainer.

Robert's aunt's company's mechanic offended the trainee.
The trainee offended Robert's aunt's company's mechanic.

Chang's daughter's attorney's partner approached the defendant.
The defendant approached Chang's daughter's attorney's partner.

Experiment 3: Multiple Semantically Biased Center-Embeddings

The lullaby that the famous country singer who the record label had signed to
    a big contract was singing yesterday was written seventy years ago.
The lullaby that the famous country singer who the record label had signed to
    a big contract was written seventy years ago.

The game that the child who the lawnmower had startled in the yard was playing
    in the morning lasted for hours.
The game that the child who the lawnmower had startled in the yard lasted for
    hours.

The crime that the gangster who the story had profiled had planned for weeks
    was quickly solved.
The crime that the gangster who the story had profiled was quickly solved.

The apartment that the maid who the service had sent over was cleaning every
    week was well decorated.
The apartment that the maid who the service had sent over was well decorated.

The shirt that the seamstress who the immigration officer had investigated last
    week was carefully mending needed to be dry cleaned.
The shirt that the seamstress who the immigration officer had investigated last
    week needed to be dry cleaned.

The monologue that the actor who the movie industry had snubbed repeatedly
    was performing last month was extremely well written.
The monologue that the actor who the movie industry had snubbed repeatedly
    was extremely well written.

Experiment 4: Multiple Semantically Neutral Center-Embeddings

The chef who the waiter who the busboy offended appreciated admired the
    musicians.
The chef who the waiter who the busboy offended frequently admired the
    musicians.

The spider that the bullfrog that the turtle followed chased ate the fly.

The spider that the bullfrog that the turtle chased mercilessly ate the fly.

The governor who the secretary who the senator called answered introduced the ambassador.

The governor who the secretary who the senator called often introduced the ambassador.

The chipmunks that the man that the rats feared avoided liked the food.

The chipmunks that the man that the rats feared deeply liked the food.

The baker who the butcher who the shoemaker paid congratulated despised the mayor.

The baker who the butcher who the shoemaker congratulated today despised the mayor.

The dog that the cat that the bird outwitted fought approached the girl.

The dog that the cat that the bird outwitted repeatedly approached the girl.

The detective who the scientist who the lawyer confused questioned told the truth.

The detective who the scientist who the lawyer confused profoundly told the truth.

The clerk that the typist that the receptionist assisted teased thanked the boss.

The clerk that the typist that the receptionist assisted regularly thanked the boss.

The woman who the boy who the policeman found saw hid the evidence.

The woman who the boy who the policeman found yesterday hid the evidence.

The person that the guest that the doorman watched disliked forgot the key.

The person that the guest that the doorman watched briefly forgot the key.

Language Learning   ISSN 0023-8333

Evolution of Brain and Language

P. Thomas Schoenemann

Indiana University

The evolution of language and the evolution of the brain are tightly interlinked. Language evolution represents a special kind of adaptation, in part because language is a complex behavior (as opposed to a physical feature) but also because changes are adaptive only to the extent that they increase either one's understanding of others, or one's understanding to others. Evolutionary changes in the human brain that are thought to be relevant to language are reviewed. The extent to which these changes are a cause or consequence of language evolution is a good question, but it is argued that the process may best be viewed as a complex adaptive system, in which cultural learning interacts with biology iteratively over time to produce language.

A full accounting of the evolution of language requires an understanding of the brain changes that made it possible. Although our closest relatives, the apes, have the ability to learn at least some critical aspects of language (Parker & Gibson, 1990), they never learn language as completely or as effortlessly as do human children. This means that there must be some important differences between the brains of human and nonhuman apes. A fair amount is known about the ways in which human brains differ from the other apes, and we know

---

Several parts of this review were adapted from my contribution to the IIAS International Seminar on Language, Evolution, and the Brain held in Kyoto, Japan in April 2007 (Schoenemann, 2009). I wish to thank John Holland for inviting me to the Language Evolution Workshop at the Santa Fe Institute in March 2007, which served as the genesis for thinking about language from a complex adaptive system approach. I also thank Nick Ellis for organizing the Language as a Complex Adaptive System Conference and the special issue of *Language Learning* devoted to this topic. This article has also benefited from various discussions with William Wang, James Minett, Vince Sarich, Jim Hurford, Morten Christensen, and Terry Deacon, as well as from suggestions by Nick Ellis, Diane Larsen-Freeman, and two anonymous reviewers.

Correspondence concerning this article should be addressed to P. Thomas Schoenemann, Department of Anthropology, Indiana University, Bloomington, Indiana 47405. Internet: toms@indiana.edu

much about specific functions of different parts of the brain. These two fields of study, combined with an understanding of general evolutionary processes, allow us to draw at least the broad outlines of the evolutionary history of brain and language.

There is a complex interplay between language evolution and brain evolution. The existence of language presupposes a brain that allows it. Languages must, by definition, be learnable by the brains of children in each generation. Thus, language change (a form of cultural evolution) is constrained by the existing abilities of brains in each generation. However, because language is critical to an individual's adaptive fitness, language also likely had a fundamental influence on brain evolution. Humans are particularly socially interactive creatures, which makes communication central to our existence. Two interrelated evolutionary processes therefore occurred simultaneously: Language adapted to the human brain (cultural evolution), while the human brain adapted to better subserve language (biological evolution). This coevolutionary process resulted in language and brain evolving to suit each other (Christiansen, 1994; Christiansen & Chater, 2008; Deacon, 1992).

The coevolution of language and brain can be understood as the result of a complex adaptive system. Complex adaptive systems are characterized by interacting sets of agents (which can be individuals, neurons, etc.), where each agent behaves in an individually adaptive way to local conditions, often following very simple rules. The sum total of these interactions nevertheless leads to various kinds of emergent, systemwide orders. Biological evolution is a prime example of a complex adaptive system: Individuals within a species (a "system") act as best they can in their environment to survive, leading through differential reproduction ultimately to genetic changes that increase the overall fitness of the species. In fact, "evolution" can be understood as the name we give to the emergent results of complex adaptive systems over time. One can also view the brain itself as a complex adaptive system. This is because brain circuits are not independent of each other. Processing in one area affects processing in connected areas; therefore, processing changes in one area—whether due to biological evolution or learning—influence (and select for over evolutionary time) changes in other areas.

A number of neural systems relevant specifically to language interact with and influence each other in important ways. Syntax depends fundamentally on the structure of semantics, because the function of syntax is to code higher level semantic information (e.g., who did what to whom). Semantics in turn depends on the structure of conceptual understanding, which—as will be reviewed later—is a function of brain structure. These structures are in turn the result of biological adaptation: Circuits that result in conceptual understanding that is relevant and useful to a given individual's (ever-changing) environmental realities will be selected for and will spread over evolutionary time.

For some species (e.g., primates, in general, and humans, in particular) the relevant selective environment for biological evolution is largely a function of the behavior of other individuals within one's social group. This means that the adaptiveness (reproductive benefit) of an individual's particular behavior at any given moment in time depends crucially on the flexible responses of others in the group, who are at the same time attempting to behave in an adaptive manner in response. Language, in its role as a communication system, is a prime example of such an interactive, adaptive set of behaviors. Because an individual's linguistic ability is a function of (and is constrained by) their own brain circuitry, understanding language evolution (and language itself) ultimately involves understanding how the repeated complex communicative interactions of individuals influences not only cultural change but also biological change. The evolution of brain circuits, therefore, cannot be understood independent of the evolution of language, and vice versa, which means the coevolution of brain and language—and, in fact, language itself—can be understood as a complex adaptive system.

By its very nature, language evolution constrains changes in both brain and language in predictable ways. Because the evolutionary benefits of language for an individual are not independent of that individual's existing social environment, language evolution is therefore inherently more complex than the typical evolutionary scenarios for physical characteristics. Natural selection involves the biased survival of individuals who have some variation (mutation) that benefits them in their environment. Biologists therefore speak of the environment "selecting for" certain traits (e.g., longer thicker fur in cold environments). Because the relevant environment doing the "selecting" for language is not something external to and independent of the species, but rather the social group itself, the benefit of any particular mutation affecting linguistic ability is therefore dependent on the existing cognitive abilities of others in one's social group. Being "better" than others linguistically is not an evolutionary benefit if it means that others cannot understand you as well. Changes are adaptive only if they increase your ability to make maximal advantage of the preexisting abilities of others. This is unlike having thicker fur in a cold environment, in which the advantage to an individual is independent of the fur thickness of others.

It is possible for mutations relevant to language evolution to be adaptive strictly at the individual level (and therefore spread) even if they are not immediately useful for communication, but only if they are beneficial for some other reason. In this case, they would simply be *inadvertently* useful for future changes in the communication system. For example, it might be that mutations responsible for circuits involved in increasing recursion, types of memory, or concept-symbol mapping abilities were initially selected for because of their usefulness for some nonlinguistic cognitive functions, perhaps by making reasoning or thought more efficient or useful. In this case, however, these circuits would necessarily be nonlinguistic (and noncommunicative), initially. Once they spread sufficiently throughout the population, language could evolve (through cultural evolution) to make use of them. This would represent a case of preadaptation, in which language adapted to preexisting brain circuitry, rather than causing the creation of wholly new language-specific circuitry.

Therefore, language evolution itself will be strongly constrained by preexisting cognitive abilities within each generation. Changes affecting the perception of linguistically relevant signals would have been favored only to the extent that they increase the individual's ability to perceive and rapidly process the acoustic signals *already used by others for language*. Changes affecting the production of linguistically relevant signals would be favored only to the extent that they could be understood by the preexisting perceptual abilities of others. Signals too complicated or subtle for others to process would not be adopted and, hence, mutations influencing them would not likely spread.

The fact that language evolution is constrained by the preexisting abilities of individuals in the population means that any changes in brain circuitry relevant to language in a given generation would likely consist of slight modifications of circuits that already exist, rather than major changes in the ways language is processed by the brain. Because this would be true for every generation, language evolution in the long run would necessarily be continually biased toward the modification of preexisting mechanisms, rather than the accumulation of wholly new components (Schoenemann, 2005). As a consequence, we should expect language circuits in modern humans to show extensive homologies with preexisting systems in closely related animals. Even if language evolved to use circuits not originally linguistic in function, these hijacked circuits would likely also represent modifications of nonhuman-specific circuitry. Thus, studying brain and behavior in nonhuman primates is actually central to understanding human language evolution.

What changes in the brain itself are likely the result of this coevolutionary process involving both language and brain? Inferences about these changes are constructed from knowledge of how language is processed in the brain, combined with knowledge of how our brains are different from those of our closest evolutionary relatives. To the extent that a particular area relevant to language appears to have changed significantly, we are justified in inferring that this area was important for language evolution. It is possible for the area to have evolved for other reasons, only to be co-opted later for (or by) language—particularly to the extent that language has adapted to the human brain. Evolutionary inferences will also involve thinking about the interplay of different behavioral abilities over our history. Both evolutionary and complex adaptive systems perspectives predict that language evolution is not independent of the evolution of other aspects of cognition.

Language processing does not appear to be highly compartmentalized into unique circuits independent of those serving other behavioral functions but instead depends heavily on the integration of a large number of abilities that are processed in widely dispersed circuits across the brain (Damasio & Damasio, 1992; Mueller, 1996). Therefore, assessing the coevolution of language and brain requires a broad focus on a number of brain regions.

Interpreting Evolutionary Changes in Size

In order to properly understand the significance of changes in the human brain, it is important to recognize that that there must have been some sort of benefit to increasing amounts of neural tissue. There are very high evolutionary costs to maintaining large brains. The human brain accounts for about 20% of the total basal metabolic resources in adults and up to approximately 50% for young children (Hofman, 1983). Larger brains are also associated with longer maturation periods in primates (Harvey & Clutton-Brock, 1985), which—everything else being equal—means fewer offspring per unit time. Because of these evolutionary costs, increases in neural resources would not be selected for unless there were clear counterbalancing benefits (Smith, 1990).

There are several kinds of comparisons one can make between species with respect to their brains. The simplest involves simply comparing absolute size differences of either the whole brain or some specific part of the brain. Because brain size varies with the size of the body across mammals (and other groups of animals), various indexes of relative brain size have been proposed to attempt to take account of body size difference—the most commonly used being Jerison's (1973) "encephalization quotient" (EQ; a ratio of a species actual brain size to the average brain size for a mammal that size). The problem with measures like EQ, however, is that their behavioral relevance is ambiguous (Schoenemann, 2006; Striedter, 2005). Larger bodies, having greater muscle mass, presumably require greater neural connectivity to these muscles, but it is not clear why we should expect a greater muscle mass to *also* require more neurons for nonmotor cognitive tasks, such as logical reasoning or language. It seems more reasonable to suppose that more neural tissue allows for more complex processing—regardless of the size of the body. A number of empirical studies show that relative brain size is not as good a predictor of behavioral differences as absolute brain size (reviewed in Schoenemann, 2006). Intriguingly with respect to language evolution, this is also true for various types of learning tasks, including "transfer learning," in which the subject is required to generalize a task away from a specific context (Beran, Gibson, & Rumbaugh, 1999). The importance of learning to human evolution in general, and language in particular, is discussed further below.

Although absolute amounts of neural tissue are likely behaviorally important, this does not mean that relative increases (i.e., controlling for body size) are therefore *irrelevant*. Both types are potentially important.

Evolutionary Changes in the Brain Relevant to Language

Overall Brain Size
At approximately 1,350 cc, human brains are about five times as large as one would expect for the average mammal of our body size (i.e., EQ = ~5) and are about three times as large as they are in the average primate of our body size (including our closest relatives: chimpanzees and gorillas; reviewed in Schoenemann, 2006). Focusing solely on overall brain size is an oversimplification, however. Some parts of our brain are larger than expected and others smaller (although some controversy exists about specific areas; Deacon, 1988; Rilling, 2006; Schoenemann, 2006; Semendeferi, Armstrong, Schleicher, Zilles, & Van Hoesen, 2001). Nevertheless, there are some interesting correlates of overall brain size that are likely relevant to language evolution.

Not only does brain size correlate strongly with length of maturation (Harvey & Clutton-Brock, 1985), but it also correlates with overall life span (Allman, McLaughlin, & Hakeem, 1993). This means that the larger the brain, the greater the potential for behavioral learning to be a central part of the organism's behavioral repertoire. Larger brained animals do in fact tend to rely on learning much more so than smaller brained animals (Deacon, 1997), and larger brained primates do better at a variety of experimental learning tasks (see above).

Given the large increase in brain size during human evolution, we should expect learned behavior specifically to have played an important role. Although

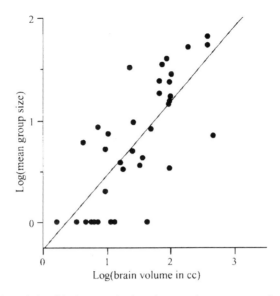

Figure 1 The relationship between brain volume and mean group size in primate species. $N = 36$, $r = .75$, $p < .0001$. Data from Dunbar (1995).

learning can be biased in particular ways by evolved innate influences, human behavioral evolution is better characterized by increasing behavioral flexibility rather than greater numbers of hardwired, innate circuits. Learning language obviously depends on being able to understand changing, fluid contingencies between constituents and meaning. Because language is fundamentally creative, it would be impossible to learn it solely through stimulus-response associations (as Chomsky has long argued, e.g., Chomsky, 1959). To the extent that language depends on learning, as well as that learning itself can be facilitated by language, the extensive changes in brain size made language increasingly possible.

Larger brained animals also show a strong tendency toward interactive sociality (Dunbar, 2003). Brain size across primates correlates strongly with the size of a species' typical social group (Figure 1), which is assumed to be an index of the complexity of the species' social existence. Larger social groups have increasingly complicated social interactions, and successful social living depends on learning how best to navigate them. Human social complexity appears to be particularly complex. Given that language is an inherently social activity, the usefulness of language (its selective value) would be greatest in the human species.

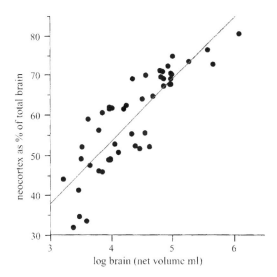

Figure 2 The relationship between log brain volume and proportion of total that is neocortex in primate species. $N = 48$, $r = .85$, $p < .0001$. Data from Stephan, Frahm, and Baron (1981).

Larger brains are also associated with disproportionate increases in the size of the neocortex, which plays a key role in conscious awareness generally, as well as mediating a number of complex cognitive functions, including language (Figure 2). Over 80% of the entire human brain is neocortex; in smaller brained primates, it averages about half that.

Furthermore, the areas of the neocortex directly devoted to the primary processing of sensory information, as well as the conscious control of muscle movement, make up a *decreasing* proportion of the entire neocortex as it increases in size (Figure 3, from Nieuwenhuys, 1994). Proportionately more of the neocortex is devoted to integrating different types of information. The larger these "association areas" are, the greater the likely potential for increasingly complex types of integrative processing (Schoenemann, 2009).

Furthermore, these association areas are composed of numerous relatively specialized processing areas. Larger brains have greater numbers of identifiably distinct cortical areas (Changizi & Shimojo, 2005; Northcutt & Kaas, 1995). This turns out to be a predictable consequence of increasing brain size: Specific areas of the neocortex tend to be less directly connected to each other in larger brains than they are in smaller brains (Ringo, 1991). This means that areas are

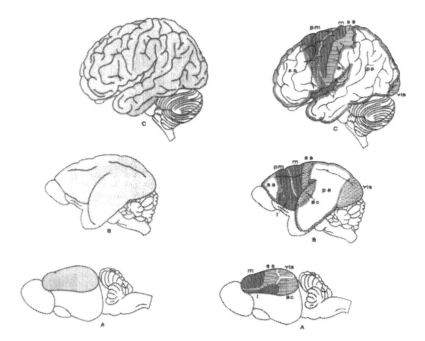

Figure 3 Size of "association" cortex in mammals of different brain size. These drawings represent lateral views of the cortex of hedgehog (**A**), galago (prosimian primate) (**B**), and human (**C**). The gray area of the figures on the left identify the cortex as a whole; the white areas of the cortex in the figures on the right identify "association" cortex, which is not devoted to processing primary sensory or motor (muscle movement) information. **aa**, anterior association cortex; **pa**, posterior association cortex; **pm**, premotor area; **m**, primary motor area; **ss**, somatosensory area; **vis**, primary visual area; **ac**, primary auditory area; **I**, insula. From Nieuwenhuys (1994), used with permission.

able to carry out tasks increasingly independently of each other, leading easily to increasing functional localization.

This has obvious implications for the development of language areas in humans, but there is a more interesting (and potentially more important) consequence: Greater numbers of specialized processing areas will result in richer, more complex, more subtle conceptual understanding (Gibson, 2002; Schoenemann, 1999, 2005). Because language semantics require a conceptual structure for words and grammar to map onto, a rich conceptual world translates into the potential for more complicated language. The functional neuroanatomy of conceptual understanding is, therefore, fundamental to understanding language evolution.

In fact, much of the brain appears to be involved with processing conceptual information (Damasio & Damasio, 1992; Schoenemann, 2005). When a subject imagines an object that is not actually present, similar areas of their brain are activated as when the object *is* being viewed (Damasio et al., 1993; Kosslyn et al., 1993). Different kinds of sensory inputs—visual, auditory, olfactory, taste, somatosensory (touch, temperature, pain, body position)—are processed with different neural pathways. Whereas some basic concepts involve only a single sensory modality (e.g., [red], or [rough (texture)]), most concepts require the integration of more than one sense. For example, the concept [coffee] typically invokes not just a particular taste, but also a smell, a visual image of a mug, the sensation of warmth, and so forth (Damasio & Damasio, 1992). For these sensory impressions to be bound in some way into the concept [coffee], the different areas that process these impressions must be connected. A complete list of areas that are relevant to just the basic features of conceptual awareness would be very long, involving all the visual (color, shape, motion, etc), spatial, auditory, temporal organization, olfactory, taste, somatosensory, and limbic system (emotion) areas.

Given that conceptual awareness forms the very foundation of language (Hurford, 2003a), that larger brains appear to give rise to more complex conceptual universes (and, hence, more interesting things to communicate about), and that humans are intensely socially interactive, increasing brain size is likely a good proxy for language evolution (Gibson, 2002; Schoenemann, 1999, 2005).

Classical Language Areas

Broca's and Wernicke's areas were the first cortical regions to be associated with specific linguistic abilities. Broca's aphasics display nonfluent, effortful, and agrammatical speech, whereas Wernicke's aphasics display grammatical but meaningless speech in which the wrong words (or parts of words) are used (Bear, Connors, & Paradiso, 2007; Damasio et al., 1993). Broca's area is located in the posterior-inferior frontal convexity of the neocortex, whereas Wernicke's area is localized to the general area where parietal, occipital, and temporal lobes meet. For most people, these areas are functional for language primarily in the left hemisphere.

Additional areas, adjacent to, but outside these classic language areas, appear to be important for these aspects of language processing as well. Broca's and Wernicke's aphasias (i.e., the specific types of language deficits themselves) are not exclusively associated with damage to Broca's and Wernicke's cortical areas (Dronkers, 2000). Damage to the caudate nucleus, putamen, and internal capsule (structures of the cerebral hemispheres that are deep to the cortex) also appear to play a role in Broca's aphasia, including aspects of syntactic processing (Lieberman, 2000).

The evolutionary histories of these areas are quite curious, as homologues to both Broca's and Wernicke's areas have been identified in nonhuman primate brains (Striedter, 2005). Exactly what function they play in other species is not currently known, but an evolutionary perspective would predict that they likely process information in ways that would be useful to language (Schoenemann, 2005), consistent with the view of language adapting to the human brain by taking advantage of circuits that already existed. The presence of these areas in nonlinguistic animals is a glaring anomaly for models that emphasize the evolution of completely new language-specific circuits in the human lineage (e.g., Bickerton, 1990; Pinker, 1995). In any case, although detailed quantitative data on these areas in nonhuman primates have not been reported, it does appear that they are significantly larger both in absolute and relative terms in humans as compared to macaque monkeys (Petrides & Pandya, 2002; Striedter, 2005).

Given that Broca's and Wernicke's areas mediate different but complementary aspects of language processing, they must be able to interact. A tract of nerve fibers known as the arcuate fasciculus directly connects these areas (Geschwind, 1974). The arcuate fasciculus in humans tends to be larger on the left side than on the right side, consistent with the lateralization of expressive language processing to the left hemisphere for most people (Nucifora, Verma, Melhem, Gur, & Gur, 2005).

The arcuate fasciculus appears to have been elaborated in human evolution. The homologue of Wernicke's area in macaque monkeys does project to prefrontal regions that are *close* to their homologue of Broca's area, but apparently not directly to it (Aboitiz & Garcia, 1997). Instead, projections directly to their homologue of Broca's area originate from a region just *adjacent* to their homologue of Wernicke's area (Aboitiz & Garcia, 1997). Thus, there appears to have been an elaboration and/or extension of projections to more directly connect Broca's and Wernicke's areas over the course of human (or ape) evolution. Recent work using diffusion tensor imaging (which delineates approximate white matter axonal connective tracts *in vivo*) suggest that both macaques and chimpanzees have tracts connecting areas in the vicinity of Wernicke's area to regions in the vicinity of Broca's area (Rilling et al., 2007). However, connections between Broca's area and the middle temporal regions (important to semantic processing; see below) are only obvious in chimpanzees and humans and appear to be most extensive in humans (Rilling et al., 2007).

Presumably these connections were elaborated during human evolution specifically for language (Rilling et al., 2007).

Prefrontal Cortex

Areas in the prefrontal cortex (in addition to Broca's area) appear to be involved in a variety of linguistic tasks, including various semantic aspects of language (Gabrieli, Poldrack, & Desmond, 1998; Kerns, Cohen, Stenger, & Carter, 2004; Luke, Liu, Wai, Wan, & Tan, 2002; Maguire & Frith, 2004; Noppeney & Price, 2004; Thompson-Schill et al., 1998), syntax (Indefrey, Hellwig, Herzog, Seitz, & Hagoort, 2004; Novoa & Ardila, 1987), and higher level linguistic processing, such as understanding the reasoning underlying a conversation (Caplan & Dapretto, 2001).

There appears to have been a significant elaboration of the prefrontal cortex during human evolution, with cytoarchitectural data pointing to an approximately twofold increase over what would be predicted for a primate brain as large as ours (Brodmann, 1909; Deacon, 1997). Recent comparative studies using magnetic resonance imaging to quantify volumes generally support these older data although there is still some debate (reviewed in Schoenemann, 2006). Our own study found that connective tracts (white matter areas composed mostly of axons) seem to account for the lion's share of the increase (Figure 4, Schoenemann, Sheehan, & Glotzer, 2005). The degree to which language was specifically and directly responsible for these changes is not clear, because the prefrontal also mediates other important nonlinguistic behavioral dimensions that likely also played a key role in human behavioral evolution, such as planning, maintaining behavioral goals, social information processing, temporary storage/manipulation of information ("working memory"), memory for serial order and temporal information, and attention (see Schoenemann, 2006, for references). Teasing out the relative contributions of these various behavioral domains (including language) to prefrontal elaboration during evolution will likely be very difficult, in part because they almost surely all contributed as part of a complex adaptive system involving many aspects of human behavior.

There are two specific areas of the prefrontal for which we have comparative information: Area 13 (involved in processing information relevant to the emotional aspects of social interactions) and area 10 (involved in planning and organizing thought for future actions) differ with respect to their apparent degrees of evolutionary modification. Area 13 seems to have lagged behind the overall increase in brain size, being only approximately 1.5 times larger than the average ape (pongid) value, whereas the brain as a whole is approximately 3 times larger (Semendeferi, Armstrong, Schleicher, Zilles, & Van Hoesen,

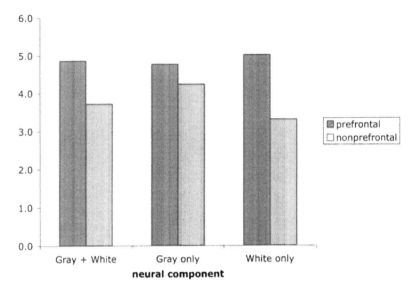

Figure 4 Ratio of the size of prefrontal cortex (anterior to the corpus callosum) between human and chimpanzee (average of common and bonobo chimps, *Pan troglodytes* and *Pan paniscus*). Prefrontal areas are disproportionately larger than nonprefrontal areas in humans, particularly for white matter (primarily connective fibers). Data from Schoenemann, Sheehan, & Glotzer (2005).

1998). However, the fact that it is absolutely larger in humans likely requires a functional explanation, presumably related to the elaboration of social complexity in humans.

Area 10, which also shows activity in linguistic tasks that require selection of appropriate words given a specific semantic context (Gabrieli et al., 1998; Luke et al., 2002), is approximately 6.6 times larger than the corresponding areas in pongids (Semendeferi et al., 2001). Although this increase is actually close to what one would expect given how this area seems to scale with the size of our brain as a whole (Holloway, 2002), it is difficult to believe that this increase did not also have functional implications for language evolution.

Concepts and Semantic Processing

Connecting conceptual understanding to specific linguistic codes is obviously central to language. As discussed earlier, conceptual understanding itself appears to depend on a wide network of many different areas of the brain. Humans (and primates generally) are particularly biased toward visual

information, which, as a consequence, forms an important component of conceptual understanding for most people (blind people being an exception). Visual
information processing starts in the retina of the eye and is transferred through
intermediate nuclei to the primary visual cortex, located in the occipital lobe,
where it first becomes available to conscious awareness (Bear et al., 2007).
Visual information is subsequently processed along two major pathways: the
dorsal stream (extending up into the parietal lobe), which processes information
regarding the location and motion of an object, and the ventral stream (extending
to the anterior tip of the temporal lobe), which processes information regarding
the characteristics of the objects themselves independent of their location and
motion (e.g., shape, color, etc., Bear et al., 2007). Because of this functional
distinction, the dorsal stream is often referred to as the "where" pathway, and the
ventral stream as the "what" pathway (Bear et al., 2007). Thus, broadly speaking, these two pathways correspond to objects (which get mapped as nouns)
and actions/orientations/directions (which are central to concepts mapped as
verbs) (cf. Hurford, 2003b).

Within the "what" pathway, the understanding of proper nouns appears to
depend on anterior and medial areas of the temporal lobe, whereas understanding common nouns appears to depend on the lateral and inferior temporal lobes
(Damasio & Damasio, 1992). These areas have been elaborated during human
evolution. Overall, the human temporal lobe is 23% larger than predicted based
on how large our brain is, and it is almost four times larger in absolute volume
than the temporal lobe of chimpanzees (data from Rilling & Seligman, 2002).
The difference appears greatest for the portions corresponding to connectivity
(i.e., white matter axonal tracts; Rilling & Seligman, 2002), consistent with
the fact that concepts critically depend on interconnectivity with other cortical
areas.

The primary auditory cortex of the temporal lobe (where conscious awareness of auditory information first occurs) appears to be only approximately
6% larger than predicted based on our overall brain size. Immediately adjacent
areas also involved in processing auditory information appear to be only approximately 17% larger (Deacon, 1997). In absolute terms, these areas would
still be more than three times larger than the equivalent area in apes, however. Thus, it seems likely that important enhancements occurred with respect
to auditory processing. Because these auditory areas are a subset of the entire temporal lobe, the rest of the temporal lobe (important to the semantics of
nouns) must have increased even more than the approximately 23% for the temporal lobe as a whole. This points, again, to the elaboration of circuits involved

in conceptual and semantic processing and suggests that this was particularly important during our evolution.

One area of the temporal lobe that has been of particular focus has been the planum temporale, located in the superior portion of the temporal lobe (just posterior to the primary auditory cortex). Studies showing a tendency for the planum temporale to be larger on the left side (e.g., Geschwind & Levitsky, 1968) were initially assumed to reflect a functional anatomical correlate of language evolution (the expressive parts of which are usually localized to the left hemisphere). However, it turns out that apes show a similar asymmetry in this region also (Gannon, Holloway, Broadfield, & Braun, 1998). Exactly what the asymmetry indicates is not clear, but it obviously cannot be specific to language. It may be that it has a general role in processing auditory information for communication (not just language). If so, it would be yet another example of brain preadaptations for language.

With respect to the "where" pathway, which likely grounds concepts central to most verbs, there is some indication of an evolutionary expansion of this area during human evolution, based on analyses of brain endocasts of fossil hominins (Bruner, 2004). Detailed comparative anatomical studies among primates have not been reported, however. The semantic generation of verbs (the actual words themselves) seems to involve Broca's area (Damasio & Damasio, 1992; Posner & Raichle, 1994), which also appears to have been elaborated during human evolution, as discussed earlier.

Right Hemisphere
Although the cortical language areas discussed so far are localized to the left hemisphere in most people, there is substantial evidence that the right hemisphere also contributes importantly to language. The right hemisphere understands short words (Gazzaniga, 1970) and entertains alternative possible meanings for particular words (Beeman & Chiarello, 1998), suggesting that it is better able to interpret multiple intended meanings of a given linguistic communication. The right hemisphere also plays a greater role in a variety of types of spatial processing in most people (Tzeng & Wang, 1984; Vallar, 2007), thus presumably grounding the semantics of spatial terms. The right frontal lobe mediates aspects of prosody (Alexander, Benson, & Stuss, 1989; Novoa & Ardila, 1987), which is critically important to understanding intended meaning (consider sarcasm, in which the intended meaning is directly opposite the literal meaning).

There are, however, no comparative analyses of right versus left hemisphere differences across primates that I am aware of, so the extent to which there has been biased evolutionary changes for one or the other hemisphere is not known. The right hemisphere in humans is not significantly different in size than the left (Allen, Damasio, & Grabowski, 2002), suggesting that it probably has increased approximately threefold along with the cortex as a whole.

Basal Ganglia

Although the cortex is heavily involved in language processing, cerebral nuclei deep to the cortex also appear to play important roles. A group of interconnected nuclei, collectively known as the basal ganglia, participate in an important circuit loop that functions in the selection and initiation of willed movements (Bear et al., 2007). The circuit starts with signals from a variety of areas of the cortex that are sent to the putamen and caudate nucleus (part of the basal ganglia). These, in turn, connect to the globus pallidus (another part of the basal ganglia), which then connects to the thalamus (ventral lateral nucleus), which finally send signals back up to the cortex (Bear et al., 2007). A variety of studies have implicated these circuits not just in language production (which makes sense given that language requires willed movements) but also in language comprehension (see references in Hochstadt, Nakano, Lieberman, & Friedman, 2006). Diseases affecting the basal ganglia, notably Parkinson's and Huntington's, result not only in motor (muscle movement) problems but also in problems understanding complicated syntax (e.g., center-embedded clauses), as well as processing semantic information (Hochstadt et al., 2006). As mentioned above Broca's aphasia (the behavioral syndrome) can be caused by damage not just to Broca's area (as was traditionally held), but also to areas deep to it, likely including circuits involving the basal ganglia (Lieberman, 2002).

Comparative studies of the relative size of the basal ganglia in humans suggest that these nuclei are only about 65% as large as predicted for a primate brain as large as ours (Schoenemann, 1997; Stephan et al., 1981). However, they are still about twice as large in absolute terms as predicted based on body size. If the basal ganglia were solely involved in motor functions, we would expect them to scale closely with overall body size. Because they are significantly larger than this and because humans do not appear to have significantly more sophisticated motor abilities than apes (with the exception being those related to vocalization), it is reasonable to suggest that the increase in absolute size of the basal ganglia indicates an important role supporting higher cortical functions like language.

Cerebellum

The primary function of the cerebellum was long thought to be monitoring and modulating motor signals from the cortex (Carpenter & Sutin, 1983).

However, more recent work has implicated the cerebellum in a whole range of higher cognitive functions, including goal organization and planning, aspects of memory and learning, attention, visuo-spatial processing, modulating emotional responses, and language (Baillieux, De Smet, Paquier, De Deyn, & Marien, 2008). The cerebellum appears to play a role in speech production and perception, as well as both semantic and grammatical processing (Ackermann, Mathiak, & Riecker, 2007; Baillieux et al.; De Smet, Baillieux, De Deyn, Marien, & Paquier, 2007). The cerebellum also seems to play a role in timing mechanisms generally (Ivry & Spencer, 2004), which may explain its functional relevance to language (given the importance temporal information plays in language production and perception).

Comparative studies suggest that the human cerebellum overall is slightly smaller than one would predict for how large our brain is (Rilling & Insel, 1998), but is approximately 2.9 times larger than predicted based on our body size (the largest increase of all brain regions besides portions of the neocortex). The higher cognitive functions of the cerebellum appear to be localized specifically to the lateral hemispheres (lobes) of the cerebellum, which are more evolutionarily recent (although present in primates; MacLeod, Zilles, Schleicher, Rilling, & Gibson, 2003). The lateral hemispheres of the cerebellum appear to have undergone a significant shift in proportions in apes and humans (hominoids) compared to monkeys: These areas are 2.7 times larger in hominoids than in monkeys, based on the size of the (evolutionarily older) cerebellar vermis region (MacLeod et al., 2003). Humans fall comfortably with apes in this measure, however, but they do differ significantly from apes with respect to overall body weight (human lateral cerebellar hemispheres are approximately 2.9 times larger than predicted based on body weight; MacLeod et al., 2003). These increases in cerebellar size therefore cannot be explained by, for example, greater muscle mass in humans, and as a consequence must result either from some sort of tight developmental linkage relative to the rest of the brain or from selection specifically for behavioral abilities that rely on the cerebellum. Given its role in language processing, this increase (however explained) may be relevant to language evolution.

Vocalization

The muscles responsible for vocalization are directly innervated by nuclei in the brainstem, which relay signals from midbrain and higher cortical areas. The nucleus ambiguous controls the muscles of the vocal folds and is therefore responsible for producing and changing the pitch of the primary vocal signal. This signal is then filtered in various ways by manipulations in the shape of the supralaryngeal vocal tract before it exits the mouth and nose (Denes & Pinson, 1963). The vocal tract is affected by the shape and position of the tongue (whose muscles are controlled by the hypoglossal nucleus and nucleus ambiguous), lower jaw (trigeminal nucleus), and the lips (facial motor nucleus). This whole system depends on the maintenance and manipulation of air pressure in the lungs, which is accomplished by the muscles of the chest and abdomen (innervated by anterior horn areas along the spinal cord; Carpenter & Sutin, 1983).

Even though vocal production has clearly been important to language, these brainstem nuclei do not appear to be particularly enlarged. The hypoglossal nucleus in humans is large, on average, but shows substantial overlap with apes, whereas the human trigeminal and facial motor nuclei completely overlap in size with those of the great apes (Sherwood et al., 2005). Thus, there is little evidence that language evolution substantially modified these nuclei.

Because conscious muscle movement depends on the cerebral cortex, deliberate communication requires direct connections from the cortex to these brainstem nuclei. In humans there are also indirect connections to the vocal folds, tongue, and mandible routed through the reticular formation of the brainstem and to the muscles of respiration routed through the nucleus retroambiguus of the brainstem (Striedter, 2005). An additional indirect pathway starts in the cingulate gyrus of the cortex and routes through the periaqueductal gray area of the midbrain and mediates involuntary vocal responses to pain or strong emotions (Striedter, 2005).

Comparative studies of these cortical-to-brainstem language pathways are, unfortunately, lacking. Nonhuman primates do have indirect connections to the brainstem nuclei involved in vocal production (Jurgens, 2002; Jurgens & Alipour, 2002), allowing them a variety of emotionally mediated vocalizations. However, nonhuman primates have weak direct connections to the brainstem nuclei that control the tongue and respiration muscles and completely lack direct connections to the larynx (Jurgens, 2002; Jurgens & Alipour, 2002). This suggests that the evolution of language encouraged the evolution of at least some new direct cortical pathways to the brainstem specifically for deliberate conscious vocalization.

Auditory Perception

For conscious awareness of sounds, auditory information must be relayed from the cochlea (where sound is translated into neural signals), through a series of intermediate nuclei in the brainstem and midbrain, on the primary auditory cortex located in the temporal lobe. Comparative mammalian data on the size of intermediate auditory nuclei along these auditory pathways suggest that humans have somewhat smaller auditory nuclei than expected for our brain weight, although the difference is not statistically significant (Glendenning & Masterton, 1998). In absolute terms, our auditory nuclei are reasonably large, although not dramatically so (total for all auditory nuclei volumes in humans is 187 mm^3, compared to 104 mm^3 for domesticated cats, which weigh only approximately 3 kg). These data suggests only modest changes in these nuclei during human evolution.

Conclusion

Many evolutionary changes in the brain appear to have relevance to language evolution. The increase in overall brain size paved the way for language both by encouraging localized cortical specialization and by making possible increasingly complicated social interactions. Increasing sociality provided the central usefulness for language in the first place and drove its evolution. Specific areas of the brain directly relevant to language appear to have been particularly elaborated, especially the prefrontal cortex (areas relevant to semantics and syntax) and the temporal lobe (particularly areas relevant to connecting words to meanings and concepts). Broca's and Wernicke's areas are not unique to human brains, but they do appear to have been elaborated, along with the arcuate fasciculus connecting these areas. Other areas of the brain that participate in language processing, such as the basal ganglia and cerebellum, are larger than predicted based on overall body weight, although they have not increased as much as a number of language-relevant areas of the cortex. Finally, little evidence suggests that significant elaboration of the auditory processing pathways up to the cortex has occurred, but direct pathways down to the tongue and respiratory muscles have been strengthened, with new direct pathways created to the larynx, presumably specifically for speech.

These findings are consistent with the view that language and brain adapted to each other. In each generation, language made use of (adapted to) abilities that already existed. This is consistent with the fact that the peripheral neural circuits directly responsible for perceptual and productive aspects of language have shown the least change. It makes sense that languages would evolve specifically to take advantage of sound contrasts that were already (prelinguistically) relatively easy to distinguish. This perspective is also consistent with the fact that Broca's and Wernicke's areas are not unique to humans. Differences in language circuits seem mostly to be quantitative elaborations, rather than completely new circuitry.

Three major factors seem to have conspired to drive the evolution of language: first, the general elaboration of—and increasing focus on—the importance of learned behavior; second, a significant increase in the complexity, subtlety, and range of conceptual understanding that was possible; and third, an increasingly complex, socially interactive existence. Each of these is reflected by a variety of changes in the brain during human evolution. Because language itself facilitates thinking and conceptual awareness, language evolution would have been a mutually reinforcing process: Increasingly complicated brains led to increasingly rich and varied thoughts, driving the evolution of increasingly complicated language, which itself facilitated even more complex conceptual worlds that these brains would then want to communicate (Savage-Rumbaugh & Rumbaugh, 1993; Schoenemann, 2009). The interplay between internal (conceptual) and external (social) aspects of human existence that drove this coevolutionary process highlights the usefulness of thinking about language evolution as a complex adaptive system. The extent to which increasing conceptual complexity itself might have driven language evolution represents an intriguing research question for the future.

Revised version accepted 11 June 2009

References

Aboitiz, F., & Garcia, V. R. (1997). The evolutionary origin of the language areas in the human brain: A neuroanatomical perspective. *Brain Research: Brain Research Reviews, 25*(3), 381–396.

Ackermann, H., Mathiak, K., & Riecker, A. (2007). The contribution of the cerebellum to speech production and speech perception: Clinical and functional imaging data. *Cerebellum (London, England), 6*(3), 202–213.

Alexander, M. P., Benson, D. F., & Stuss, D. T. (1989). Frontal lobes and language. *Brain and Language, 37,* 656–691.

Allman, J., McLaughlin, T., & Hakeem, A. (1993). Brain weight and life-span in primate species. *Proceedings of the National Academy of Sciences of the United States of America, 90*(1), 118–122.

Allen, J. S., Damasio, H., & Grabowski, T. J. (2002). Normal neuroanatomical variation in the human brain: An MRI-volumetric study. *American Journal of Physical Anthropology, 118*(4), 341–358.

Baillieux, H., De Smet, H. J., Paquier, P. F., De Deyn, P. P., & Marien, P. (2008). Cerebellar neurocognition: Insights into the bottom of the brain. *Clinical Neurology and Neurosurgery, 110*(8), 763–773.

Bear, M. F., Connors, B. W., & Paradiso, M. A. (2007). *Neuroscience: Exploring the brain* (3rd ed.). Philadelphia: Lippincott Williams & Wilkins.

Beeman, M. J., & Chiarello, C. (1998). Complementary right- and left-hemisphere language comprehension. *Current Directions in Psychological Science, 7*(1), 2–8.

Beran, M. J., Gibson, K. R., & Rumbaugh, D. M. (1999). Predicting hominid intelligence from brain size. In M. C. Corballis & S. E. G. Lea (Eds.), *The descent of mind: Psychological perspectives on hominid evolution* (pp. 88–97). Oxford: Oxford University Press.

Bickerton, D. (1990). *Language & species*. Chicago: University of Chicago Press.

Brodmann, K. (1909). *Vergleichende lokalisationsiehre der grosshirnrinde in ihren prinzipien dargestellt auf grund des zellenbaues*. Leipzig: Johann Ambrosius Barth Verlag.

Bruner, E. (2004). Geometric morphometrics and paleoneurology: Brain shape evolution in the genus homo. *Journal of Human Evolution, 47*, 279–303.

Caplan, R., & Dapretto, M. (2001). Making sense during conversation: An fMRI study. *Neuroreport, 12*(16), 3625- 3632.

Carpenter, M. B., & Sutin, J. (1983). *Human neuroanatomy* (8th ed.). Baltimore: Williams & Wilkins.

Changizi, M. A., & Shimojo, S. (2005). Parcellation and area-area connectivity as a function of neocortex size. *Brain, Behavior and Evolution, 66*(2), 88–98.

Chomsky, N. (1959). A Review of B. F. Skinner's Verbal Behavior. *Language, 35*(1), 26–58.

Christiansen, M. H. (1994). *Infinite languages, finite minds: Connectionism, learning and linguistic structure*. Unpublished doctoral dissertation, University of Edinburgh, Edinburgh.

Christiansen, M. H., & Chater, N. (2008). Language as shaped by the brain. *Behavioral and Brain Sciences, 31*, 489-509.

Damasio, A. R., & Damasio, H. (1992). Brain and language. *Scientific American, 267*(3), 89–95.

Damasio, H., Grabowski, T. J., Damasio, A., Tranel, D., Boles-Ponto, L., Watkins, G. L., et al. (1993). Visual recall with eyes closed and covered activates early visual cortices. *Society for Neuroscience Abstracts, 19*, 1603.

De Smet, H. J., Baillieux, H., De Deyn, P. P., Marien, P., & Paquier, P. (2007). The cerebellum and language: The story so far. *Folia Phoniatrica et Logopaedica, 59*(4), 165–170.

Deacon, T. W. (1988). Human brain evolution: II. Embryology and brain allometry. In H. J. Jerison & I. Jerison (Eds.), *Intelligence and evolutionary biology* (pp. 383–415). Berlin: Springer-Verlag.

Deacon, T. W. (1992). Brain-language coevolution. In J. A. Hawkins & M. Gell-Mann (Eds.), *The evolution of human languages* (Vol. 11, pp. 49-83). Redwood City, CA: Addison-Wesley.

Deacon, T. W. (1997). *The symbolic species: The co-evolution of language and the brain*. New York: W.W. Norton.

Denes, P. B., & Pinson, E. N. (1963). *The speech chain*. Garden City, NY: Anchor Press/Doubleday.

Dronkers, N. F. (2000). The pursuit of brain-language relationships. *Brain and Language, 71*(1), 59–61.

Dunbar, R. I. M. (1995). Neocortex size and group size in primates: A test of the hypothesis. *Journal of Human Evolution, 28*, 287–296.

Dunbar, R. I. M. (2003). The social brain: Mind, language, and society in evolutionary perspective. *Annual Review of Anthropology, 32*, 163–181.

Gabrieli, J. D., Poldrack, R. A., & Desmond, J. E. (1998). The role of left prefrontal cortex in language and memory. *Proceedings of the National Academy of Sciences of the United States of America, 95*(3), 906–913.

Gannon, P. J., Holloway, R. L., Broadfield, D. C., & Braun, A. R. (1998). Asymmetry of chimpanzee planum temporale: Humanlike pattern of Wernicke's brain language area homolog. *Science, 279*(5348), 220–222.

Gazzaniga, M. S. (1970). *The bisected brain*. New York: Appleton-Century-Crofts.

Geschwind, N. (1974). *Selected papers on language and the brain*. Boston: Reidel.

Geschwind, N., & Levitsky, W. (1968). Human brain: Left-right asymmetries in temporal speech region. *Science, 161*(837), 186–187.

Gibson, K. R. (2002). Evolution of human intelligence: The roles of brain size and mental construction. *Brain, Behavior and Evolution, 59*(1–2), 10–20.

Glendenning, K. K., & Masterton, R. B. (1998). Comparative morphometry of mammalian central auditory systems: Variation in nuclei and form of the ascending system. *Brain, Behavior and Evolution, 51*(2), 59–89.

Harvey, P. H., & Clutton-Brock, T. H. (1985). Life history variation in primates. *Evolution, 39*, 559–581.

Hochstadt, J., Nakano, H., Lieberman, P., & Friedman, J. (2006). The roles of sequencing and verbal working memory in sentence comprehension deficits in Parkinson's disease. *Brain and Language, 97*(3), 243–257.

Hofman, M. A. (1983). Energy metabolism, brain size, and longevity in mammals. *Quarterly Review of Biology, 58*, 495–512.

Hofman, M. A. (2001). Brain evolution in hominids: Are we at the end of the road? In D. Falk & K. R. Gibson (Eds.), *Evolutionary anatomy of the primate cerebral cortex* (pp. 113–127). Cambridge: Cambridge University Press.

Holloway, R. L. (2002). Brief communication: How much larger is the relative volume of area 10 of the prefrontal cortex in humans? *American Journal of Physical Anthropology, 118*(4), 399–401.

Hurford, J. R. (2003a). The language mosaic and its evolution. In M. H. Christiansen & S. Kirby (Eds.), *Language evolution* (pp. 38–57). Oxford: Oxford University Press.

Hurford, J. R. (2003b). The neural basis of predicate-argument structure. *The Behavioral and Brain Sciences, 26*(3), 261–283; discussion 283–316.

Indefrey, P., Hellwig, F., Herzog, H., Seitz, R. J., & Hagoort, P. (2004). Neural responses to the production and comprehension of syntax in identical utterances. *Brain and Language, 89*(2), 312–319.

Ivry, R. B., & Spencer, R. M. (2004). The neural representation of time. *Current Opinion in Neurobiology, 14*(2), 225–232.

Jerison, H. J. (1973). *Evolution of the brain and intelligence.* New York: Academic Press.

Jurgens, U. (2002). Neural pathways underlying vocal control. *Neuroscience and Biobehavioral Reviews, 26*(2), 235–258.

Jurgens, U., & Alipour, M. (2002). A comparative study on the cortico-hypoglossal connections in primates, using biotin dextranamine. *Neuroscience Letters, 328*(3), 245–248.

Kerns, J. G., Cohen, J. D., Stenger, V. A., & Carter, C. S. (2004). Prefrontal cortex guides context-appropriate responding during language production. *Neuron, 43*(2), 283–291.

Kosslyn, S. M., Alpert, N. M., Thompson, W. L., Maljkovic, V., Weise, S. B., Chabris, C. F., et al. (1993). Visual mental imagery activates topographically organized visual cortex: PET investigations. *Journal of Cognitive Neuroscience, 5*, 263–287.

Lieberman, P. (2000). *Human language and our reptilian brain: The subcortical bases of speech, syntax, and thought.* Cambridge, MA: Harvard University Press.

Lieberman, P. (2002). On the nature and evolution of the neural bases of human language. *Yearbook of Physical Anthropology, 45*, 36–62.

Luke, K. K., Liu, H. L., Wai, Y. Y., Wan, Y. L., & Tan, L. H. (2002). Functional anatomy of syntactic and semantic processing in language comprehension. *Human Brain Mapping, 16*(3), 133–145.

MacLeod, C. E., Zilles, K., Schleicher, A., Rilling, J. K., & Gibson, K. R. (2003). Expansion of the neocerebellum in hominoidea. *Journal of Human Evolution, 44*(4), 401–429.

Maguire, E. A., & Frith, C. D. (2004). The brain network associated with acquiring semantic knowledge. *NeuroImage, 22*(1), 171–178.

Mueller, R.-A. (1996). Innateness, autonomy, universality? Neurobiological approaches to language. *Behavioral and Brain Sciences, 19*(4), 611–675.

Nieuwenhuys, R. (1994). The neocortex: An overview of its evolutionary development, structural organization and synaptology. *Anatomy and Embryology, 190*(4), 307–337.

Noppeney, U., & Price, C. J. (2004). Retrieval of abstract semantics. *NeuroImage, 22*, 164–170.

Northcutt, R. G., & Kaas, J. H. (1995). The emergence and evolution of mammalian neocortex. *Trends in Neurosciences, 18*(9), 373–379.

Novoa, O. P., & Ardila, A. (1987). Linguistic abilities in patients with prefrontal damage. *Brain and Language, 30*, 206–225.

Nucifora, P. G., Verma, R., Melhem, E. R., Gur, R. E., & Gur, R. C. (2005). Leftward asymmetry in relative fiber density of the arcuate fasciculus. *Neuroreport, 16*(8), 791–794.

Parker, S. T., & Gibson, K. R. (Eds.). (1990). *"Language" and intelligence in monkeys and apes: Comparative developmental perspectives.* Cambridge: Cambridge University Press.

Petrides, M., & Pandya, D. N. (2002). Comparative cytoarchitectonic analysis of the human and the macaque ventrolateral prefrontal cortex and corticocortical connection patterns in the monkey. *The European Journal of Neuroscience, 16*(2), 291–310.

Pinker, S. (1995). Facts about human language relevant to its evolution. In J.-P. Changeux & J. Chavaillon (Eds.), *Origins of the human brain* (pp. 262–283). Oxford: Clarendon.

Posner, M. I., & Raichle, M. E. (1994). *Images of mind.* New York: W. H. Freeman.

Rilling, J. K. (2006). Human and nonhuman primate brains: Are they allometrically scaled versions of the same design? *Evolutionary Anthropology, 15*, 65–77.

Rilling, J. K., Glasser, M. F., Preuss, T. M., Ma, X., Zhang, X., Zhao, T., et al. (2007). A comparative diffusion tensor imaging (DTI) study of the arcuate fasciculus language pathway in humans, chimpanzees and rhesus macaques. *American Journal of Physical Anthropology, 132*(S44), 199–200.

Rilling, J. K., & Insel, T. R. (1998). Evolution of the cerebellum in primates: Differences in relative volume among monkeys, apes and humans. *Brain, Behavior and Evolution, 52*(6), 308–314.

Rilling, J. K., & Seligman, R. A. (2002). A quantitative morphometric comparative analysis of the primate temporal lobe. *Journal of Human Evolution, 42*(5), 505–533.

Ringo, J. L. (1991). Neuronal interconnection as a function of brain size. *Brain, Behavior and Evolution, 38*, 1–6.

Savage-Rumbaugh, E. S., & Rumbaugh, D. M. (1993). The emergence of language. In K. R. Gibson & T. Ingold (Eds.), *Tools, language and cognition in human evolution* (pp. 86–108). Cambridge: Cambridge University Press.

Schoenemann, P. T. (1997). *An MRI study of the relationship between human neuroanatomy and behavioral ability.* Unpublished doctoral dissertation, University of California, Berkeley.

Schoenemann, P. T. (1999). Syntax as an emergent characteristic of the evolution of semantic complexity. *Minds and Machines, 9*, 309–346.

Schoenemann, P. T. (2005). Conceptual complexity and the brain: Understanding language origins. In W. S.-Y. Wang & J. W. Minett (Eds.), *Language acquisition, change and emergence: Essays in evolutionary linguistics* (pp. 47–94). Hong Kong: City University of Hong Kong Press.

Schoenemann, P. T. (2006). Evolution of the size and functional areas of the human brain. *Annual Review of Anthropology, 35*, 379–406.

Schoenemann, P. T. (2009). Brain evolution relevant to language. In J. W. Minett & W. S.-Y. Wang (Eds.), *Language, evolution, and the brain* (pp. 191–223). Hong Kong: City University of Hong Kong Press.

Schoenemann, P. T., Sheehan, M. J., & Glotzer, L. D. (2005). Prefrontal white matter volume is disproportionately larger in humans than in other primates. *Nature Neuroscience, 8*(2), 242–252.

Semendeferi, K., Armstrong, E., Schleicher, A., Zilles, K., & Van Hoesen, G. W. (1998). Limbic frontal cortex in hominoids: A comparative study of area 13. *American Journal of Physical Anthropology, 106*(2), 129–155.

Semendeferi, K., Armstrong, E., Schleicher, A., Zilles, K., & Van Hoesen, G. W. (2001). Prefrontal cortex in humans and apes: A comparative study of area 10. *American Journal of Physical Anthropology, 114*(3), 224–241.

Sherwood, C. C., Hof, P. R., Holloway, R. L., Semendeferi, K., Gannon, P. J., Frahm, H. D., et al. (2005). Evolution of the brainstem orofacial motor system in primates: A comparative study of trigeminal, facial, and hypoglossal nuclei. *Journal of Human Evolution, 48*(1), 45–84.

Smith, B. H. (1990). The cost of a large brain. *Behavioral and Brain Sciences, 13*, 365–366.

Stephan, H., Frahm, H., & Baron, G. (1981). New and revised data on volumes of brain structures in insectivores and primates. *Folia Primatologica, 35*, 1–29.

Striedter, G. F. (2005). *Principles of brain evolution.* Sunderland, MA: Sinauer Associates.

Thompson-Schill, S. L., Swick, D., Farah, M. J., D'Esposito, M., Kan, I. P., & Knight, R. T. (1998). Verb generation in patients with focal frontal lesions: A neuropsychological test of neuroimaging findings. *Proceedings of the National Academy of Sciences of the United States of America, 95*(26), 15,855–15,860.

Tzeng, O. J. L., & Wang, W. S.-Y. (1984). Search for a common neurocognitive mechanism for language and movements. *American Journal of Physiology (Regulatory Integrative Comparative Physiology), 246*(15), R904–R911.

Vallar, G. (2007). Spatial neglect, Balint-Homes' and Gerstmann's syndrome, and other spatial disorders. *CNS Spectrums, 12*(7), 527–536.

Language Learning   ISSN 0023-8333

Complex Adaptive Systems and the Origins of Adaptive Structure: What Experiments Can Tell Us

Hannah Cornish

The University of Edinburgh

Monica Tamariz

The University of Edinburgh

Simon Kirby

The University of Edinburgh

Language is a product of both biological and cultural evolution. Clues to the origins of key structural properties of language can be found in the process of cultural transmission between learners. Recent experiments have shown that iterated learning by human participants in the laboratory transforms an initially unstructured artificial language into one containing regularities that make the system more learnable and stable over time. Here, we explore the process of iterated learning in more detail by demonstrating exactly how one type of structure—compositionality—emerges over the course of these experiments. We introduce a method to precisely quantify the increasing ability of a language to systematically encode associations between individual components of meanings and signals over time and we examine how the system as a whole evolves to avoid ambiguity in these associations and generate adaptive structure.

Hannah Cornish is funded by an ESRC postgraduate studentship. Monica Tamariz was funded by a Leverhulme Early Career Fellowship. Monica Tamariz and Simon Kirby are supported by ESRC Grant Number RES-062-23-1537 and by AHRC Grant Number AH/F017677/1. The work presented here benefited from discussion among the members of the University of Edinburgh's Language Evolution and Computation Research Unit, and constructive comments from two anonymous referees.

Correspondence concerning this article should be addressed to Simon Kirby, Language Evolution and Computation Research Unit, The University of Edinburgh, 3 Charles Street, Edinburgh, EH8 9AD, UK. Internet: simon@ling.ed.ac.uk

Introduction

The position paper in this issue (Beckner et al.) sets out a powerful motivating picture of language as a complex adaptive system. It presents us with a way of thinking not only about the dynamics of language as we know it now but also the emergence of language in the first place. More specifically, in this article, we suggest that the very fact that language persists through multiple repeated instances of usage can explain the origins of key structural properties that are universally present in language. Because of this, taking a complex adaptive systems perspective on language lifts the burden of explanation for these properties from a putative richly structured domain-specific substrate, of the sort assumed by much of generative linguistics (e.g., Chomsky, 1965). Ultimately, this alters our view of what biological evolution must provide in order to get language off the ground.

Much of the work over the past 20 years or so in modeling the evolution of language has taken this complex adaptive systems perspective (see, e.g., Brighton, Smith, & Kirby, 2005; Kirby, 2002b; Steels, 2003, for review). One particular strand of work has focused on the adaptation of language through a repeated cycle of learning and use within and across generations, where adaptation is taken to mean a process of optimization or *fitting* of the structure of language to the mechanisms of transmission (Kirby, 1999).[1]

A particular subset of models have looked extensively at the impact of repeated learning on the process of emergence. They investigate how a form of cultural evolution known as *iterated learning* affects the structure of language (e.g., Batali, 1998; Brighton, 2002; Griffiths & Kalish, 2007; Hurford, 2000; Kirby, 1999; Kirby, Dowman, & Griffiths, 2007; Kirby & Hurford, 2002; A. Smith, 2005; K. Smith, 2002; Vogt, 2005; Zuidema, 2003). In these models, each agent (i.e., simulated individual) must acquire a set of (initially random) mappings between meanings and signals by observing the behavior of agents in the previous generation. Once this mapping is acquired, the learner becomes a teacher, and the process repeats. Crucially there is a bottleneck in the transmission process that puts pressure on the system to be generalizable (Deacon, 1997). This bottleneck models the data-sparsity present in real language acquisition and is typically enforced in the simulations by the learner only being exposed to signals for a subset of the total meanings during training.

Overall, two consistent conclusions have been drawn from this computational research: Over time, iterated learning ensures languages evolve to (a) become easier to learn and (b) become more structured. These two facts are not unrelated: One of the ways in which a language can evolve to become more learnable is by becoming structured. This is because there are only two ways to survive the transmission bottleneck: be heard (and remembered) by the next generation or be easily inferable from what is heard. This latter solution can only occur when there is some kind of regularity to be exploited in the system. The exact form this regularity takes can vary, which is something we explore later.

The regularity that emerges gradually in the computational simulations justifies our use of the term "adaptive" in this case. This is because the kinds of linguistic structures that evolve show the hallmarks of *apparent design*. For example, in some models (e.g., Batali, 2002; Kirby, 2002a), recursive compositional syntax evolves that clearly enables the simulated agents to successfully convey meanings in an open-ended way. This kind of adaptive structure in language might lead researchers to conclude that it must reflect innate constraints that are the result of biological evolution by natural selection (e.g., Pinker & Bloom, 1990). However, this conclusion is not justified. In most of these models, there is no biological evolution. Indeed, individuals are essentially clones throughout. Rather, the adaptation arises purely from the iterated learning process itself. Language transmission is a complex adaptive system.

Recently, we developed a method for studying this process of adaptive evolution in the laboratory, extending experimental studies of iterated learning in the nonlinguistic domain by Griffiths and Kalish (2007) and Kalish, Griffiths, and Lewandowsky (2007). By combining two experimental techniques—artificial language learning (e.g., Esper, 1925, 1966; Fitch & Hauser, 2004; Gómez & Gerkin, 2000; Saffran, Aslin, & Newport, 1996) and diffusion chains (e.g., Bangerter, 2000; Bartlett, 1932; Horner, Whiten, Flynn, & de Waal, 2006; Mesoudi, Whiten, & Dunbar, 2006; Whiten, Horner, & de Waal, 2005)—we were able to track the evolution of a miniature language over "generations" of experimental participants from an initially random, unstructured state, to one showing clear evidence of adaptive structure (Kirby, Cornish, & Smith, 2008).[2] In this article, we provide a new analysis of the results of this study to examine in more detail the way structure emerges as a result of competition between linguistic variants.

Human Iterated Learning: An Overview

Before we move onto the details of the studies, it is necessary to familiarize ourselves with the general methodology and key parameters of the experiments that follow. A participant is trained on an "alien" language consisting of a set of meanings (usually presented as pictures) paired with signals (a string of letters, or possibly sounds) drawn from a finite set. After being trained on some proportion of these meanings, the participant is then presented with a series of meanings without signals and asked to provide the correct description in the alien language. These meanings and signals are recorded and become the new set of training pairs for the next participant, who forms the next "generation" of the chain. This procedure is repeated until the chain is complete (i.e., until the desired number of generations has been reached).

Participants involved in the study are only asked to learn the language as best they can: They are not told anything about the iterated nature of the study or that their responses will be given to future participants. During each training round, participants are shown a picture drawn at random from the set of meanings, and below it, a string of letters that they are told represents how the alien would describe that picture in its own language. Training occurs via a computer, and each exposure is timed to ensure no training item (meaning-signal pair) is seen for longer than any other and continues until all training items have been seen. During the final test, the participant is shown each picture in the language once, one after another, and asked to type in the missing descriptions. These responses are then randomly sampled from to generate the new training items for the next generation.

Clearly, this experimental setup represents a highly simplified idealization of the real process of linguistic transmission. In particular, the population model is the simplest that we could construct (in line with the other diffusion chain experiments mentioned previously). Three parameters characterize possible population models: direction of transmission (vertical or horizontal), the size of the population, and who learns from whom (network structure). For the rest of this article we focus on just one scenario: vertical transmission, involving 10 people, with each person learning from just 1 other person. However, it is important to remember that there are many other scenarios that could be explored within this framework.

Learnability, Expressivity, and Adaptation

As stated in the introduction, the main finding to have emerged over the past decade or so of research into this area is that languages themselves adapt to be better learnable and transmissible by us over time (see, e.g., Christiansen & Chater, 2008, for a review). However, it should be recognized that this pressure toward greater learnability must be tempered somewhat in order for structure to emerge. The reason for this is simple: The most easily learnable language might be one in which there is one word for everything (or possibly, no words at all). It is only when we also have a pressure for expressivity, for meanings to actually be distinguished from one another, that we are likely to see the emergence of structure.

The first application of this new experimental methodology set about investigating this tension between expressivity and learnability (Kirby et al., 2008). In this study, the meaning space consisted of 27 pictures showing a scene that varied along three features and three values: color of object (blue, black, red), shape of object (circle, triangle, square), and a dotted line indicating the movement of object (bouncing, spiralling, moving horizontally). Two different experimental conditions were explored, with four chains of 10 people in each. In one condition there was a "hidden" pressure for each of the meanings in the meaning space to be expressed uniquely: Participants' input was filtered in such a way as to ensure they never perceived different meanings with the same signal. In the other, there was no such pressure. Participants could not be aware of the experimental condition in which they were included.

The chains in each condition both began with random initial languages, and a transmission bottleneck was imposed by exposing each generation with just half (14) of the meaning-signal pairs during training (the particular meanings that they would be exposed to were chosen randomly each generation). Example (1) shows a sample of the initial randomly generated language in one of the chains to illustrate what is meant by the claim that they are unstructured with respect to their meanings.[3] In spite of the fact that these meanings in the world are similar (triangles of every color that either move horizontally or in a spiral), the signals used to describe them are all idiosyncratic, with no consistently repeating subparts.

(1) a. kapihu   b. luki
         "black triangle horizontal"   "black triangle spiral"

     c. humo   d. namola
         "blue triangle horizontal"   "blue triangle spiral"

     e. lahupiki   f. lumoka
         "red triangle horizontal"   "red triangle spiral"

After training, participants were tested on all 27 meanings, and it is from this output set that the new training set is sampled for the participant in the next generation.

The main findings can be summarized as follows (see Kirby et al., 2008, for more details). First, by looking at the learning errors made between adjacent generations, it was shown that the languages in both conditions were being acquired significantly more faithfully toward the end of the chains than they were at the beginning. Second, this increase in learnability over time occurred as a result of the languages becoming more structured over time.

What is interesting about this last fact, however, is that the way in which the languages were structured differed markedly between the two experimental conditions. In the first condition, for which there was no filtering of the participants' input, systems emerged that were characterized by *underspecification*. This involved a reduction in the total number of distinct signals, introducing ambiguity with respect to the meanings. However, this ambiguity was not complete, as it did not affect all meaning dimensions. In one chain for instance, a system emerged [of which a sample is reproduced as Example (2)] whereby everything that moved horizontally was called *tuge*, everything that moved in a spiral was named *poi*, and there was a three-way distinction of bouncing items dependent on shape: for bouncing squares, *tupim* for bouncing triangles, *tupin*, and for bouncing circles, *miniku*. This system proved to be highly adaptive in the sense that, once it emerged, it was stable and faithfully acquired by subsequent generations without error.[4]

(2)	a.	tuge "black triangle horizontal"	b.	poi "black triangle spiral"
	c.	tuge "blue triangle horizontal"	d.	poi "blue triangle spiral"
	e.	tuge "red triangle horizontal"	f.	poi "red triangle spiral"

As Kirby et al. (2008) pointed out, underspecification is not an unusual feature of human languages, but taken to extremes, it would lead to an inexpressive and communicatively disfunctional language (albeit one that would be easy to learn). The second experimental condition, whereby items were removed from a participant's input if they should lead to the same string being assigned to more than one meaning, was designed to introduce a hidden pressure against underspecification. With this modification in place, the systems that emerged appear much closer to what we might expect a communicatively useful system to look like. These systems were characterized by *compositionality*, whereby the meaning of a given string could be inferred by the meaning of subparts of that string (morphemes) and the way they are put together. Example (3) again shows a sample of this.[5]

(3)	a.	nekeki "black triangle horizontal"	b.	nekipilu "black triangle spiral"

c.	lakeki	d.	lakipilu
	"blue triangle horizontal"		"blue triangle spiral"
e.	raheki	f.	rahopilu
	"red triangle horizontal"		"red triangle spiral"

These results are very exciting, as they experimentally verify the main findings to have emerged from computational models of iterated learning for the first time: that languages adapt purely by virtue of transmission through iterated learning. Moreover, the kind of adaptation is determined, in part, by constraints placed on the transmission of the languages about which participants could not be aware. However, although it has been shown that the languages in these experiments *do* adapt, it has not yet been established *how* they adapt. It is to this question that we now turn.

The Evolution of Signals During Iterated Learning

In this subsection we will focus on the utterances, leaving aside the meanings for the moment, and construct phylogenies demonstrating the evolution of linguistic forms over iterations. We used one of the languages [part of which was reproduced in Example (2)], taken from Kirby et al. (2008) to construct the coalescent tree shown in Figure 1. These trees are a standard way to represent phylogenetic descent in evolutionary biology (Barton, 2007; Hein, Schierup, & Wiuf, 2005), although here we have amended them to also include frequency information in brackets. Bold lines show perfect replication of an utterance, whereas other lines show possible relationships of descent between utterances across generations.

As we can see in Figure 1, the number of different utterances decreases over time as we start to observe perfect replication of select utterances, along with a general tendency for utterances to become shorter. In the early history of this language, the process of transmission is principally one of generating new recombinations of signal substrings. We observe only one instance of replication of a whole utterance but many replications of parts of the utterances, such as unigrams or bigrams, and even larger n-grams. For example, the introduction of the form miniku in generation 2 could be the result of a blend between miniki and miweniku.[6] There is still much variation in the language at this point. In the final generations, however, the frequencies of the few remaining units stabilize around multiples of 3, suggesting adaptation to a meaning space containing three dimensions.

In the case of the language in Figure 1, given the nondecomposable utterances that survived into the final stable system, it was appropriate to analyze

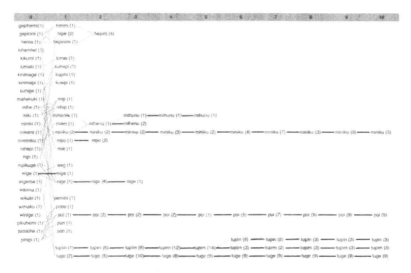

Figure 1 Coalescent tree showing lineages of signals for all 27 items over generations of one of the languages obtained by Kirby et al. (2008) exhibiting systematic underspecification. Columns correspond to generations; horizontal bold lines indicate the perfect replication of the whole signal; all other lines indicate some of the possible relationships of descent between signals that share some features. Numbers shown in brackets indicate the frequency with which variants were produced at each generation. The number of variant types decreases over time, although the number of tokens remains fixed at 27 throughout. Among these surviving variants there are clear relationships of descent, sometimes with modification. The frequency information is suggestive of the fact that signal variants may be adapting to express a meaning space composed of multiples of 3.

replication at the level of the whole utterance. However, in a compositional system, the meaning of a complex utterance is a function of the meanings of the elements of the utterance and the way they are arranged. The tree in Figure 1 illustrates adaptation of the whole signals to the structure of the meaning space; in a compositional language, we expect the same phenomena to occur but this time at the level of signal elements. We will now quantify compositionality using a different language (part of which is shown in Example (3)] from Kirby et al. (2008).

First, we need to segment the signals into element units. To do this, we first examined the language of the final participant in the chain to find the most parsimonious segmentation of the strings into elements that corresponded to aspects of the meanings (e.g., "the signal endings reliably encode motion" or "signal-initial 'la' consistently encodes colour blue"). This resulted in each

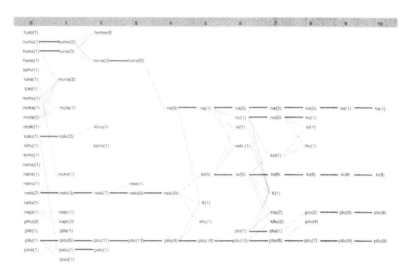

Figure 2 Coalescent tree showing lineages of signal ending variants for all 27 items over 10 generations of one of the languages obtained by Kirby et al. (2008), referred to in (3). Numbers shown in brackets indicate the frequency with which variants were produced at each generation. The number of variant types decreases over time, although the number of tokens remains fixed at 27 throughout. Among these surviving variants there are clear relationships of descent, sometimes with modification. The frequency information is suggestive of the fact that signal variants may be adapting to express a meaning space consisting of three meaning elements (see generations 4, 9, and 10).

string being divided into three substrings, and this segmentation pattern was carried back to all previous generations in order to allow for a consistent analysis. Figure 2 shows the coalescent tree for the word-final signal element (although similar trees can be constructed for both initial and middle positions also).

As earlier, we observe a marked reduction in the number of variants over time, as just a few become selected to be reused more often. Furthermore, we can see that the variants that appear at each generation are not random; we can trace the genealogy of the surviving variants back in time. Even over this minute timescale, many of the changes observed appear to follow paths that are well attested in cases of natural language change, such as single segment replacements (nepi → napi; pilu → pilo), reductions (hona → na, neki → ki, pilu → plu), metathesis (neki → nike), and blends (humo & huna → homa & hona; na & ki → neki).

It is significant to notice that at generation 4 we have three variants (na, neki, pilu), each with a frequency of 9 and that for the final two generations, this pattern repeats (now for variants ki, plo, pilu) broken only by a single instance of na. This, again, suggests that these lineages are adapting to a three-element meaning space. Obviously, we know that this is indeed the case; the interesting thing is that the signals alone suggest it. In the next subsection, we show how we can precisely quantify regularities in the mappings between signal and meaning elements in order to objectively confirm this.

Quantifying the Emergence of Compositionality

We now have an analysis of all the languages in terms of the following: *signal segments*—in this case, the word beginning, middle, or end; *signal segment variants*—actual tokens residing in a segment position, such as pilu or ki. Similarly, we can define the following: *meaning elements*—aspects of meaning, such as motion, shape, and color; *meaning element variants*—actual instances of a meaning element, for instance, "blue," or "circle," or "bounce."

Kirby et al. (2008) quantified the emergence of structure using a pairwise distance correlation (Shillcock, Kirby, McDonald, & Brew, 2001). This measures the extent to which similar meanings are expressed using similar forms—or more precisely, whether there is a correlation between the structure of the meaning and signal spaces. Although this is valuable in showing that structure emerges, it does not allow us to track the evolution of the compositional structure of the languages directly: As a measurement, the pairwise distance correlation is very general and cannot distinguish between compositionality and other kinds of structures (such as underspecification). Here, we apply a new method of analysis to one of the chains[7] reported in Kirby et al. (2008) to tackle this problem. We use *RegMap* (Tamariz & Smith, 2008), an information-theoretic metric that combines the conditional entropy of meanings given signals and of signals given meanings and normalizes the result to make it comparable across systems of different sizes. Informally, what *RegMap* (short for regularity of the mappings) does is return the degree of confidence that a signal element consistently predicts a meaning element (for instance, the degree to which we can be sure that the beginning of the signal encodes color).

More formally, $H(X \mid Y)$, the conditional entropy, is the Shannon entropy (Shannon, 1948) but replacing $p(x)$ with $p(x \mid y)$. The *RegMap* for a meaning element (M) and a signal segment (S) is given by

$$RegMap = \sqrt{\left(1 - \frac{H(S \mid M)}{\log(n_s)}\right) \times \left(1 - \frac{H(M \mid S)}{\log(n_m)}\right)}. \qquad (1)$$

$H(S \mid M)$ is the conditional entropy of the signal segment given the meaning feature, or the uncertainty about the meaning when we know the segment. This relates to comprehension. For example, for shape and first signal segment, $H(S \mid M)$ quantifies how uncertain we are on average about what shape an object is if we hear the first segment of its corresponding signal. $H(M \mid S)$ is the conditional entropy of the meaning feature given the signal segment, or the uncertainty about the segment when we know the meaning. This relates to production. Still, in the case of shape and first signal segment, $H(M \mid S)$ quantifies how uncertain we are, on average, about what first segment to produce if we know the shape of an object. The logs of n_m and n_s normalize the values between 0 and 1; n_m is the number of different meaning values (e.g., triangle, circle, square for shape); n_s is the number of different segment variants in the relevant segment position. Subtracting the conditional entropies from Equation 1 returns levels of confidence instead of uncertainty.

Figure 3 shows the *RegMap* values for all combinations of signal and meaning elements both with and without a bottleneck for the 10 generations. The "input" data shown in Figure 3 (upper) reflects the extent to which signals predict meanings in the subset of the language (taken from the previous generation) that was actually transmitted to the current generation, after the bottleneck was applied. The "output" data shown in Figure 3 (lower) is obtained from the complete languages that participants actually produced at a given generation, before the bottleneck was applied. The significance of the obtained *RegMaps* was established with a Monte Carlo analysis involving 10,000 randomizations of the correspondences between meanings and signals and are shown as boxplots.

Focusing first on the bottom graphs of Figure 3, obtained from the participants' output languages, we see that, starting from values indistinguishable from random at generation 1, *RegMap* becomes massively increased to highly statistically significant levels; specifically, by the third generation, motion is consistently encoded by the final signal segment; by the fourth generation, color is encoded by the initial segment, and by the ninth generation, shape is encoded by the middle segment (all $p < .001$).

Second, a comparison of the input (upper) and output (lower) results in Figure 3 reveals the effect of the bottleneck. The *RegMap* values are, in the majority of cases, amplified by the bottleneck (the absolute value of *RegMap* increases). Moreover, the lower the input *RegMap*, the more likely it is to be amplified by the bottleneck. How is this happening? The answer is potentially counterintuitive; randomly occurring patterns are more likely to be perceived the smaller the system is. At least in the early generations, a subset drawn from a language is more likely to accidentally contain more regular patterns than the

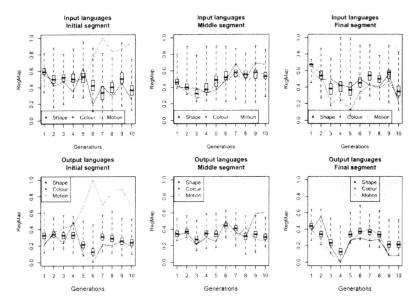

Figure 3 Regularity of the associations between signal and meaning elements, measured as *RegMap*, changes over time in the direction of maximizing compositionality, whereby signal elements are consistently associated with distinct meaning elements. The continuous colored lines represent *RegMap* values obtained with all nine segment-meaning feature pairs in the 10 generations of a language family from the study by Kirby et al. (2008), referred to in Example (3). The boxplots show the distributions of values obtained with 10,000 randomized languages. The upper graphs show *RegMap* values from the subset of language (taken from the previous generation) that was actually transmitted to the current generation, after the "bottleneck" was applied. The lower graphs show *RegMap* values obtained from the complete languages that participants actually produced at a given generation, before the bottleneck was applied.

entire language. Implicit in this, and by the same token, a given subset will also tend to contain less counterevidence against such patterns. This explains why we observe such a dramatic difference between the ranges shown in the boxplots in the upper and lower graphs in Figure 3. The large range of *RegMap* values in the input languages directly reflects the fact that participants are sensitive to this reduced number of observations when they are inferring the mappings between meanings and signals. Together, this accounts for the structure-generating effect of the bottleneck on language: The input to each generation is only a fraction of (and therefore tends to be more systematic than) the total output of the previous generation.

Third, the graphs show cases of competition between meanings all vying to be expressed by the same signal element. For example, motion and shape are both equally encoded in the final signal segment in the input to generation 3, but generation 3 resolves this conflict by ignoring one of the associations (shape) and amplifying the other (motion) to a significance level of $p < .01$. Conversely, we also see cases of competition between signals vying to express the same meaning: In the input of generation 5, color is equally encoded in the initial and middle signal segments (similar absolute values and levels of significance); in this case, the conflict is resolved by massively amplifying the association with the initial segment to a significance level of $p < .001$ and reducing the association with the middle one. These processes are adequately explained by the standard evolutionary mechanisms of variation, replication, and selection applied to the mappings between signals and meanings elements. Selection, in this case, can be hypothesized to be guided by perceptual and attentional biases such as higher salience of certain signal and meaning elements over others. Unfortunately, a detailed discussion of these biases is outside the scope of the present work.

Summary

Kirby et al. (2008) found that the languages that emerge through a repeated cycle of learning and production in a laboratory setting show evidence of adaptation to the bottleneck placed on their transmission. Making even minor changes to the way in which language is culturally transmitted can produce radically different types of structures. Given only a bottleneck on transmission preventing a proportion of the language from being seen by the next generation, language can adapt in such a way that ensures that it is stably transmitted to future generations. However, this occurs at the expense of being able to uniquely refer to every meaning. When they introduced the additional pressure of having to use a unique signal for each meaning, the language once again adapted to cope with these new transmission constraints, this time by becoming compositional. Having a compositional system ensures that both signals and meanings survive the bottleneck.

Because the participants could not know which condition they were in, it is impossible that the resulting languages were intentionally designed as adaptive solutions to the transmission bottleneck. Rather, the best explanation for the result is that in these experiments, just as in the computational models, linguistic adaptation is an inevitable consequence of the transmission of linguistic variants under particular constraints on replication. The result is apparent design, but without an intentional designer.

Whereas Kirby et al. (2008) analyzed their results at the level of whole signals and whole meanings, in this subsection we have developed new techniques to analyze the same results in terms of the component parts of linguistic signals. An analysis of how signal variants and their frequencies change over time showed relationships of descent with modification among them. It also suggested that signal variants are adapting to the structure of the meaning space. This intuition was verified by the application of *RegMap*, a tool designed to objectively measure compositionality. Using this method, we showed that individual signal elements come to encode individual meaning elements, whereas the whole system evolves to avoid ambiguity (i.e., more than one meaning being encoded in the same signal element or vice versa). Moreover, we were able to more precisely describe the role of the bottleneck in bringing about compositionality: The smaller subsets sampled as inputs to the next generation may locally contain more systematicity than the entire language. Iterating this learning process using these smaller samples therefore provides a platform that allows systematic patterns to be noticed, remembered, and replicated preferentially, thereby allowing them to gradually accumulate in the language as a whole.

It seems clear from all of this that, first, cultural transmission alone is capable of explaining the emergence of languages that exhibit that appearance of design and, second, experimental studies of the iterated learning of artificial languages are a potentially useful methodological tool for those interested in studying cultural evolution.

Conclusion

This article has extended previous work on iterated language learning experiments by showing, using data obtained from an earlier study, exactly how compositional structure emerges over time as a result of cultural transmission. Using a recently developed analytical technique that calculates the regularity of mapping between signal and meaning elements (Tamariz & Smith, 2008), we were able to precisely quantify changes in the language's ability to systematically encode such associations between meaning and signal components. From this we were able to explain the amplification effect the bottleneck seems to have on systematicity in language, arguing that the sampling of smaller subsets of the language for training input to the next generation tends to make weaker patterns that are not visible at the level of the entire language appear stronger locally.

One obvious criticism of the experimental work described here is that it necessarily involves participants who already speak a language. As such, can it tell us anything about the original evolution of language, as we are claiming? The sceptical position might be that we are simply seeing the evolution of structure that reflects the native language of the participants as opposed to any adaptive logic of the iterated learning process itself. This criticism faces a number of problems, however. Most importantly, the experimental results are backed up by the computational simulations and mathematical models surveyed in the introduction. In these models we can be sure that there is no influence of prior language, as the models have none initially. Furthermore, the structure that arises depends on aspects of the transmission bottleneck that are hidden from our participants (given our two experimental conditions) and the particular properties of the language appear more dramatically shaped by these than any similarity to the language of the participants. The most parsimonious explanation, then, is that we are seeing adaptation to the transmission bottleneck rather than an emerging simple first language influence. However, a more subtle point can be made: We fully expect that language evolution through iterated learning will involve adaptation to all aspects of the transmission bottleneck, and this will include the biases of language learners. In our experiment, participants bring to bear a mixture of biologically basic biases and those that arise from their acquired cultural heritage. We can see no principled way to separate these out. This means that our experiments should not be taken to be a "discovery procedure" for uncovering our evolutionary ancient learning biases but rather as a tool for understanding the fundamental adaptive dynamics of the cultural transmission of language by iterated learning.

We started this article by noting that a complex adaptive systems perspective shifts the burden of explanation away from a richly structured domain-specific innate substrate for language in our species. Although we have talked a great deal about linguistic structure as an adaptation, this is adaptation by the language itself rather than biological evolution of the faculty of language. The relevant explanatory mechanisms relate to *cultural* as opposed to *natural* selection. However, of course, this does not mean that biology is irrelevant to the evolution of language.

Rather than seeking evolutionary explanations for innate constraints that determine language structure, the work presented in this article strongly suggests a different approach. The iterated learning models on which we base our experiments start with agents who can (a) learn complex signals and (b) infer complex meanings. Humans belong to an unusual set of species, called the "vocal learners" (Jarvis, 2004), that can learn sequential signals (others include most notably the songbirds). We are also unusually adept in inferring intentionality (Tomasello, Carpenter, Call, Behne, & Moll, 2005). By taking into account the power of language as a complex adaptive system to generate structure itself, future work on the biological evolution of language in our species should focus on how we came to have these two crucial preadaptations for language. Without the combination of vocal learning and meaning inference, iterated learning of the sort we are studying would not be possible at all (Okanoya, 2002). Once they are in place, on the other hand, the emergence of structure is inevitable.

Revised version accepted 11 June 2009

Notes

1 Underlying this work is a typically unstated assumption that modern languages are already optimized for transmission (i.e., all extant languages are both learnable by children and meet the expressive needs of their users); thus, further change is driven not so much by inherent properties of linguistic variants but rather sociolinguistic factors (e.g., Croft, 2000). However, when looking at the origins of language, we necessarily need to consider a different state of affairs, one in which language has not yet reached equilibrium and the *inherent* structural properties of linguistic variants are relevant. A related point is the likelihood that intergenerational transmission is less important in ongoing language change than it is in language emergence. Where social status, for example, is the primary driving force behind selection of variants, the impact of learners' innovations is likely to be lower than where those innovations actually make language transmissible at all.

2 There are other experimental approaches to the origins of language, such as Galantucci (2005) and Selten and Warglien (2007), but note that these rely on participants intentionally and consciously designing a communicative system. Our interest is in whether the adaptive structure of language can arise without intentional design.

3 The glosses here are given as English words; recall that in the experiment, visual stimuli were used. This example is taken from Chain 3 in Experiment 2 in the study by Kirby et al. (2008).

4 This is not a trivial result considering the rather narrow bottleneck applied during training meant that each generation was being trained on a (different) random subset of half of the total language.

5 Taken from generation 9, chain 3, experiment 2 in the study by Kirby et al. (2008). Note that whereas color and motion are consistently expressed (ne for black, la for blue, ra for red, ki for horizontal, and pilu for spiral), shape is more haphazardly encoded (ke when blue/black and horizontal, ki when blue/black and spiral, he when red and horizontal, and ho when red and spiral).

6 It is perhaps interesting to note that the investigation of this type of phenomenon, historically referred to as analogical change, was what prompted the very first application of this methodology by Esper in 1925.

7 Specifically, we examine chain 3 in experiment 2, but similar results can be obtained wherever compositionality clearly emerges.

References

Bangerter, A. (2000). Transformation between scientific and social representations of conception: The method of serial reproduction. *British Journal of Social Psychology, 39*, 521–535.

Bartlett, F. (1932). *Remembering: A study in experimental and social psychology.* Cambridge: Cambridge University Press.

Barton, N. H. (2007). *Evolution.* Cold Spring Harbor, NY: Cold Spring Harbor Laboratory Press.

Batali, J. (1998). Computational simulations of the emergence of grammar. In J. Hurford, M. Studdert-Kennedy, & C. Knight (Eds.), *Approaches to the evolution of language: Social and cognitive bases* (pp. 405–426). Cambridge: Cambridge University Press.

Batali, J. (2002). The negotiation and acquisition of recursive grammars as a result of competition among exemplars. In T. Briscoe (Ed.), *Linguistic evolution through language acquisition: Formal and computational models* (pp. 111–172). Cambridge: Cambridge University Press.

Brighton, H. (2002). Compositional syntax from cultural transmission. *Artificial Life, 8*(1), 25–54.

Brighton, H., Smith, K., & Kirby, S. (2005). Language as evolutionary system. *Physics of Life Reviews, 2*, 177–226.

Chomsky, N. (1965). *Aspects of the theory of syntax.* Cambridge, MA: MIT Press.

Christiansen, M. H., & Chater, N. (2008). Language as shaped by the brain. *Behavioral and Brain Science, 31*(5), 489–509.

Croft, W. (2000). *Explaining language change: An evolutionary approach.* London: Longman.

Deacon, T. W. (1997). *The symbolic species: The co-evolution of language and the brain.* New York: W.W. Norton.

Esper, E. A. (1925). *A technique for the experimental investigation of associative interference in artificial linguistic material.* Philadelphia: Linguistic Society of America.

Esper, E. A. (1966). Social transmission of an artificial language. *Language, 42*(3), 575–580.

Fitch, T., & Hauser, M. (2004). Computational constraints on syntactic processing in a non-human primate. *Science, 303*, 377–380.

Galantucci, B. (2005). An experimental study of the emergence of human communication systems. *Cognitive Science, 29*, 737–767.

Gómez, R. L., & Gerken, L. A. (2000). Infant artificial language learning and language acquisition. *Trends in Cognitive Sciences, 4*(5), 178–186.

Griffiths, T. L., & Kalish, M. L. (2007). Language evolution by iterated learning with Bayesian agents. *Cognitive Science, 31*(3), 441–480.

Hein, J., Schierup, M. H., & Wiuf, C. (2005). *Gene genealogies, variation and evolution: A primer in coalescent theory*. Oxford: Oxford University Press.

Horner, V., Whiten, A., Flynn, E., & de Waal, F. B. M. (2006). Faithful replication of foraging techniques along cultural transmission chains by chimpanzees and children. *PNAS, 103*(37), 13,878–13,883.

Hurford, J. (2000). Social transmission favours linguistic generalization. In J. R. H. Chris Knight & M. Studdert-Kennedy (Eds.), *The evolutionary emergence of language: Social function and the origins of linguistic form* (pp. 324–352). Cambridge: Cambridge University Press.

Jarvis, E. (2004). Learned birdsong and the neurobiology of human language. *Annals of the New York Academy of Sciences, 1016*, 749–777.

Kalish, M. L., Griffiths, T. L., & Lewandowsky, S. (2007). Iterated learning: Intergenerational knowledge transmission reveals inductive biases. *Psychonomic Bulletin and Review, 14*(2), 288–294.

Kirby, S. (1999). *Function, selection and innateness: The emergence of language universals*. Oxford: Oxford University Press.

Kirby, S. (2002a). Learning, bottlenecks and the evolution of recursive syntax. In T. Briscoe (Ed.), *Linguistic evolution through language acquisition: Formal and computational models* (pp. 173–204). Cambridge: Cambridge University Press.

Kirby, S. (2002b). Natural language from artificial life. *Artificial Life, 8*(2), 185–215.

Kirby, S., & Hurford, J. (2002). The emergence of linguistic structure: An overview of the iterated learning model. In A. Cangelosi & D. Parisi (Eds.), *Simulating the evolution of language* (pp. 121–148). London: Springer-Verlag.

Kirby, S., Dowman, M., & Griffiths, T. (2007). Innateness and culture in the evolution of language. *Proceedings of the National Academy of Sciences of the United States of America, 104*, 5241–5245.

Kirby, S., Cornish, H., & Smith, K. (2008). Cumulative cultural evolution in the laboratory: An experimental approach to the origins of structure in human language. *Proceedings of the National Academy of Sciences of the United States of America, 105*, 10,681–10,686.

Mesoudi, A., Whiten, A., & Dunbar, R. (2006). A bias for social information in human cultural transmission. *British Journal of Psychology, 97*, 405–423.

Okanoya, K. (2002). Sexual display as a syntactical vehicle: The evolution of syntax in birdsong and human language through sexual selection. In A. Wray (Ed.), *The transition to language* (pp. 46–63). Oxford: Oxford University Press.

Pinker, S., & Bloom, P. (1990). Natural language and natural selection. *Behavioral and Brain Sciences, 13*(4), 707–784.

Saffran, J., Aslin, R., & Newport, E. (1996). Statistical learning by 8-month olds. *Science, 274*, 1926–1928.

Selten, R., & Warglien, M. (2007). The emergence of simple languages in an experimental co-ordination game. *PNAS, 104*(18), 7361–7366.

Shannon, C. E. (1948). A mathematical theory of communication. *Bell Systems Technical Journal, 27*, 379–423, 623–656.

Shillcock, R., Kirby, S., McDonald, S., & Brew, C. (2001, August). Filled pauses and their status in the mental lexicon. In *Proceedings of the 2001 conference on disfluency in spontaneous speech*, Edinburgh, UK.

Smith, A. (2005). The inferential transmission of language. *Adaptive Behavior, 13*(4), 311–324.

Smith, K. (2002). The cultural evolution of communication in a population of neural networks. *Connection Science, 14*(1), 65–84.

Steels, L. (2003). Evolving grounded communication for robots. *Trends in Cognitive Science, 7*(7), 308–312.

Tamariz, M., & Smith, A. D. M. (2008). Regularity in mappings between signals and meanings. In A. D. M. Smith, K. Smith, & R. Ferrer i Cancho (Eds.), *The evolution of language: Proceedings of the 7th international conference (EVOLANG7)* (pp. 315–322). Singapore: World Scientific.

Tomasello, M., Carpenter, M., Call, J., Behne, T., & Moll, H. (2005). Understanding and sharing intentions: The origins of cultural cognition. *Behavioral and Brain Sciences, 28*, 675–691.

Whiten, A., Horner, V., & de Waal, M. (2005). Conformity to cultural norms of tool use in chimpanzees. *Nature, 437*, 737–740.

Vogt, P. (2005). The emergence of compositional structures in perceptually grounded language games. *Artificial Intelligence, 167*, 206–242.

Zuidema, W. (2003). How the poverty of the stimulus argument solves the poverty of the stimulus argument. In S. Becker, S. Thrun, & K. Obermayer (Eds.), *Advances in neural information processing systems 15 (Proceedings of NIPS'02)* (pp. 51–58). Cambridge, MA: MIT Press.

Language Learning   ISSN 0023-8333

Meaning in the Making: Meaning Potential Emerging From Acts of Meaning

Christian M. I. M. Matthiessen
The Hong Kong Polytechnic University

This article is concerned with how meaning potential, in particular an individual's personalized meaning potential, emerges from acts of meaning. This happens during different time frames: logogenetic—the creation of meaning in text; ontogenetic—the learning of a personalized meaning potential; and phylogenetic—the evolution of the collective meaning potential. Logogenetically, a person learns through text in interaction with others, distilling meaning potential from the instantial acts of meaning and constantly revising their own personalized meaning potential, both qualitatively and quantitatively. This learning involves both learning language and learning "content" through language, locally within a single text or cumulatively over many texts. I will model both these aspects of learning and show how they vary registerially according to the contexts in which texts unfold.

Introduction

My contribution to the discussion of "language as a complex adaptive system" is based on Systemic Functional Linguistics (SFL; for recent overviews, see Hasan, Matthiessen & Webster, 2005, 2007; Matthiessen, 2007). Since its inception in the early 1960s, SFL has been concerned with language as a complex adaptive system, although the current terminology is, of course, more recent than SFL.

In SFL, language is modeled as a complex adaptive system of the fourth order of complexity in an ordered typology of systems (see, e.g., Halliday & Matthiessen, 1999; Matthiessen, 2007), "inheriting" properties from systems of lower orders through which it is manifested: *physical* (first order); *biological* (second order: + "life"); *social* (third order: + "value," or social order);

Correspondence concerning this article should be addressed to Christian M. I. M. Matthiessen, Department of English, PolySystemic Research Group, Faculty of Humanities, The Hong Kong Polytechnic University, Hong Kong. Internet: egcmim@inet.polyu.edu.hk

© 2009 Language Learning Research Club, University of Michigan

semiotic (fourth order: + "meaning"). Language is a higher order semiotic system: It is a system not only for carrying meaning, the central property of primary semiotic systems, but also for creating meaning. We hypothesize that it evolved out of a *primary* semiotic system, protolanguage (see Matthiessen, 2004); researchers have shown how it develops out of such a primary semiotic in the early life of a child (discussed later).

Like other kinds of system, language is both system and instance. These are not separate phenomena but rather different phases of a unified phenomenon extended along a *cline of instantiation* from potential to instance. Because the central characteristic of language is that it is a resource for making meaning, we can say that the *acts of meaning* that make up a text unfolding in time instantiate a *meaning potential*, noting that these are simply different phases of language as a meaning-making resource: acts instantiate potential, and potential emerges from acts. This is where we can locate *learning*: Learning takes place when instances are distilled into potential higher up along the cline of instantiation.

In this article, I will first explore how texts unfold as patterns of meaning at the instance pole of the cline and I will then turn to learning, outlining the picture of language learning that has emerged in recent years.

The Cline of Instantiation

Regions Along the Cline of Instantiation

As just noted, the *cline of instantiation* is a continuum extending from *instances*, from *texts* in contexts of situation, unfolding over fairly short intervals of time (e.g., Halliday, 1977; Matthiessen, 2002b), to the *potential*, to the *system* of language in the context of culture, evolving over long intervals of time (e.g., Halliday, 1973; Halliday & Matthiessen, 1999; Matthiessen, 2004).

Because the cline is a continuum, we find intermediate patterns of meaning between the two poles. These can be modeled as subsystemic patterns that operate under certain contextual conditions: *registers* operating in institutional settings, or they can be explored as instance types that emerge over time; *text types* operating in situation types. Registers are functional varieties of language that have evolved as adaptations to different institutional settings— different uses of language according to the nature of the context of use; they are the subsystems of language that operate in these contexts (e.g., Gregory, 1967; Halliday, McIntosh, & Strevens, 1964; Hasan, 1973; Matthiessen, 1993). The contexts of use have been characterized since the mid-1960s in terms of *field* (what is going on in the context), *tenor* (who is taking part in these

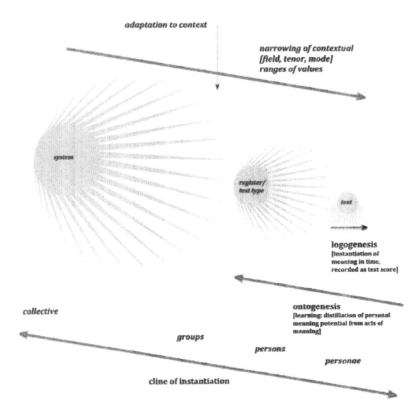

Figure 1 The cline of instantiation, extended from the potential pole (the system of language) via subpotentials (registers)/instance types (text types) to instances (texts).

activities), and *mode* (what role language is playing in the context). Registers thus represent constrained uses of the overall potential, but we can also view them from the point of view of instances as recurrent patterns in texts that emerge over time as distinctive text types. Figure 1 provides a diagrammatic summary of key concepts to be discussed in this and the next section. It shows the cline of instantiation with the two poles—potential (system) and instance (texts)—together with intermediate patterns (registers/text types). It also indicates the location of *persons* in relation to the cline as members of different groups making up the collective: Learners are persons building up repertoires of registers through their processing of texts in different roles (personae).

Text Unfolding at the Instance Pole as Systemic Selections

At the instance pole, texts unfold as ongoing selections from the system—instantiations of options in the meaning potential of language (see Halliday, 1977). For example, we can examine successive selections in the system of MOOD, recording these selections clause by clause: see Figure 2. The diagram shows how the selections represent different *paths* through the grammatical systems of MOOD; in each clause, a certain part of the system is activated or instantiated (cf. our computational modeling of this process discussed in, e.g., Matthiessen & Bateman, 1991). The selections can be represented as a *text score* (adopting Weinreich's, 1972, German term *Textpartitur*; see Matthiessen, 1995, 2002b).

The system is always in flux—in a process of continuous change; it is not fixed or frozen. Thus, every time selections are made in the system, they may perturb it ever so slightly. This is, of course, not immediately apparent from the diagram in Figure 2 because the system of MOOD seems to be fixed: There are no qualitative changes in the system in the course of this short passage of dialogue, but quantitatively a good deal is happening. Every selection of a term in a system, such as the selection of "declarative" as opposed to "interrogative" in the system of indicative type contributes to the *relative frequency* of that term in a text and, thus, to the *probability* that that this term will be selected over "interrogative" in the system (see, e.g., Halliday, 1959, 2004; Matthiessen, 2006b). Even in the short passage represented in Figure 2, the probabilistic status of "declarative" as the unmarked term in the mood system (cf. Halliday, 1984; König & Siemund, 2007; Teruya et al., 2007) is evident.

The relative frequencies of selection could, of course, change dramatically within the next phase of the dialogue. Such changes do in fact often occur, and they are indicative of transitions between *phases* in the unfolding of a text (see, e.g., Cloran, Stuart Smith & Young, 2007, on the phasal analysis developed by Michael Gregory; see also Matthiessen, 2002b). For example, as a narrative text unfolds, we can expect to see changes in the frequencies of selections of terms in the system of LOGICO-SEMANTIC TYPE (see Halliday & Matthiessen, 1999, Ch. 3, 2004, Ch. 7; Matthiessen, 2002a; Teruya, 2006), the system concerned with the nature of links between clauses combined into clause complexes; this is illustrated for a retelling for children of the Noah's Ark tale from Genesis: see Figure 3.[1] Figure 3 shows selections in the system of LOGICO-SEMANTIC TYPE of different types of relation for linking clauses together into clause complexes by projection (one clause quoting or reporting another), elaboration (one clause exemplifying, characterizing, or restating another), extension (one clause adding to, providing an alternative to, or contrasting with another), or

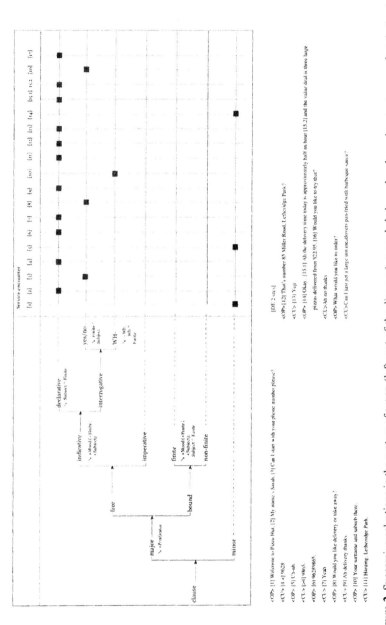

Figure 2 Successive selections in the system of MOOD (left part of the diagram), recorded clause by clause in a text score of a telephonic service encounter (right part of the diagram).

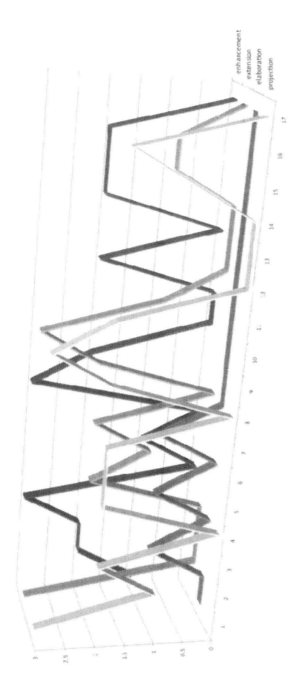

Figure 3 Frequencies of selections of LOGICO-SEMANTIC TYPES in linking of clauses into clause complexes in the course of the unfolding of a traditional narrative ("Noah's Ark"), shown in successive spans of five clause complexes.

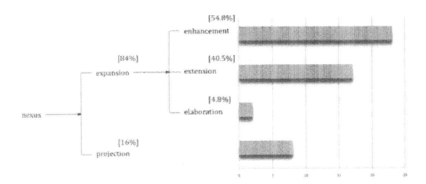

Figure 4 Instantial profile of the system of LOGICO-SEMANTIC TYPE at the completion of the "Noah's Ark" text ($N = 50$ clause nexuses).

enhancement (one clause relating to another in terms of time, cause-condition, manner, or some other circumstantial feature). These selections are shown for the unfolding text, from left to right on the x-axis, in spans of five clause complexes. For example, by tracking selections of "projection," we can get a sense of when reporting or quoting clauses are used to create passages of dramatic dialogue in the narrative.

Locally, the frequencies with which the different terms are instantiated through selections from the system thus keep varying. As the text comes to an end, the frequencies can be *distilled* in an *instantial version* of the system of LOGICO-SEMANTIC TYPE, as shown in Figure 4. This instantial profile of the system is at it were the *systemic memory* of the text—the quantitative effect of the successive selections in the course of the unfolding of the text. The instantial version of the system of LOGICO-SEMANTIC TYPE that emerges from the creation of clause linkages in "Noah's Ark" clearly favors enhancing relations over the other LOGICO-SEMANTIC TYPES (i.e., relations involving some circumstantial feature such as one of time, space, or cause). It is hardly surprising that, in a narrative text, clauses are often combined by means of such relations because they construe the sequence of events of the narrative (as in *When all had been done as God had ordered, Noah closed the door.*).

Language as Aggregate of Registers; Adaptive Variation

More generally, the probabilistic profiles of systems vary according to register: A key aspect of the adaptive nature of language is that it adapts to its contexts of use, and this is reflected quantitatively. In different registers, certain meanings are "at risk": Certain terms are more likely to be selected because of the nature

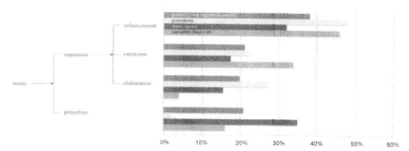

Figure 5 Instantial profile of the system of LOGICO-SEMANTIC TYPE at the completion of the "Noah's Ark" text compared with profiles of this system for sample of texts from a range of other registers. Bars represent from top to bottom for each systemic term: general sample of different registers ($N = 6536$ clause nexuses), procedure, news reports, and the Noah's Ark narrative.

of the context in which the selections are made, whereas other terms are less likely to be selected (see Halliday, 1978). This can be illustrated for the system of LOGICO-SEMANTIC TYPE. Figure 5 shows the relative frequencies for the terms in the system for the Noah's Ark narrative together with counts from a general sample of texts from a variety of registers, a subsample from this sample of procedural texts and another subsample of news reporting texts. The details are not important here, of course (cf. Matthiessen, 2002a, 2006b, for some discussion of the details); the important point is the how *registerial variation* in language—or what we might also call *adaptive variation*—in relation to context of use shows up quantitatively as variation in systemic probabilities of instantiation (or, seen from the point of view of the instance, as frequencies of instantiation in texts within different registers): compare Figure 1.

Thus, language is *inherently variable*, and this variation can be observed, measured, and modeled in quantitative terms as systemic patterns of instantiation.[2] These patterns can be observed and recorded in the course of the unfolding of a text (as in Figures 2, 3) or at the completion of this unfolding (as in Figure 4), or they can be induced as generalizations beyond particular instances, higher up the cline of instantiation, for larger samples of texts representative of one register or another. The inherent registerial variability is a central condition for language learning: People learn language through texts belonging to particular registers, and they expand their own meaning potential by adding registers to their repertoires of registers. Because different meanings are "at risk" in different registers, what they learn by adding a register to their registerial repertoires will depend on the nature of that register.[3]

Learning

Individual learning starts at the instance pole of the cline and takes place if instances leave a trace in the learner's system (personalized meaning potential): a systemic memory. Learning language means learning how to mean by learning a complex, adaptive, inherently variable system (cf. Halliday, 1993). However, although learning a complex system may sound forbidding, learnability has, of course, always been a central feature of language. Language has evolved as a learnable system: Its adaptiveness and inherent variability make it easier to learn because we do not have to learn it in one fell swoop; we learn it in a cumulative way, building up the complexity gradually from texts instantiating different registers.

Phases in Learning How to Mean

Whether people learn how to mean in their mother tongue or in a second/foreign language, their most important material for building up their own personal meaning potentials is text in context: Learning means distilling meaning potential from the acts of meaning that make up text. With respect to the learning of the mother tongue, the general outline is now fairly clear, although a great deal of research remains to be done to fill in significant gaps. Salient features of this are outlined in Table 1.

According to Halliday (e.g., 1975, 2004), children learn how to mean in three phases (see also Painter 1984, 1999; Painter, Derewianka, & Torr, 2007; Torr, 1997):

- **Phase I: protolanguage (child tongue) [primary semiotic]:** Children begin learning how to mean by developing a simple bistratal (content plus expression planes) primary semiotic system in interaction with their immediate caregivers, starting around the middle of their first year of life and continuing on this track for around 6–9 months. Protolanguage consists of a few micro-functional meaning potentials (initially, interactional, personal, regulatory, instrumental), each of which operates in a particular context of use (each of which that we can recognize as a critical context of socialization).[4]
- **Phase II: transition from protolanguage to mother tongue:** Somewhere around the middle of their second year of life, children begin to expand their meaning potential more rapidly, adding more systems and options within systems. This marks the beginning of their transition from protolanguage to the mother tongue spoken around them. Building on their experience with learning how to mean in protolanguage, children now

Table 1 Phases in learning how to mean

Phase	Approximate age	Learning environment	Knowledge	Function[a]	Stratification	Lexico-grammar	Varieties[b]
(prelinguistic)	0–0;5	Home & neighborhood		— (communicative acts, but no semiotic acts)	— (no semiotic acts)	—	0–¾: protoconversation
Phase I: protolanguage	0;5–1;6 (6–9 months)	Home & neighborhood	Commonsense (folk)	Microfunctional (personal/ interactional/ regulatory/ instrumental)	Bistratal: content/ expression	—	¾–1½: protolanguage
Phase II: transition	1;6–	Home & neighborhood		Macrofunctional (mathetic/ pragmatic)	*Bifurcation* of content (emergence of lexicogrammar) and of expression (emergence of phonology)	(emergence)	1½–2: protonarrative, protodialogue

Table 1 Continued

Phase	Approximate age	Learning environment	Knowledge	Function[a]	Stratification	Lexico-grammar	Varieties[b]
Phase III: adult language (mother tongue)	2– (remainder of life)	Home & neighborhood		Metafunctional (ideational ~ interpersonal ~ textual)	Quadri-stratal (content [semantics ~ lexicogrammar] ~ expression: [phonology ~ phonetics]	2–5: elementary	2–5: protodiscourse
	5–9	+ school [primary]	Gradually uncommonsense (educational)		expression [+ graphology ~ graphetics]	5–9: intermediate	5–9: discourse; + written mode (beginning of written registers)
	9–13	[late primary/ secondary]		+ grammatical metaphor (ideational)		9–13: advanced	9–13: turn-taking
	13(–18)						13(–18) variation, registers (disciplinary)
	18	+ university	Uncommonsense (scientific)				18– continued expansion of registerial repertoire: academic
	21–	+ workplace					Continued expansion of registerial repertoire: professional

[a]See Halliday (2004, p. 52).
[b]See Halliday (2004, p. 139).

begin to transform their protolinguistic system into a more complex but also a more powerful semiotic system. They generalize the microfunctions into two macrofunctions: The instrumental and regulatory microfunctions are generalized as the pragmatic macrofunction (language as action) and the personal and heuristic microfunctions are generalized as the mathetic macrofunction (language as reflection), whereas the interactional microfunction is split between these two macrofunctions. At the same time, the content planes and expression planes begin to bifurcate (cf. Steel's, 1998, notion of level formation in the evolution of language). Within the content plane, lexicogrammar begins to emerge as a distinct stratum of wording.

- **Phase III: mother tongue (postinfancy, adult language) [higher order semiotic]:** At the end of Phase II, children have made the transition from their own child tongues to the mother tongues spoken around them. This marks the beginning of Phase III: learning how to mean in the mother tongue. They are now operating with a semiotic system that is metafunctional rather than macrofunctional; in other words, they can now mean more than one thing at the same time. The mathetic macrofunction has given rise to the ideational metafunction, the pragmatic macrofunction has given rise to the interpersonal metafunction, and at the same time as these are now becoming simultaneous systems of choice, the textual metafunction emerges as an enabling metafunction—a resource for turning ideational and interpersonal meanings into a flow of discourse.

Phase III begins around the age of 2 and continues throughout life. Any notion that language learning has come to a completion at some early age such as 4 is simply a reflection of a theoretically limited view of what constitutes language. However, the nature of language learning does change from the early stages of Phase III to later ones. Leading up to the transition into the mother tongue, learning how to mean has meant transforming the functional and stratal organization of language; but once the "adult" system of the mother tongue is in place, learning how to mean is essentially a continuous expansion of a person's *registerial repertoire*: Learners keep mastering new registers, thereby expanding their personal meaning potential.[5]

Phase III
Until recently, we had only a fairly partial picture of the developments during Phase III: language development during postinfancy childhood, during the transition from childhood to adolescence, and then during the transition from adolescence to early adulthood. However, research in the last two decades has

produced a much clearer outline of developments: Lemke (1990), Derewianka (1995), Christie and Martin (1997), Christie and Derewianka (2008), Colombi and Schleppegrell (2002), Schleppegrell (2004), Parodi (in press).

Based on previous contributions to educational linguistics and their own large-scale research project, Christie and Derewianka (2008) documented the development of the registers of writing throughout primary and secondary school. They tracked both the development of the genres of English, history, and science and the development of lexico-grammatical resources. They showed the progression from simpler genres to more complex ones—for example, in history from personal recounts to historical recounts to historical explanations to historio-graphical exposition and discussion (see also, e.g., Coffin, 2006)—and at the same time, they identified lexico-grammatical features that are developed further as part of this progression. For example, they pointed out that learning projection nouns such as *opinion*, *thesis*, and *view* (Halliday & Matthiessen, 2004, p. 469) is an important part of learning historio-graphical argumentation in late adolescence. This is also the period when students learn to use verbs of proof such as *show*, *indicate*, and *demonstrate* in identifying relational clauses.

Christie and Derewianka's (2008) work is an account of language development in the written mode throughout the primary and secondary school years. In a sense, Parodi (in press) picked up where they leave off[6]: he and his colleagues reported on another remarkable cartographic project, a corpus-based study of the written texts that university students in four different disciplines engage with during their undergraduate years (their "PUCV-2006 Corpus").

Parodi and his colleagues (in press) provided registerial profiles of these four different disciplines, revealing striking differences between the two disciplines in their sample that are close to the sciences end of the scholarly spectrum (construction engineering and industrial chemistry) and the two disciplines in their sample that are closer to the humanities end (psychology and social work). In our contextual terms (see Figure 6), the center of registerial gravity in the natural sciences (i.e., the sciences of the material world, in our ordered typology of systems) is in the "expounding" sector of field (what Parodi and his colleagues called "text book" texts), but the center of registerial gravity in the humanities and social sciences (i.e., the sciences of the immaterial world) is in the "exploring" sector (what they call "disciplinary texts").[7]

In addition to profiling the four different university disciplines, Parodi and his colleagues (in press) have also investigated the professional contexts in different institutions that the university students are likely to move into after graduating. They found considerable differences between the range of registers that the students would be exposed to during their university education and the range of registers that they would be likely to have to master as they move into the professional world (see Parodi, Ibáñez, & Venegas, in press).

Learning (Through) Registers

So what kind of fundamental insight into language learning can we gain from these recent pathbreaking studies? The general principle is this: A language is an aggregate of registers (see above, and Halliday, 1978; Matthiessen, 1993), so once the basic Phase III system has emerged during the transitional Phase II from Phase I, we continue to learn language in an ever-growing range of contexts through the different registers that we come to engage with (listen to, speak, read and write) in these contexts. A language is a meaning potential in the first instance, but it is a collective meaning potential, so what each person learns is a "personalized" version of this collective meaning potential (cf. Matthiessen, 2006a). A person's personalized meaning potential is thus the aggregate of those registerial meaning potentials that he or she has mastered.[8]

During the first 5 years or so of life, the contexts will be those that occur in the family and neighborhood (including, of course, also family outings to various professional contexts such as visits to the doctor, to restaurants, and to recreational institutions). Once children have entered the institution of formal education, the contexts will also include those of structured learning created by the educational establishment.[9] The child's engagement with a growing range of registers in different institutional settings can, in principle, be charted through a combination of the diary and cartographic methods used by Halliday (1975) and Gu (2001); for a sample of one child's learning journey, see the CD accompanying Halliday (2004).

When children, adolescents, and adults learn new registers, they learn all aspects of the language of those registers and, of course, also all aspects of the context (institutional setting) in which the registers operate. Thus, they learn the semantic strategies that are characteristic of a given register, and they learn to deploy the lexico-grammatical resources that they need in order to realize options in these semantic strategies.[10] Let me just give one example from lexico-grammar: the deployment of the resources of "relational" clauses to realize semantic strategies for sorting out our experience of the world by categorizing, naming, classifying, and defining phenomena. Based on the work by Painter (1999) and Christie and Derewianka (2008), we can identify some of the "milestones" in the mastering of the resources of "relational" clauses (of the "intensive" type; see Halliday & Matthiessen, 2004):

- [categorization, naming:] *that's a circle* (c. $2\frac{1}{2}$ years)>
- [classification:] *a platypus is a mammal* > (c. $3\frac{1}{2}$ years)

- [definition of abstractions:] *balance means you hold it on your fingers and it doesn't go* (c. 4 years) >
- ... >
- [interpretation and proof:] *these relationships demonstrated ... aspects of the characters' worlds* (c. 16–18 years)

In other words, children learn early on to use "relational" clauses to categorize some external phenomenon in the field of vision they share with their interlocutors (e.g., *that's a circle*). Later, they learn to use "relational" clauses to probe and construct classificatory taxonomies (e.g., *a platypus is a mammal*). Still later, they advance beyond such "attributive" clauses and begin to use "identifying" ones to define abstract concepts (not until around the age of 4; e.g., *balance means you hold it on your fingers and it doesn't go* ["fall"]). Having learned to use the resources of "identifying" "relational" clauses to define concepts, they are, in principle, ready to tackle the definitions that they will meet once they enter the institution of formal education. Many years later, they will be able to build on their early mastery of "identifying" clauses used in definitions by expanding these resources to interpret and produce "identifying" clauses of interpretation and of proof using a number of lexically more specific verbs than *be*, such as *show, demonstrate, indicate, reveal, suggest,* and *prove*.

Learning Paths: Registerial Progression

Using the school subject of history as an example (as described by Christie & Derewianka, 2008; see also Coffin, 2006; Martin, 2009), I have charted the progression of (written) registers that students learn in Australian schools from early primary school to late secondary school: see Figure 6. I have represented the progression in terms of the field parameter within context,[11] more specifically the *socio-semiotic process* undertaken by those involved in the context (their activity: "what's going on" in the context). There are eight primary socio-semiotic processes (for other educational applications of this typology, see, e.g., Matthiessen, 2006a; Teruya, 2006, 2009, pp. 71–75), represented by the labeled sectors in Figure 6: *expounding* knowledge about general classes of phenomena according to some theory (explaining or characterizing these phenomena), *reporting* on particular phenomena (chronicling events, describing entities or surveying places), *re-creating* some aspect of experience (typically imaginary), *sharing* personal values and experiences, *doing* some social activity, with language coming in to facilitate this activity, *recommending* some course of action (advising or promoting it), *enabling* some course of action (instructing or regulating), and *exploring* (typically public) values and ideas (evaluating and comparing them).

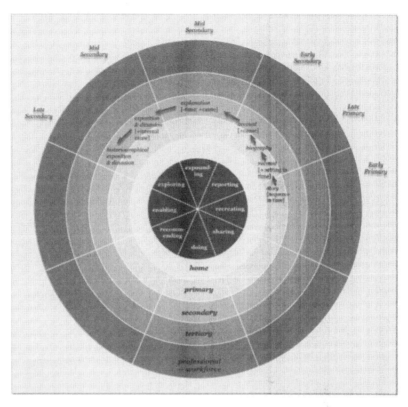

Figure 6 Progression of registers in history from early primary school to late secondary school (represented by the concentric circles, ranging from "home" to "professional—workforce").

In history, learners in primary school start with the transition from stories in the "re-creating" sector of Figure 6 to recounts in the "reporting" sector, as shown by the arrow crossing the border between "re-creating" and "reporting" in the figure. Both stories and recounts are, of course, concerned with sequence in time, but recounts are also concerned with settings in time, including eras and epochs used to "scaffold" history. The same is true of biographies (including both of the types found in Australian schools: biographical recounts and empathetic autobiographies), but when learners move on to historical accounts in early secondary school, they have to go beyond temporal sequences to master causal ones as well: "chronicling infused with causal links," as Christie and Derewianka (2008, p. 101) put it. By the middle of secondary school, they have to add explanations (factorial and consequential ones) to their registerial repertoire; here, cause is foregrounded over time and they are now operating in the "expounding" sector (which is the main registerial niche of physics and other science subjects): They are explaining history instead of only chronicling it. In late secondary school, learners move into the exploring sector (which is one of the two main registerial niches of English), learning first historical expositions and discussions and then historio-graphical expositions and discussions. Both of these involve internal cause (reasons why one should believe a statement about what happened) rather than simply external clause (reasons why something happened).

The progression through the registerial terrain shown in Figure 6 is, of course, specific to history, but the research carried out, and summarized, by Christie and Derewianka (2008) has revealed similar learner paths through the registerial terrain in other subjects. As they move through the educational system, students learn how to operate in new contexts with new registers. Different subjects have different centers of registerial gravity.[12]

In a similar way, we can map out children's pre-primary-school paths through the (spoken) registers of different contexts in the sectors shown in Figure 6, taking note of how their registerial repertoires expand and identifying potential bridge heads to registers they will engage with once they enter the educational system. Additionally, we can do the same for universities and workplaces, drawing on the findings presented by Parodi and his colleagues in Parodi (in press).[13]

Second/Foreign Languages

At some point or points during the school years, students will begin to learn one or more second or foreign languages.

1. In many places, this will happen as they start school: They will have to learn a second language as the medium of instruction while their mother tongue remains the language of the home and the neighborhood. In such cases, their registerial repertoires will be partitioned into two or even more languages. Here, there are interesting questions about the complementary roles that the different languages can play in the process of learning, in different registers, and about the degree to which the mother tongue is valued and supported in the processes of formal education. The mother tongue has been the resource for learning until school age, and it can continue to serve as a rich resource for learning throughout the school years and beyond.

2. In other places, they will learn one or more foreign languages as additional languages. Although these do not take on the role of medium of instruction, the possibility exists that students would learn relevant content from across the curriculum through these languages as they master them.

In either case, learners are developing multilingual meaning potentials, which can be modeled in interesting ways in SFL (see, e.g., Bateman, Matthiessen, & Zeng, 1999). How such multilingual meaning potentials are developed as aggregates of registerial subpotentials will become much clearer through longitudinal studies of second/foreign language learning: see Ortega and Byrnes (2008).

Conclusion

In this contribution, I have been concerned with "meaning in the making"— with the question of how language is learned as a meaning potential through the acts of meaning that make up a text. Referring to studies of language learning in SFL, I have suggested that a learner's meaning potential of a language is distilled from innumerable acts of meaning as he or she moves through life. However, a language is not a monolithic system; it is (among other things) an aggregate of registerial subsystems—of meaning subpotentials that have evolved, and operate, in particular types of contexts.

When people learn languages, they build up their own personalized meaning potentials as part of the collective meaning potential that constitutes the language, and they build up these personal potentials by gradually expanding their own registerial repertoires—their own shares in the collective meaning potential. As they expand their own registerial repertoires, they can take on roles in a growing range of contexts, becoming semiotically more empowered and versatile. This kind of learning starts before children enter the institutions of formal education, and it continues after adolescents or young adults leave these institutions (at the secondary or tertiary level). It continues as adults take on new roles in their working lives and in other aspects of their adult lives. With today's emphasis on lifelong learning, on a succession of university degrees throughout life, and on professional training in the workplace, people's registerial repertoires are constantly changing in makeup and they typically keep expanding.

We need many more longitudinal studies; we need more discourse diaries and more discourse biographies so that we can flesh out the picture. However, the general outlines are clear enough for us to formulate research questions and to discern some central implications for the organization of educational processes and the development of educational materials. This is indeed what the work by Heidi Byrnes and her colleagues at Georgetown University has demonstrated on constructing a text and context based collegiate foreign language curriculum: see, for example, Rinner and Weigert (2006).

Revised version accepted 13 July 2009

Notes

1 There are many interesting details here. For example, the frequencies in the selections of "projection"—i.e., of quoted or report speech or thought—vary considerably throughout the text; and as it unfolds, a pattern of "peaks" and "troughs" begins to emerge. This reflects the fairly regular appearance of passages of dramatic dialogue in the construction of this narrative (between God and Noah, and between Noah and his family, as in *"'We must hurry and collect the animals,' said Noah."*).

2 In addition to the kind of variation I can illustrate within this article, there are the other well-known types of variations: dialectal variation and codal variation (see, e.g., Gregory. 1967; Halliday et al., 1964; Halliday, 1978; Hasan, 1973; Matthiessen, 1993).

3 For example, learners can process huge volumes of casual conversation in contexts in which there are personal values and experiences with others without coming across any instances of *shall* as a modal auxiliary of obligation, but even a few legal texts regulating people's behavior are likely to give them enough instances of *shall* as a modal of obligation to begin to integrate it into their own systems.

4 It is only possible to select within one of these meaning potentials at a given time. During Phase I, children gradually expand their meaning potential by adding systems and terms within systems. At certain points, new microfunctions appear (in particular, the heuristic and the imaginative); but the development is still fairly gradual.

5 There are two apparent exceptions to this generalizations. (a) As children make the transition from the "unstructured" learning of the home and neighborhood to the structured learning of primary school, they expand their expression plane by learning a new mode of expression—graphology and graphetics. (b) As children make the transition from primary school to secondary school (around the age of puberty), they begin to learn a more complex relationship between semantics and lexico-grammar within the ideational metafunction—grammatical metaphor of the ideational kind. However, both of these apparent exceptions are directly related to children's continuing registerial expansion of their meaning potential—to move into the registers of the written mode, and to the registers of uncommonsense, disciplinary knowledge, respectively. In this way, they follow the general principle

of language learning: The complexity of the meaning potential increases as a function of new demands that are placed on it in new contexts.

6 Here, we must switch from English to Spanish as the language being investigated; but registers of modern standard languages of nation states such as English and Spanish are typically comparable and intertranslatable, particularly in internationally oriented institutions such as universities.

7 At the same time, their research also shows that psychology and social work are registerially considerably more varied than construction engineering and industrial chemistry.

8 A person's personalized version of the collective meaning potential is, of course, never the full meaning potential of the collective; it is a personal subpotential consisting of those registers that he or she has become familiar with—his or her registerial repertoire, as I put it earlier.

9 Naturally, a learner may leave the educational system at various points; see Rose (1998) for the social and educational significance.

10 Although there is no space to expand on the point that registers are semantic strategies in the first instance, it is important to promote this understanding and to describe and model registers as networks of strategic options (cf. Halliday, 1973, Ch. 4). When we learn a new register, we learn the semantic strategies we need to take on a new role in some institutional setting. Such strategies constitute new ways of using existing lexico-grammatical resources, or ways of expanding on existing resources to meet the new needs.

11 It is, of course, also important to take account of the other contextual parameters—tenor (who's taking part) and mode (what role is played by language); but to keep the discussion short enough, I have selected field for present purposes.

12 For example, in physics, it is located in the "expounding" sector; here, key registers are explanations and reports. However, another motif in physics is experimentation: Lab experiments fall in the "enabling" sector, and lab reports fall in the "reporting" sector. In English, there are two centers of registerial gravity. One is located in the "re-creating" sector; here, key registers are different types of narratives, starting with personal recounts and gradually increasing in complexity. The other is located in the "exploring" sector; here, key registers are (in developmental sequence) personal responses, reviews, character analyses, and thematic interpretations. Obviously, the picture that has emerged from the investigations of the registers of writing needs supplementing by investigations of the registers of speaking, as in group work in school or homework sessions at Starbuck's. We need to map out the complete discursive learning experience.

13 As already noted, their research shows that the center of registerial gravity in psychology and social work is located in the "exploring" sector, whereas the center of registerial gravity in industrial chemistry and construction engineering is located in the "expounding" sector. Like the school subjects of secondary school, these academic disciplines differ significantly in what kinds of semiotic work they do.

References

Bateman, J. A., Matthiessen, C. M. I. M., & Zeng, L. (1999). Multilingual language generation for multilingual software: A functional linguistic approach. *Applied Artificial Intelligence: An International Journal, 13*(6), 607–639.

Christie, F., & Derewianka, B. (2008). *School discourse: Learning to write across the years of schooling*. London: Continuum.

Christie, F., & Martin, J. R. (Eds.). (1997). *Genre and institutions: Social processes in the workplace and school*. London: Cassell.

Cloran, C., Stuart-Smith, V., & Young, L. (2007). Models of discourse. In R. Hasan, C. M. I. M. Matthiessen, & J. J. Webster (Eds.), *Continuing discourse on language: A functional perspective* (Vol. 2, pp. 645–668). London: Equinox.

Coffin, C. (2006). *Historical discourse*. London: Continuum.

Derewianka, B. (1995). *Language development in the transition from childhood to adolescence: The role of grammatical metaphor*. Unpublished doctoral dissertation, Macquarie University Sydney, Australia.

Gregory, M. J. (1967). Aspects of varieties differentiation. *Journal of Linguistics, 3*, 177–198.

Gu, Y.-G. (2001). Towards an understanding of workplace discourse: A pilot study for compiling a spoken Chinese corpus of situated discourse. In C. Candlin (Ed.), *Theory and Practice of Professional Discourse* (pp. 137–185). Hong Kong: CUHK Press.

Halliday, M. A. K. (1959). *The language of the Chinese SECRET HISTORY of the Mongols*. Oxford: Blackwell.

Halliday, M. A. K. (1973). *Explorations in the functions of language*. London: Edward Arnold.

Halliday, M. A. K. (1975). *Learning how to mean: Explorations in the development of language*. London: Edward Arnold.

Halliday, M. A. K. (1977). Text as semantic choice in social contexts. In T. van Dijk & J. Petöfi (Eds.), *Grammars and descriptions* (pp. 176–225). Berlin: Walter de Gruyter.

Halliday, M. A. K. (1978). *Language as social semiotic: The social interpretation of language and meaning*. London: Edward Arnold.

Halliday, M. A. K. (1984). Language as code and language as behaviour: A systemic-functional interpretation of the nature and ontogenesis of dialogue. In M. A. K. Halliday, R. P. Fawcett, S. Lamb, & A. Makkai (Eds.), *The semiotics of language and culture* (Vol. 1, pp. 3–35). London: Frances Pinter.

Halliday, M. A. K. (1993). Towards a language-based theory of learning. *Linguistics and Education, 5*(2), 93–116.

Halliday, M. A. K. (2004). *The language of early childhood*. In J. J. Webster (Ed.), *Collected works of M. A. K. Halliday: Vol. 4. The language of early childhood*. London: Continuum.

Halliday, M. A. K., & Matthiessen, C. M. I. M. (1999). *Construing experience through meaning: A language-based approach to cognition.* London: Cassell. Study edition, 2006. London: Continuum.

Halliday, M. A. K., & Matthiessen, C. M. I. M. (2004). *An introduction to functional grammar* (3rd ed.). London: Arnold.

Halliday, M. A. K., McIntosh, A., & Strevens, P. (1964). *The linguistic sciences and language teaching.* London: Longman.

Hasan, R. (1973). Code, register and social dialect. In B. Bernstein (Ed.), *Class, codes and control: Applied studies towards a sociology of language* (pp. 253–292). London: Routledge & Kegan Paul.

Hasan, R., Matthiessen, C. M. I. M., & Webster, J. J. (Eds.). (2005). *Continuing discourse on language: A functional perspective* (Vol. 1). London: Equinox Publishing.

Hasan, R., Matthiessen, C. M. I. M., & Webster, J. J. (Eds.). (2007). *Continuing discourse on language: A functional perspective* (Vol. 2). London: Equinox Publishing.

König, E., & Siemund, P. (2007). Speech act distinctions in grammar. In T. Shopen (Ed.), *Language typology and syntactic description.* Cambridge: Cambridge University Press.

Lemke, J. L. (1990). *Talking science: Language, learning and values.* Norwood, NJ: Ablex.

Martin, J. R. (2009). Genre and language learning: A social semiotic perspective. *Linguistics and Education 20*(1), 10–21.

Matthiessen, C. M. I. M. (1993). Register in the round: Diversity in a unified theory of register analysis. In M. Ghadessy (Ed.), *Register analysis: Theory and practice* (pp. 221–292). London: Pinter Publishers.

Matthiessen, C. M. I. M. (1995). *Lexicogrammatical cartography: English systems.* Tokyo: International Language Sciences Publishers.

Matthiessen, C. M. I. M. (2002a). Combining clauses into clause complexes: A multi-faceted view. In J. Bybee & M. Noonan (Eds.), *Complex sentences in grammar and discourse: Essays in honor of Sandra A. Thompson* (pp. 237–322). Amsterdam: Benjamins.

Matthiessen, C. M. I. M. (2002b). Lexicogrammar in discourse development: Logogenetic patterns of wording. In G. Huang & Z. Wang (Eds.), *Discourse and language functions* (pp. 91–127). Shanghai: Foreign Language Teaching and Research Press.

Matthiessen, C. M. I. M. (2004). The evolution of language: A systemic functional exploration of phylogenetic phases. In G. Williams & A. Lukin (Eds.), *Language development: Functional perspectives on evolution and ontogenesis* (pp. 45–90). London: Continuum.

Matthiessen, C. M. I. M. (2006a). Educating for advanced foreign language capacities: Exploring the meaning-making resources of languages systemic-functionally. In H.

Byrnes (Ed.), *Advanced instructed language learning: The complementary contribution of Halliday and Vygotsky* (pp. 31–57). London: Continuum.

Matthiessen, C. M. I. M. (2006b). Frequency profiles of some basic grammatical systems: An interim report. In S. Hunston & G. Thompson (Eds.), *System and corpus: Exploring connections* (pp. 103–142). London: Equinox Publishing.

Matthiessen, C. M. I. M. (2007). The architecture of language according to systemic functional theory: Developments since the 1970s. In R. Hasan, C. M. I. M. Matthiessen, & J. J. Webster (Eds.), *Continuing discourse on language* (Vol. 2, pp. 505–561). London: Equinox Publishing.

Matthiessen, C. M. I. M., & Bateman, J. A. (1991). *Systemic linguistics and text generation: Experiences from Japanese and English*. London: Frances Pinter.

Ortega, L., & Byrnes, H. (Eds.). (2008). *The longitudinal study of advanced L2 capacities*. London: Routledge.

Painter, C. (1984). *Into the mother tongue: A case study in early language development*. London: Frances Pinter.

Painter, C. (1999). *Learning through language in early childhood*. London: Cassell.

Painter, C., Derewianka, B., & Torr, J. (2007). From microfunctions to metaphor: Learning language and learning through language. In R. Hasan, C. M. I. M. Matthiessen, & J. J. Webster (Eds.), *Continuing discourse on language: A functional perspective* (Vol. 2, pp. 563–588). London: Equinox Publishing.

Parodi, G. (Ed.). (in press). *Discourse genres in Spanish: Academic and professional connections*. Amsterdam: Benjamins.

Parodi, G., Ibáñez, R., & Venegas, R. (in press). Academic and professional genres: Variations and commonalities in the PUCV-2006 Corpus of Spanish. In G. Parodi (Ed.), *Discourse genres in Spanish: Academic and professional connections*. Amsterdam: Benjamins. pp. 39–68.

Rinner, S., & Weigert, A. (2006). From sports to the EU economy: Integrating curricula through genre-based content courses. In H. Byrnes, H. D. Weger-Gunthrap, & K. A. Sprang (Eds.), *Educating for advanced foreign language capacities: constructs, curriculum, instruction, assessment* (pp. 136–151). Washington, DC: Georgetown University Press.

Rose, D. (1998). Science discourse and industry hierarchy. In J. R. Martin & R. Veel (Eds.), *Reading science: Critical and functional perspectives of discourses of science* (pp. 236–265). London: Routledge.

Schleppegrell, M. J. (2004). *The language of schooling: A functional linguistics approach*. Mahwah, NJ: Lawrence Erlbaum.

Schleppegrell, M. J., & Colombi, C. M. (Eds.). (2002). *Developing advanced literacy in first and second languages: Meaning with power*. Mahwah, NJ: Lawrence Erlbaum.

Steels, L. (1998). Synthesizing the origins of language and meaning using coevolution, self-organization and level formation. In J. R. Hurford, M. Studdert-Kennedy, & C.

Knight (Eds.), *Approaches to the evolution of language: Social and cognitive bases* (pp. 384–404). Cambridge: Cambridge University Press.

Teruya, K. (2006). Grammar as resource for the construction of language logic for advanced language learning in Japanese. In H. Byrnes (Ed.), *Advanced instructed language learning: The complementary contribution of Halliday and Vygotsky* (pp. 109–133). London: Continuum.

Teruya, K. (2009). Grammar as a gateway into discourse: A systemic functional approach to SUBJECT, THEME, and logic. *Linguistics and Education, 20*(1), 67–79.

Teruya, K., Akerejola E., Andersen, T. H., Caffarel, A., Lavid, J., Matthiessen, C. M. I. M., et al. (2007). Typology of MOOD: A text-based and system-based functional view. In R. Hasan, C. M. I. M. Matthiessen, & J. J. Webster (Eds.), *Continuing discourse on language: A functional perspective* (Vol. 1, pp. 859–920). London: Equinox Publishing.

Torr, J. (1997). *From child tongue to mother tongue: A case study of language development in the first two and a half years.* Nottingham, UK: University of Nottingham.

Weinreich, H. (1972). Die Textpartitur als heuristische Methode. *Der Deutschunterricht, 24*(4), 43–60.

Language Learning   ISSN 0023-8333

Individual Differences: Interplay of Learner Characteristics and Learning Environment

Zoltán Dörnyei

University of Nottingham

The notion of language as a complex adaptive system has been conceived within an agent-based framework, which highlights the significance of individual-level variation in the characteristics and contextual circumstances of the learner/speaker. Yet, in spite of this emphasis, currently we know relatively little about the interplay among language, agent, and environment in the language acquisition process, which highlights the need for further research in this area. This article is intended to pursue this agenda by discussing four key issues in this respect: (a) conceptualizing the agent, (b) conceptualizing the environment and its relationship to the agent, (c) operationalizing the dynamic relationship among language, agent, and environment, and (d) researching dynamic systems.

In their position paper, the "Five Graces Group" (this issue; henceforth FGG) proposed that the complex adaptive system (CAS) of language should be conceived within an *agent-based* framework, in which "different speakers may exhibit different linguistic behavior and may interact with different members of the community (as happens in reality)." This highlights the significance of individual-level variation in the characteristics and contextual circumstances of the learner/speaker. Accordingly, a key principle of the proposed approach is that from the point of view of language acquisition and behavior, the interaction between the language learner/user and the environment matters. This, of course, is in stark contrast to the traditional approach of generative linguistics dominating the second half of the 20th century, for which the cognitive system underlying language was conceptualized as largely context and user independent.

I would like to thank Peter MacIntyre for his helpful comments on a previous version of this article.

Correspondence concerning this article should be addressed to Zoltán Dörnyei, School of English Studies, University of Nottingham, University Park, Nottingham NG7 2RD, UK. Internet: zoltan.dornyei@nottingham.ac.uk

In the light of the above, a curious feature of the FGG paper is that in spite of the emphasis on the agent-based framework, there is very little said about the agent, and even the discussion of the role of the environment is limited to highlighting a few selected points only, such as social networks or the language input generated by the learner's social experience. It is clear that further research is needed to elaborate on the interplay among language, agent, and environment, and the current article is intended to pursue this agenda by discussing four key areas in this respect: (a) conceptualizing the agent, (b) conceptualizing the environment and its relationship to the agent, (c) operationalizing the dynamic relationship among language, agent, and environment, and (d) researching dynamic systems.

Conceptualizing the Agent

Learner characteristics in applied linguistics have traditionally been investigated within the context of *individual differences* (IDs), which are conceived to be attributes that mark a person as a distinct and unique human being. Of course, people differ from each other in respect of a vast number of traits, of which ID research has traditionally focused only on those personal characteristics that are enduring, that are assumed to apply to everybody, and on which people differ by degree. In other words, ID factors concern stable and systematic deviations from a normative blueprint (Dörnyei, 2005).

Individual differences have been well established in SLA research as a relatively straightforward concept: They have usually been seen as background learner variables that modify and personalize the overall trajectory of the language acquisition processes; thus, in many ways, IDs have been typically thought of as the systematic part of the background "noise" in SLA. Particularly, four ID factors have received special attention in past second language (L2) research (see, e.g., Dörnyei, 2005; Dörnyei & Skehan, 2003; Robinson, 2002a; Skehan, 1989): *motivation, language aptitude, learning styles,* and *learning strategies.* Broadly speaking, *motivation* was seen to concern the affective characteristics of the learner, referring to the direction and magnitude of learning behavior in terms of the learner's choice, intensity, and duration of learning. *Language aptitude* determines the cognitive dimension, referring to the capacity and quality of learning. *Learning styles* refer to the manner of learning, and *learning strategies* are somewhere in between motivation and learning styles by referring to the learner's proactiveness in selecting specific made-to-measure learning routes. Thus, the composite of these variables has been seen to answer *why, how long, how hard, how well, how proactively,* and *in what way* the learner engages in the learning process.

In a recent overview of the psychology of SLA, I have proposed (Dörnyei, 2009) that the seemingly comprehensive and straightforward picture of IDs being stable and monolithic learner traits that concern distinct learner characteristics is part of an idealized narrative that may not hold up against scientific scrutiny. The core of the problem is that if we take a situated and process-oriented perspective of SLA, we cannot fail to realize that the various learner attributes display a considerable amount of variation from time to time and from situation to situation. Indeed, one of the main conclusions of my 2005 review of individual differences (Dörnyei, 2005) was that the most striking aspect of nearly all the recent ID literature was the emerging theme of *context*:

> It appears that cutting-edge research in all these diverse areas has been addressing the same issue, that is, the situated nature of the ID factors in question. Scholars have come to reject the notion that the various traits are context-independent and absolute, and are now increasingly proposing new dynamic conceptualizations in which ID factors enter into some interaction with the situational parameters rather than cutting across tasks and environments. (p. 218)

Thus, language aptitude, for example, has been found to impact different tasks and learning contexts differently (e.g., Robinson, 2007), and motivation usually shows considerable ongoing fluctuation with regular ebbs and flows (e.g., Dörnyei, 2000). More generally, most ID researchers would now agree that the role of learner characteristics can only be evaluated with regard to their interaction with specific environmental and temporal factors or conditions. In their recent analysis of SLA, Ellis and Larsen-Freeman (2006, p. 563) summed up this issue as follows: "To attribute causality to any one variable (or even a constellation of variables) without taking time and context into account is misguided." This view is also supported by the results of genetics research, which reveal that not even our inherited genes are context independent but exert their influence through their interaction with the environment: According to Bouchard and McGue (2003), for example, genetic influences account for approximately 40–55% of the variance in personality and Modell (2003) explained that environmental influences make the brains of even identical twins appreciably different.

Thus, ID effects cannot be identified accurately without taking into account the idiosyncratic features of the specific temporal and situational context we are investigating, and the picture gets even more complicated with the recognition that rather than being monolithic, most learner characteristics are complex, higher order mental attributes, resulting from the integrated operation of several subcomponents and subprocesses. Indeed, higher order ID variables such as aptitude and motivation involve, at one level or another, the cooperation of components of very different nature (e.g., cognitive, motivational, or emotional), resulting in "hybrid" attributes.

A good illustration of this componential mixture has been provided by a recent study by Dörnyei and Tseng (2009), which examined the question of motivational task processing by empirically testing a theoretical model that I proposed in 2003 (Dörnyei, 2003). As I suggested then, the motivational dynamics of learning tasks is dependent on how the participating learners process the various motivational stimuli they encounter and, as a result, how they activate certain necessary motivational strategies. The construct suggests that L2 learners are engaged in an ongoing appraisal and response process, involving their continuous monitoring and evaluating how well they are doing in a task and then making possible amendments if something seems to be going amiss. This process can be represented through a dynamic system that consists of three interrelated mechanisms: "task execution," "appraisal," and "action control."

Task execution refers to the learners' engagement in task-supportive learning behaviors in accordance with the task goals and the action plan that were either provided by the teacher (through the task instructions) or drawn up by the student or the task team. In other words, this is the level of actual "learning." *Task appraisal* refers to the learner's continuous processing of the multitude of stimuli coming from the environment regarding the progress made toward the action outcome, comparing the actual performance with the predicted or hoped-for ones or with the likely performance that alternative action sequences would offer. *Action control* processes denote self-regulatory mechanisms that are called into force in order to enhance, scaffold, or protect learning-specific action; active use of such mechanisms may "save" the action when ongoing monitoring reveals that progress is slowing, halting, or backsliding.

Dörnyei and Tseng's (2009) validation study involved a structural equation modeling (SEM) analysis of the proposed construct and has confirmed a circular relationship of the three components (see Figure 1): Signals from the appraisal system concerning task execution trigger the need to activate relevant action control strategies, which, in turn, further facilitate the execution process. An example of this process would involve someone, say Martin, listening to a rather boring lecture and noticing that his concentration is flagging. This recognition, in turn, initiates a search in his repertoire of relevant action control

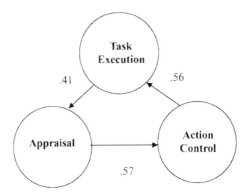

Figure 1 Structural equation diagram of motivational task processing (from Dörnyei & Tseng, 2009).

or self-motivating strategies, and if Martin finds a way that would help him to refocus his attention (e.g., reminding himself of the significance of the topic or of the need to listen or else he will not be able to write a required report of the content of the presentation), then he executes this troubleshooting strategy, thereby restoring the necessary level of attention. Thus, a process that is primarily motivational in nature relies on a cognitive appraisal component. This is in fact not an uncommon combination, as most theoretical conceptualizations of emotion, for example, contain a cognitive appraisal component that is responsible for the evaluation of the situation that evokes an emotional response (Lewis, 2005).

Addressing this issue more generally, Dörnyei (2009) provided a detailed argument that given the complex and interlocking nature of higher order human functioning, individual differences in mental functions typically involve a blended operation of cognitive, affective, and motivational components—a convergence that becomes even more obvious if we take a neuropsychological perspective, because at the level of neural networks it is difficult to maintain the traditional separation of different types of functions. The question, then, is whether in this light there is any justification for proposing any macro-structuring principles to individual variation in human mental functions (such as "cognitive" or "motivational" functions)?

I believe that there is one perspective according to which the main types of mental functions can be separated: the *phenomenological* (i.e., experiential) view: People can phenomenally distinguish three areas of mental functioning— *cognition, motivation*, and *affect* (or emotions)—which is, in fact, a traditional division going back to Greek philosophy, often referred to as the "trilogy of the mind" (see Mayer, Chabot, & Carlsmith, 1997). Plato proposed that the human soul contained three components: *cognition* (corresponding to thought and reason and associated with the ruling class of philosophers, kings, and statesmen), *emotion/passion* (corresponding to anger or spirited higher ideal emotions and associated with the warrior class), and *conation/motivation* (associated with impulses, cravings, desires and associated with the lower classes) (for a review, see Scherer, 1995).

I believe that it is useful to maintain this tripartite view and think of these three dimensions of the mind as three subsystems. However, it is also clear that the three subsystems have continuous dynamic interaction with each other and cannot exist in isolation from one another; as Buck (2005, p. 198) put it: "In their fully articulated forms, emotions imply cognitions imply motives imply emotions, and so on." Therefore, I have argued (Dörnyei, 2009) that instead of conceptualizing learner characteristics in a modular manner (i.e., in terms of distinct ID factors), future research should try and take a systemic approach by identifying higher level amalgams or constellations of cognition, affect, and motivation that act as "wholes." Two examples of such composite factors in SLA research are Robinson's (2002b, 2007) notion of *aptitude complexes* and Dörnyei's concept of *ideal and ought-to selves* (e.g., Dörnyei, 2005, 2009).

Conceptualizing the Environment and Its Relationship With the Agent

The FGG paper clearly states that "Language has a fundamentally social function" and reiterates later that "Language is used for human social interaction, and so its origins and capacities are dependent on its role in our social life." Indeed, currently most scholars would agree that the individual's experience in the social environment affects every aspect of human functioning, including language acquisition and use. This is in fact a relatively old issue, going back to at least the 1930s; as Funder (2006) has summarized in a recent article devoted to the analysis of the personal and situational determination of behavior,

> Since at least the 1930s, deep thinkers as diverse as Allport (1937) and Lewin (1951) have argued that invidious comparisons miss the point because behavior is a function of an interaction between the person and the situation. By the 1980s this recognition had deteriorated into a truism. Nowadays, everybody is an interactionist. (p. 22)

In spite of this seeming agreement, the social issue is a hotbed of disagreement and debates. In psychology, this dispute has often been referred to as the "person situation debate," and a recent Focus Issue of *The Modern Language Journal* (Lafford, 2007) has articulated well the tension between cognitive and social agendas in applied linguistics (for good summaries of the cognitive-social debate, see Larsen-Freeman, 2007b; Zuengler & Miller, 2006). Thus, we seem to have a curious situation whereby everybody appears to agree with certain general principles, and yet when these principles are put into practice, the issue becomes oddly divisive.

One of the main reasons for the divergent views is, I believe, the challenge of conceptualizing the environment and its relationship with the agent in particular. In psychology, the field specialized in the study of how the individual interacts with the surrounding social world is *social psychology*. This field has been deeply divided by a basic disagreement about how to approach the issue of the individual embedded in society: from the individual's or from the society's perspective (for an overview, see Abrams & Hogg, 1999). The *individualistic perspective*—best represented by the "social cognition" paradigm—considers the social or cultural context through the individual's eyes. Accordingly, the complexity of the social environment is only important inasmuch as it is reflected in the individual's mental processes and the resulting attitudes, beliefs and values; that is, the focus is on how people process social information and make sense of social situations. This perspective, therefore, offers a cognitive representation of the social world.

In contrast, the *societal perspective*—best represented by "social identity" theory—focuses on broad social processes and macro-contextual factors, such as sociocultural norms, intergroup relations, acculturation/assimilation processes, and cross-cultural or interethnic conflicts. From this perspective, the individual's behavior is seen to be largely determined by the more powerful forces at large; that is, social identity is often seen to override personal identity as exhibited, for example, by the individual's submission to normative pressures imposed by specific reference groups of cultural expectations.

This individual-societal tension can be seen as a good reflection of the inherent challenge of relating the agent to the environment in a coherent theoretical or research framework. For example, within the context of quantitative research, Byrne (2002, p. 9) explained that "Conventional statistical reasoning in the social sciences is incapable of dealing with relationships among levels—or relating individuals to social collectivities—other than by regarding social collectivities as mere aggregates of individuals with no emergent properties." The individualistic-societal contrast also manifests itself clearly in the often mixed selection of variables, metaphors, and research approaches to link the agent and the environment. The FGG paper mentions, for example, the learner/speaker's "prior experience," which is at the individualistic end of the cline, and the learner's position in a "social network structure," which is further toward the societal end. Else, as the abstract of the paper summarizes, "A speaker's behavior is the consequence of competing factors ranging from perceptual constraints to social motivations," which, again, reflects a prominent individual-social contrast. There is, in fact, a great variety of approaches along the individualistic-societal cline, depending on how we identify and select the relevant environmental factors to be integrated in a particular research paradigm. In this respect, Funder (2006) drew attention to the specific difficulty of identifying the key parameters of the "social situation":

it is difficult to pin down just how situations are important, in part because of the common but unilluminating practice of assigning "the situation" responsibility for all the behavioral variance not accounted for by a particular personality trait, *without* specifying what aspects of the situation are psychologically essential. There is a good deal of confusion concerning how situations should be conceptualized. (p. 27)

A good illustration of the confusing complexity that Funder is talking about is offered by the way one of the main types of instructional contexts—the "classroom situation"—has been theorized in educational psychology. As Turner and Meyer (2000) summarized, classroom environments have been variously studied in terms of the "beliefs, goals, values, perceptions, behaviors, classroom management, social relations, physical space, and social-emotional and evaluative climates that contribute to the participants' understanding of the classroom" (p. 70). Furthermore, it is common to distinguish at least two broad dimensions of the classroom environment: the "instructional context,", which concerns the influences of the teacher, students, curriculum, learning tasks, and teaching method, among other things, and the "social context," which is related to the fact that the classroom is also the main social arena for students, offering deeply intensive personal experiences such as friendship, love, or identity formation. These two contexts are interdependent and also interact with the complex process of learning.

In the study of SLA, there have been several initiatives to situate research and thus capture environmental effects, for example in classroom ethnography (e.g., Harklau, 2005; Toohey, 2008; Watson-Gageo, 1997), the microanalysis of classroom discourse (e.g., Zuengler & Mori, 2002), the interaction hypothesis (e.g., Gass, 2003; Gass & Mackey, 2007; Mackey & Polio, 2009), the group dynamics of language learning and teaching (e.g., Dörnyei & Murphey, 2003; Ehrman & Dörnyei, 1998), sociocultural theory (e.g., Lantolf & Thorne, 2006), and language socialization (e.g., Schieffelin & Ochs, 1986; Watson-Gegeo, 2004; Zuengler & Cole, 2005). In fact, even the general issues of language instruction and how language input becomes intake concern the interaction of the learner and the environment.

In sum, the availability of diverse multiple approaches to conceptualizing the environment relative to the agent indicates the inherent difficulty of establishing a parsimonious system of valid and generalizable parameters to describe contextual characteristics. Therefore, challenge for future research is to find ways of identifying the key factors determining the joint operation of the agent-environment dyad. In Larsen-Freeman's (2007a, p. 37) words, "The answer, I believe, lies in finding the optimal interconnected units of analysis depending on what we are seeking to explain." Additionally, as she elaborates, the challenge will lie in "cultivating a dialectical relation between parts and wholes in order to identify the appropriate functional units of analysis, which is of course something that is likely to require ongoing redefinition, depending on the inquiry." Because different aspects of the agent's development are possibly affected by different aspects of the environment, the initial understanding of the agent-environment link is likely to be established primarily through exploratory qualitative investigations, a question I will come back to in the last section of this article.

Operationalizing the Dynamic Relationship Among Language, Agent, and Environment

A basic principle of the CAS approach in the FGG paper is that the process of language acquisition and use is taken to be *dynamic*. The term "dynamic" is used here in a specific sense, as a technical term to signify the relevance of *complexity theory* and two trends within this broad approach—*dynamic systems theory* and *emergentism*. These approaches share in common their central objective of describing development in complex, dynamic systems that consist of multiple interconnected parts and in which the multiple interferences between the components' own trajectories result in nonlinear, emergent changes in the overall system behavior (for overviews, see, e.g., de Bot, 2008; de Bot, Lowie, & Verspoor, 2007; Dörnyei, 2009; Ellis & Larsen-Freeman, 2006; Larsen-Freeman & Cameron, 2008a; van Geert, 2008). Ellis (2007, p. 23) argued that from this dynamic view language can be seen as a complex dynamic system where cognitive, social and environmental factors continuously interact, where creative communicative behaviors emerge from socially co-regulated interactions, where there is little by way of linguistic universals as a starting point in the mind of *ab initio* language learners or discernable end state, where flux and individual variation abound, where cause-effect relationships are nonlinear, multivariate and interactive, and where language is not a collection of rules and target forms to be acquired, but rather a by-product of communicative processes.

Complex, dynamic systems are in constant interaction with their environment, so much so that the context is seen as part of the system, with neither the internal development of the organism nor the impact of the environment given priority in explaining behavior and its change. Equilibrium in this sense means a smooth, ongoing adaptation to contextual changes (Larsen-Freeman & Cameron, 2008a). The following summary by de Bot et al. (2007) provides a good illustration of the intricacy of this dynamic conceptualization:

a language learner is regarded as a dynamic subsystem within a social system with a great number of interacting internal dynamic sub-sub systems, which function within a multitude of other external dynamic systems. The learner has his/her own cognitive ecosystem consisting of intentionality, cognition, intelligence, motivation, aptitude, L1, L2 and so on. The cognitive ecosystem in turn is related to the degree of exposure to language, maturity, level of education, and so on, which in turn is related to the SOCIAL ECOSYSTEM, consisting of the environment with which the individual interacts. . . . Each of these internal and external subsystems is similar in that they have the properties of a dynamic system. They will always be in flux and change, taking the current state of the system as input for the next one. (p. 14)

Such a complex setup is admittedly not easy to work with and our natural tendency has been to focus on selected aspects of the system such as the nature of input, particular learner characteristics, or some social aspect of the environment and then examine the system outcome (e.g., language attainment) in this particular light. De Bot et al. (2007), however, warned that such accounts will provide a gross oversimplification of reality, because only the integrated consideration of all factors can form an appreciation of the actual complexity. Although this might be true, the authors also add that "it is a matter of fact that it is very difficult to get a grip on complex interactions" (p. 18).

Interestingly, even Larsen-Freeman and Cameron (2008a), who have written a whole book on complexity theory, admitted that developing the new perspective has posed a real language challenge, as it is "easy to fall back into old ways of thinking, and requires continual monitoring to ensure that ways of talking (or writing) reflect complex dynamic ways of thinking" (p. x). One important factor that may explain why it is relatively easy to become complacent about describing the language system in sufficiently dynamic terms is that although there are several aspects of first language (L1) acquisition that point to the relevance of a dynamic, emergent systems approach, the existence of some powerful forces—or in dynamic systems terms, *attractors*—appear to override much of this dynamic variation, to the extent that L1 acquisition is one of the most homogeneous and predictable of all the higher level cognitive processes. Indeed, *in spite of* all the individual differences and experience-based variation, L1 speakers uniformly master their mother tongue to an extent that they become indistinguishable from other members of the L1 community in terms of their language-based membership (which is often referred to as being a *native speaker*). Furthermore, we find robust, predictable tendencies even with regard to social and regional stratification, such as accents and dialects. In short, we can go a long way in analyzing and understanding L1 phenomena without having to take the system dynamics into account.

However, coming from a SLA background— like I do —one becomes more alert to dynamic variation, because one of the main differences between L1 and L2 acquisition is the significantly increased variability of the latter process. Without any doubt, L2 development is far more exposed to the impact of system complexity than mother-tongue learning, which is reflected in the heterogeneity of the (typically limited) end state of adult learners' language attainment. When discussing SLA, we simply cannot provide adequate explanations without considering a number of learner-based or environmental factors such as the learner's age and motivation or the amount and nature of instructional language input.

Researching Dynamic Systems

The final challenge in giving the language-agent-environment dynamics its due importance is related to the general uncertainty in the social sciences about how to conduct empirical studies in a dynamic systems vein. The FGG paper recognizes this issue very clearly: "In the various aspects of language considered here, it is always the case that form, user, and use are inextricably linked. But such complex interactions are difficult to investigate in vivo." Indeed, there are obvious problems with (a) modeling nonlinear, dynamic change (especially quantitatively), (b) observing the operation of the whole system and the interaction of the parts rather than focusing on specific units in it, and

(c) replacing conventional quantitative research methodology and statistics with alternative methods and tools (Dörnyei, 2009). In a recent article examining the research methodology on language development from a complex systems perspective, Larsen Freeman and Cameron (2008b, p. 200) summarized this issue as follows: "The dynamic, nonlinear, and open nature of complex systems, together with their tendency toward self-organization and interaction across levels and timescales, requires changes in traditional views of the functions and roles of theory, hypothesis, data, and analysis."

Thus, measuring the state of dynamic systems with precision is not at all straightforward, particularly in the light of Byrne's (2002, p. 8) assertion: "If we think of the world as complex and real we are thinking about it in a very different way from the ontological program that underpins conventional statistical reasoning and cause." Unfortunately, complexity/dynamic systems research in the social and cognitive sciences is a relatively uncharted territory and, therefore, currently we have only few research methodological guidelines on how to conduct language-specific dynamic systems studies. Key research issues in this respect, listed by Dörnyei (2009), include the following (for a detailed overview, see Larsen-Freeman & Cameron, 2008b):

- *Cause-effect relationships.* Within a dynamic systems framework there are no simple cause-effect explanations between variables examined in isolation, which is the standard research focus in most applied linguistic research, particularly in the area of individual differences. Thus, rather than pursuing such a reductionist agenda, studies in the dynamic systems vein need to emphasize the processes of self-organization with regard to the whole of the interconnected system. Byrne (2005) summarizes this issue very clearly:

  Arguments for complexity are not arguments against simplicity. Some things can be understood by the analytic and reductionist program and where that program works it has done great service in elucidating causality. The problem is that it works where it works and it does not work everywhere. Indeed in a natural/social world the range of its applicability is rather limited. The problem is that, instead of the application of the simple model being understood as something that always has to be justified by showing that what is being dealt with can be analyzed, the simple model is taken as 'the scientific model', which is always applicable. The dominant contemporary modes of statistical reasoning in the social sciences are a particular example of this (see Byrne, 2002). (pp. 101–102)

- *Qualitative rather than quantitative approach.* Although complexity/ dynamic systems theory has an extensive mathematical basis in applications in the natural sciences, a dynamic systems approach in SLA does not lend itself easily to quantitative investigations, because the number of confounding variables is extensive and some of them cannot be measured at the level of precision that is required for mathematical analyses. On the other hand, several aspects of *qualitative research* make this approach suited to complexity/dynamic systems studies because of (a) the emergent nature of data collection and analysis, (b) the thick description of the natural context, (c) the relative ease of adding longitudinal aspects to the research design, and (d) the individual-level analysis that helps to avoid the potential problem that the results derived from a group of learners are unlikely to correspond to the unique dynamic patterns characterizing the individual participants.
- *Mixed methods research.* I have argued elsewhere (Dörnyei, 2007) that *mixed methods research* (i.e., the meaningful combination of qualitative and quantitative approaches) offers a radically different new strand of research methodology that suits the multilevel analysis of complex issues, because it allows investigators to obtain data about both the individual and the broader societal context.
- *Focus on change rather than variables.* Social scientists tend to focus on well-defined and generalizable *variables* to describe the social world around them. A complexity/dynamic systems approach needs to shift the emphasis from this variable-centered, reductionist practice to studying how systems *change* in time. As van Geert (2008, p. 197) summarized, "an understanding of dynamic systems is crucial if we want to go beyond the static or structural relationships between properties or variables and wish to understand the mechanism of development and learning as it applies to individuals."
- *Longitudinal research.* In his influential book on longitudinal research, Menard (2002) argued that longitudinal research should be seen as the default when we examine any dynamic processes in the social sciences. Such dynamic processes are obviously involved in human learning/growth or social change, but they can also be associated with various interactions of different levels of an issue (e.g., micro or macro) or of different types of variables (e.g., learner traits and learning task characteristics). Indeed, it is difficult to imagine a dynamic systems study that does not have a prominent longitudinal aspect.
- *Focus on system modeling.* Modeling is an important aspect of complexity/dynamic systems theory because it considers, by definition, the

coordinated operation of the whole system and allows for various cyclical processes, feedback loops, and iterations. However, as mentioned earlier, drawing up quantitative models of complex systems may not only be mathematically too demanding but arguably also unrealistic and inadequate for cognitive and social systems (van Gelder & Port, 1995). Larsen-Freeman and Cameron (2008a) described an interesting *qualitative modeling* approach that they call "complexity thought modeling," comprising a series of steps: (a) identifying the different components of the system, (b) identifying the timescales and levels of social and human organization on which the system operates, (c) describing the relations between and among components, (d) describing how the system and context adapt to each other, and (e) describing the dynamics of the system—that is, how the components and the relations amongst the components change over time.

Conclusion

The starting point of this article was the observation that even though the FGG paper emphasizes an agent-based framework for the study of language as a complex adaptive system, it offers few specific details about the agent's role in the language acquisition process. In explaining this situation, I suggested that, currently, the dynamic interaction among language, agent, and environment is rather undertheorized and underresearched. I discussed four areas in particular where we face certain conceptual challenges with regard to doing the language-agent-environment relations justice in the study of L1 and L2 acquisition: conceptualizing the agent; conceptualizing the environment and its relationship to the agent; operationalizing the dynamic relationship among language, agent, and environment; and, finally, researching dynamic systems.

With respect to the analysis of the agent, I pointed out that applied linguistics (and educational psychology in general) has typically followed an individual difference-based approach to integrate learner characteristics into the various research paradigms. However, the traditional notion of individual difference factors, conceived as stable and monolithic learner characteristics, is outdated because it ignores the situated and multicomponential nature of these higher order attributes; the study of such complex constellations of factors requires a dynamic systems approach. If this argument is correct, then, identifying "pure" individual difference factors has only limited value both from a theoretical and a practical point of view. Instead, a potentially more fruitful approach is to focus on certain higher order combinations of different attributes that act as integrated wholes.

Understanding the functioning of the agent in the language learning process is further complicated by the fact that humans are social beings, and in an inherently social process such as language acquisition/use, the agent cannot be meaningfully separated from the social environment within which he/she operates. The significance of contextual influences has become a hot topic in several fields within the social sciences and, accordingly, conceptualizing situated constructs and research paradigms has become the dominant tendency in virtually all of contemporary SLA research. The challenge, then, is to adopt a dynamic perspective that allows us to consider simultaneously the ongoing multiple influences between environmental and learner factors in all their componential complexity, as well as the emerging changes in both the learner *and* the environment as a result of this development. This latter aspect is critical because, as Ushioda (2009) pointed out, context is generally defined in individual difference research as an independent background variable, or a static backdrop, over which the learner has no control. Such a conceptualization, Ushioda argued, sustains the basic Cartesian dualism between the mental and the material worlds, between the inner life of the individual and the surrounding culture and society. A truly dynamic systems approach will need to bridge this gap between the inner mental world of the individual and the surrounding social environment.

Although a dynamic systems approach would offer obvious benefits for the study of the complex interaction of language, agent, and environment, operationalizing this dynamic relationship in specific theoretical and measurement terms takes us into rather uncharted territories, with few specific guidelines or templates currently available to follow. In a position paper in *Developmental Review* championing dynamic systems approaches, Howe and Lewis (2005) explained the reasons why dynamic systems approaches to development remain a clear minority as follows:

> There has been a great deal of complaining in developmental journals about the constraints of conventional developmental approaches, including static or linear models and the use of averages rather than time-sensitive process accounts, and many developmentalists have espoused the value of systems thinking in theoretical articles. Yet most developmentalists continue to use conventional experimental designs and statistics to carry out their research. We think this is because the trajectory of developmental psychology, like other dynamic systems, tends toward stability much of the time. Researchers stick to well-established habits of thinking and working, and their students acquire the same habits, often

because that is the easiest road to publication and career advancement. (p. 250).

However, I would like to believe that the absence of ready-made research models and templates is not an indication of the inadequacy of a dynamic approach but only of the transitional problems that are bound to accompany a major paradigm shift. After all, I hope I am not alone in sharing Thelen and Smith's (1994, p. 341) experience:

Once we began to view development from a dynamic and selectionist approach, we found the ideas so powerful that we could never go back to other ways of thinking. Every paper we read, every talk we heard, every new bit of data from our labs took on new meaning. We planned experiments differently and interpreted old experiments from a fresh perspective. Some questions motivating developmental research no longer seemed important; other, wholly new areas of inquiry begged for further work.

Revised version accepted 19 May 2009

References

Abrams, D., & Hogg, M. A. (Eds.). (1999). *Social identity and social cognition.* Oxford: Blackwell.

Allport, G. W. (1937). *Personality: A psychological interpretation.* New York: Holt Rinehart & Winston.

Bouchard, T. J., & McGue, M. (2003). Genetic and environmental influences on human psychological differences. *Journal of Neurobiology, 54*(1), 4–45.

Buck, R. (2005). Adding ingredients to the self-organizing dynamic system stew: Motivation, communication, and higher-level emotions—and don't forget the genes! *Behavioral and Brain Science, 28*(2), 197–198.

Byrne, D. (2002). *Interpreting quantitative data.* London: Sage.

Byrne, D. (2005). Complexity, configurations and cases. *Theory, Culture & Society, 22*(5), 95–111.

de Bot, K. (2008). Second language development as a dynamic process. *Modern Language Journal, 92,* 166–178.

de Bot, K., Lowie, W., & Verspoor, M. (2007). A Dynamic Systems Theory approach to second language acquisition. *Bilingualism: Language and Cognition, 10*(1), 7–21.

Dörnyei, Z. (2000). Motivation in action: Towards a process-oriented conceptualization of student motivation. *British Journal of Educational Psychology, 70,* 519–538.

Dörnyei, Z. (2003). Attitudes, orientations, and motivations in language learning: Advances in theory, research, and applications. In Z. Dörnyei (Ed.), *Attitudes, orientations, and motivations in language learning* (pp. 3–32). Oxford: Blackwell.

Dörnyei, Z. (2005). *The psychology of the language learner: Individual differences in second language acquisition*. Mahwah, NJ: Lawrence Erlbaum.

Dörnyei, Z. (2007). *Research methods in applied linguistics: Quantitative, qualitative and mixed methodologies*. Oxford: Oxford University Press.

Dörnyei, Z. (2009). The L2 motivational self system. In Z. Dörnyei & E. Ushioda (Eds.), *Motivation, language identity and the L2 self* (pp. 9–42). Bristol, UK: Multilingual Matters.

Dörnyei, Z. (2009). *The psychology of second language acquisition*. Oxford: Oxford University Press.

Dörnyei, Z., & Murphey, T. (2003). *Group dynamics in the language classroom*. Cambridge: Cambridge University Press.

Dörnyei, Z., & Skehan, P. (2003). Individual differences in second language learning. In C. J. Doughty & M. H. Long (Eds.), *The handbook of second language acquisition* (pp. 589–630). Oxford: Blackwell.

Dörnyei, Z., & Tseng, W.-T. (2009). Motivational processing in interactional tasks. In A. Mackey & C. Polio (Eds.), *Multiple perspectives on interaction: Second language research in honor of Susan M. Gass* (pp. 117–134). Mahwah, NJ: Lawrence Erlbaum.

Ehrman, M. E., & Dörnyei, Z. (1998). *Interpersonal dynamics in second language education: The visible and in-visible classroom*. Thousand Oaks, CA: Sage.

Ellis, N. C. (2007). Dynamic systems and SLA: The wood and the trees. *Bilingualism: Language and Cognition, 10*(1), 23–25.

Ellis, N. C., & Larsen-Freeman, D. (2006). Language emergence: Implications for applied linguistics: Introduction to the special issue. *Applied Linguistics, 27*(4), 558–589.

Funder, D. C. (2006). Towards a resolution of the personality triad: Persons, situations, and behaviors. *Journal of Research in Personality, 40*, 21–34.

Gass, S. M. (2003). Input and interaction. In C. J. Doughty & M. H. Long (Eds.), *The handbook of second language acquisition* (pp. 224–255). Oxford: Blackwell.

Gass, S. M., & Mackey, A. (2007). Input, interaction, and output in second language acquisition. In B. VanPatten & J. Williams (Eds.), *Theories in second language acquisition: An introduction* (pp. 175–199). Mahwah, NJ: Lawrence Erlbaum.

Harklau, L. (2005). Ethnography and ethnographic research on second language teaching and learning. In E. Hinkel (Ed.), *Handbook of research in second language teaching and learning* (pp. 179–194). Mahwah, NJ: Lawrence Erlbaum.

Howe, M. L., & Lewis, M. D. (2005). The importance of dynamic systems approaches for understanding development. *Developmental Review, 25*, 247–251.

Lafford, B. A. (Ed.) (2007). Second language acquisition reconceptualized? The impact of Firth and Wagner (1997) [Focus issue]. *Modern Language Journal, 91*.

Lantolf, J. P., & Thorne, S. L. (2006). *Sociocultural theory and the genesis of second language development.* Oxford: Oxford University Press.

Larsen-Freeman, D. (2007a). On the complementarity of Chaos/Complexity Theory and Dynamic Systems Theory in understanding the second language acquisition process. *Bilingualism: Language and Cognition, 10*(1), 35–37.

Larsen-Freeman, D. (2007b). Reflecting on the cognitive-social debate in second language acquisition. *Modern Language Journal, 91*, 773–787.

Larsen-Freeman, D., & Cameron, L. (2008a). *Complex systems and applied linguistics.* Oxford: Oxford University Press.

Larsen-Freeman, D., & Cameron, L. (2008b). Research methodology on language development from a complex systems perspective. *Modern Language Journal, 92*(2), 200–213.

Lewin, K. (1951). *Field theory in social science.* New York: Harper & Row.

Lewis, M. D. (2005). Bridging emotion theory and neurobiology through dynamic systems modeling. *Behavioral and Brain Science, 28*(2), 169–245.

Mackey, A., & Polio, C. (Eds.). (2009). *Multiple perspectives on interaction: Second language research in honor of Susan M. Gass.* Mahwah, NJ: Lawrence Erlbaum.

Mayer, J. D., Chabot, H. F., & Carlsmith, K. M. (1997). Conation, affect, and cognition in personality. In G. Matthews (Ed.), *Cognitive science perspectives on personality and emotion* (pp. 31–63). Amsterdam: Elsevier.

Menard, S. (2002). *Longitudinal research* (2nd ed.). Thousand Oaks, CA: Sage.

Modell, A. H. (2003). *Imagination and the meaningful brain.* Cambridge, MA: MIT Press.

Robinson, P. (Ed.). (2002a). *Individual differences and instructed language learning.* Amsterdam: Benjamins.

Robinson, P. (2002b). Learning conditions, aptitude complexes and SLA: A framework for research and pedagogy. In P. Robinson (Ed.), *Individual differences and instructed language learning* (pp. 113–133). Amsterdam: Benjamins.

Robinson, P. (2007). Aptitudes, abilities, contexts, and practice. In R. M. DeKeyser (Ed.), *Practice in second language learning: Perspectives from linguistics and cognitive psychology* (pp. 256–286). Cambridge: Cambridge University Press.

Scherer, K. R. (1995). Plato's legacy: Relationships between cognition, emotion, and motivation. *Geneva Studies in Emotion and Communication, 9*(1), 1–7. Retrieved September 11, 2009, from http://www.unige.ch/fapse/emotion/publications/pdf/plato.pdf

Schieffelin, B., & Ochs, E. (Eds.). (1986). *Language socialization across cultures.* New York: Cambridge University Press.

Skehan, P. (1989). *Individual differences in second language learning.* London: Edward Arnold.

Thelen, E., & Smith, L. B. (1994). *A dynamic systems approach to the development of cognition and action.* Cambridge, MA: MIT Press.

Toohey, K. (2008). Ethnography and language education. In K. King & N. Hornberger (Eds.), *Encyclopedia of language and education: Vol. 10. Research methods* (pp. 177–188). New York: Springer.

Turner, J. C., & Meyer, D. K. (2000). Studying and understanding the instructional contexts of classrooms: Using our past to forge our future. *Educational Psychologist, 35*(2), 69–85.

Ushioda, E. (2009). A person-in-context relational view of emergent motivation and identity. In Z. Dörnyei & E. Ushioda (Eds.), *Motivation, language identity and the L2 self* (pp. 215–228). Bristol, UK: Multilingual Matters.

van Geert, P. (2008). The Dynamic Systems approach in the study of L1 and L2 acquisition: An introduction. *Modern Language Journal, 92*, 179–199.

van Gelder, T., & Port, R. F. (1995). It's about time: An overview of the dynamical approach to cognition. In R. F. Port & T. van Gelder (Eds.), *Mind as motion: Explorations in the dynamics of cognition* (pp. 1–43). Cambridge, MA: MIT Press.

Watson-Gegeo, K. A. (1997). Classroom ethnography. In N. Hornberger & D. Corson (Eds.), *Encyclopedia of language and education: Vol. 8. Research methods in language and education* (pp. 135–144). Dordrecht: Kluwer.

Watson-Gegeo, K. A. (2004). Mind, language, and epistemology: Toward a language socialization paradigm for SLA. *Modern Language Journal, 88*(3), 331–350.

Zuengler, J., & Cole, K. (2005). Language socialization and second language learning. In E. Hinkel (Ed.), *Handbook of research in second language teaching and learning* (pp. 301–316). Mahwah, NJ: Lawrence Erlbaum.

Zuengler, J., & Miller, E. R. (2006). Cognitive and sociocultural perspectives: Two parallel SLA worlds? *TESOL Quarterly, 40*(1), 35–58.

Zuengler, J., & Mori, J. (2002). Microanalyses of classroom discourse: A critical consideration of method: Introduction to the special issue. *Applied Linguistics, 22*(3), 283–288.

Language Learning   ISSN 0023-8333

If Language Is a Complex Adaptive System, What Is Language Assessment?

Robert J. Mislevy

University of Maryland

Chengbin Yin

Center for Applied Linguistics

Individuals' use of language in contexts emerges from second-to-second processes of activating and integrating traces of past experiences—an interactionist view compatible with the study of language as a complex adaptive system but quite different from the trait-based framework through which measurement specialists investigate validity, establish reliability, and ensure fairness of assessments. This article discusses assessment arguments from an interactionist perspective. We argue that the familiar concepts and methods of assessment that evolved under a trait perspective can be gainfully reconceived in terms of the finer-grained perspective of interactionism, and we illustrate how key ideas relate to familiar practices in language testing.

Introduction

An educational assessment embodies an argument from what we see people say, do, or make in a handful of particular situations, to inferences about their capabilities as more broadly construed. Although the visible elements of assessments such as tasks, scoring rubrics, and measurement models are familiar, it is a conception of capabilities that shapes their form and gives them meaning. Different conceptions give rise to markedly differently requirements

This article was presented at "Language as a Complex Adaptive System," an invited conference celebrating the 60th anniversary of *Language Learning*, at the University of Michigan, Ann Arbor, MI, November 7–9, 2008. The first author's work was supported by a grant from the Spencer Foundation.

Correspondence concerning this article should be addressed to Robert J. Mislevy, University of Maryland, 1230-C Benjamin, College Park, MD 20742. Internet: rmislevy@umd.edu

© 2009 Language Learning Research Club, University of Michigan

for what to observe and how to interpret it, in order to support markedly different claims about examinees (Mislevy, 2003, 2006; Mislevy, Steinberg, & Almond, 2003). This article considers implications for assessment of a conception of individuals' language capabilities from an interactionist perspective, a view aligned with research on language as a complex adaptive system (LaCAS; Beckner et al., this issue).

The following section reviews key ideas of interactionism, focusing on aspects that become important in assessments meant to support learning, evaluate capabilities, or make decisions about individuals' capabilities with respect to a given language. A framework for assessment arguments is then reviewed. Ways the interactionist perspective impacts assessment arguments and assessment use arguments are then discussed, drawing on current work in language testing (e.g., Chalhoub-Deville, 2003; Chapelle, 1998; Douglas, 1998, 2000).

LaCAS and an Interactionist Approach to Language Testing

Language as a CAS [complex adaptive system] involves the following key features: The system consists of multiple agents (the speakers in the speech community) interacting with one another. The system is adaptive—that is, speakers' behavior is based on their past interactions and current and past interactions together feed forward into future behavior. A speaker's behavior is the consequence of competing factors ranging from perceptual constraints to social motivations. The structures of language emerge from interrelated patterns of experience, social interaction, and cognitive mechanisms. (Beckner et al., this issue)

Studies of language as a complex adaptive system are an important contributor to an emerging integration of individual, situative, and social perspectives on cognition (Gee, 1992; Greeno, 1998). Although a review of this work is beyond the scope of the present article, this section summarizes key ideas and offers terminology in order to ground a discussion of language testing. There is broad agreement on a core set of ideas:

- Performances are composed of complex assemblies of component information-processing actions that are adapted to task requirements during performance. These moment-by-moment assemblies build on past experience and incrementally change capabilities for future action.
- A connectionist paradigm proves useful to frame the intrapersonal processes of learning, memory activation, and situated action. Not

coincidentally, this paradigm reflects neuropsychological research on the mechanisms through which brains accomplish these processes.

- The patterns through which people in communities interact shape individuals' learning, in all its linguistic, cultural, and substantive aspects. Intrapersonal learning is becoming attuned to extrapersonal patterns, in order to perceive, act in, and create situations.
- The extrapersonal patterns themselves evolve over time as individuals use them, extend them, and recombine them in novel ways. The connectionist paradigm can also be gainfully applied to study adaptations at this level.

This research holds profound implications for language testing, for it is from this perspective that we would want to design and use assessments. Language testing researchers are now seeking to develop conceptions and methodologies for language assessment that build from the start around the dynamic interaction among people, capabilities, and situations—what is called an *interactionist* approach to language testing (Bachman, 2007; Chalhoub-Deville, 2003; Chapelle, 1998). We draw on this research, as well as work in allied fields. Strauss and Quinn's (1997) cognitive theory of cultural meaning, Kintsch's (1998) construction-integration (CI) model of reading comprehension (representative from among many sources), and Young's (2002, 2008) notion of developing resources to participate in discursive practices prove useful for framing points in the discussion.

Strauss and Quinn (1997) highlighted the interplay between internal and external realms in the production of cultural, or extrapersonal, meanings. Cultural meanings (i.e., typical interpretations of an event or an object as invoked in a person) are created and maintained in such interactions in a community, the outcomes of which entail durability but allow for variation and change. Meanings are intersubjectively shared, in that people develop mental structures that, although unique in each individual, share salient aspects as their interpretation of the world develops under similar circumstances or as they need to communicate about shared experiences.

Kintsch's (1998) work dovetails with and further extends Strauss and Quinn's (1997) with regard to intrapersonal cognition. Kintsch represented knowledge as an associative net and relevant concepts as nodes. The *construction* processes activate an inconsistent, incoherent associative network on the basis of linguistic input, contextual factors, and the comprehender's knowledge base. Mutually reinforcing elements strengthen and isolated elements deactivate in the *integration* processes. The resulting "situation model" mediates understanding and action, akin to Fauconnier and Turner's (2002) notion of a "blended mental space." Kintsch argued that the CI paradigm applies more generally, so that an analogue of a situation model would build from cues and patterns (or models, as we will call them here) at all levels: linguistic, in terms of phonology, grammar, and conventions, and pragmatic, cultural, situational, and substantive.[1] We will use the abbreviation L/C/S models to stand collectively for linguistic, cultural, and substantive models.

More specifically in the context of language, Young (2000, 2008) described talk activities that people do as "discursive practices," the construction of which depends on a conglomeration of linguistic, interactional, and identity resources that enable "the ways in which participants construct interpersonal, experiential, and textual meanings in a practice" (Young, 2008, p. 71). The Strauss and Quinn (1997) and the Kintsch (1998) frameworks help us understand the nature of such resources. Developing them and being able to bring them to bear in appropriate situations is the goal of learning and what assessments are to provide information about (i.e., the inferential targets of assessment).

The Structure of Assessment Arguments

Explicating assessment as evidentiary argument brings out its underlying structure, clarifies the roles of the observable elements and processes, and guides the construction of tasks (Kane, 2006; Messick, 1994). The particular forms of the elements and processes will be shaped by a perspective on the nature of the knowledge, skills, or capabilities that are to be assessed. This section sketches that structure and, anticipating the contrast with assessment from an interactionist perspective, illustrates it with a simple example from discrete-points language testing.

Figure 1 is a of depiction Toulmin's (1958) schema for evidentiary reasoning. The *claim* (C) is a proposition that we wish to support with *data* (D). The arrow represents inference, which is justified by a *warrant* (W), a generalization that justifies the inference from the particular data to the particular claim. Theory and experience provide *backing* (B) for the warrant. In any particular case we may need to qualify our conclusions because of *alternative explanations* (A) for the data.

Figure 2 applies these ideas to assessment arguments (Mislevy, 2003, 2006). At the top appears a claim, justified by assessment data through a warrant. At the bottom is a student's action in a situation: The student says, does, or makes something, possibly extending over time, possibly interacting with others. Note that it is interpretations of the actions rather than the actions themselves that constitute data in an assessment argument, and these interpretations are

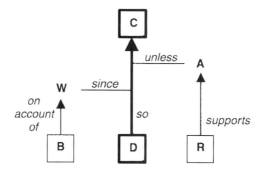

Figure 1 Toulmin's general structure for arguments.

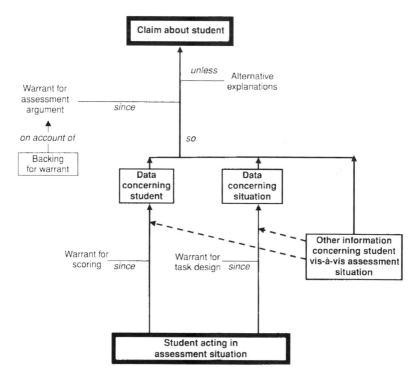

Figure 2 The structure of assessment arguments.

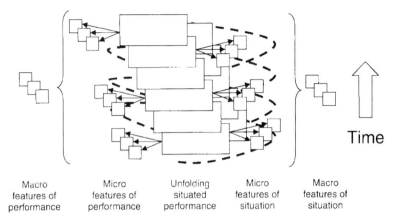

Time

Macro	Micro	Unfolding	Micro	Macro
features of	features of	situated	features of	features of
performance	performance	performance	situation	situation

Figure 3 Elaborated performance and data portion of assessment argument.

themselves inferences to be justified by warrants cast in a conception of knowledge and its use.

Figure 3 elaborates this region of the argument to bring out the interactive and evolving nature of situated action, to accommodate data that arise in more complex assessments. The situated performance is represented as a spiral through time, with arbitrary segments depicted (e.g., conversation turns, discourse topics, speech acts), because as the examinee (inter)acts, the situation evolves. The spiral indicates that the examinee's actions—and if other people are involved, their actions too, as represented by the gray rectangles—play a role in creating the situation in each next instant.

The assessment argument encompasses three kinds of data:

- aspects of the person's actions in the situation;
- aspects of the situation in which the person is acting;
- additional information about the person's history or relationship to the situation.

The last of these does not show up directly in the formal elements and processes of an assessment. We will see the crucial role that it plays in assessment from an interactionist perspective.

Figure 4 augments the assessment argument with an assessment use argument (Bachman, 2003). The *claim* of the assessment argument is *data* for the use argument. The claim of the use argument serves some educational purpose such as guiding learning, evaluating progress, or predicting performance in future (criterion) situations. In language testing, the criterion typically

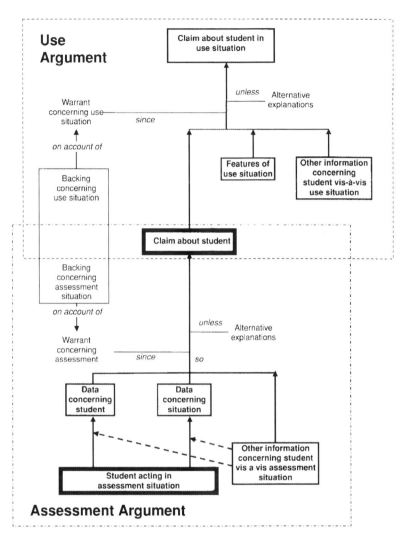

Figure 4 Toulmin diagram for assessment argument and assessment use argument combined.

concerns the use of language in particular kinds of real-world situations, or target language usage (TLU; Bachman & Palmer, 1996).

The simple example from a discrete-points grammar test illustrates these ideas. An examinee is asked to supply the form of an English verb in a sentence:

John _____ the apple yesterday.   [eat]

Context is minimal and performance is simple; the task is neither interactive nor purposeful. The task does, nevertheless, provide sufficient semantic and syntactic information to determine the targeted verb form (i.e., the data concerning the situation) and activate an aspect of English usage that is relevant in language use situations. An examinee's response of "ate" rather than "eated" provides evidence (i.e., the data concerning the performance) for a claim about the examinee's capabilities with regard to this point of grammar, although we will see that its force is limited under an interactionist perspective.

Assessment Arguments Through an Interactionist Lens

Characteristics of an interactionist perspective that hold implications for assessment are the interactive, constructive nature of language in use; the joint dependence of communication on many patterns, of many kinds, at many levels; and the dependence on previous personal experience to form long-term memory patterns that can be activated in relevant situations. Particular attention is accorded to the features of assessment situations and criterion situations in terms of L/C/S models they "should" evoke, in terms of the assessment purpose.

Illustrative Assessment Configurations

To ground a discussion of assessment from an interactionist perspective, we will consider the four typical configurations used in language testing listed below. These are not meant to be an exhaustive set of configurations or a taxonomy; they have been selected from among many possible assessment configurations because they are widely used and because they can be used to illustrate key issues in language testing from an interactionist perspective.

(C1) *Lean context, predetermined targets, to support learning.* Discrete-points tasks like "John _____ the apple yesterday" can be used to support instruction under the behaviorally cast "focus-on-forms" approach.

(C2) *Lean context, predetermined targets, for broad purposes.* Traditional language proficiency tests are large-scale, context-lean, minimally interactive, highly constrained by costs and logistics, and are meant to support broad and vaguely defined inferences. Examples include TOEFL and the Defense Language Proficiency Tests (DLPTs).

(C3) *Rich context, predetermined targets, for focused purposes.* This configuration is meant to support inferences about examinees' performance in more specified contexts. For example, the International Teaching Assistants Evaluation (ITAE) is used to qualify nonnative English speakers as teaching assistants at the University of Maryland.

(C4) *Rich context, opportunistic targets, to support learning.* Task-based language tests can be used in instructional settings to provide feedback and guide instruction for learners based on their unfolding performances. This strategy is related to the "focus-on-form" instructional approach. ITEA tasks can also be used in classroom to prepare students for the qualification examination.

A brief preliminary discussion of the first and second configurations from the perspective of behavioral and trait approaches to assessment follows immediately. New considerations that an interactionist perspective raises are then addressed and illustrated in further discussion of the second configuration and of the third and fourth configurations.

Configuration 1: Lean Context, Predetermined Targets, to Support Learning
The previous example with discrete-points language testing illustrates this configuration. Performance in a lean context provides evidence for determining whether the student has acquired the capability to carry out such tasks in previous equally lean and decontextualized learning situations or would benefit from additional practice. Although the behaviorist pedagogical approach can be debated, the "lean context, predetermined targets, to support learning" configuration clearly illustrates a coherent coupling of an assessment and a purpose.

Configuration 2: Lean Context, Predetermined Targets, for Broad Purposes
In this configuration, the assessment context is again lean, but the contexts of use for which inferences are intended are complex although vaguely specified: a variety of real-world language use situations as might be encountered in higher education in a North American university in the case of TOEFL, or in the case of the DLPTs, a range of settings encountered by military personnel in country, foreign service workers doing diplomatic or bureaucratic functions, or intelligence analysts. Every situation within these criterion settings draws upon not only linguistic but also cultural, social, and substantive patterns. Each is interactive in its own way, each involves its own goals and actors, and there are great variations among them.

For any particular criterion situation, then, much that determines success in that situation, in terms of other L/C/S models the examinee would need to bring to bear, will not be present in the assessment situation. Some make successful use of the targeted language models *more* likely (e.g., affinities with the situations in which they were learned and practiced), whereas some make successful use *less* likely (e.g., unfamiliar situations, high stress). The limitation arises from applying the same assessment evidence to all use situations—even when, from a formal view, it is common to them all—when it is stripped of the context of any of them.

From the perspective of educational and psychological measurement, the problem is *construct underrepresentation* with respect to any particular use situation. From the perspective of assessment arguments, it raises alternative explanations for both good and poor assessment performance as a prediction of performance in the use situations. From the interactionist perspective, the context lean assessment situations do not adequately reflect the language use situations that are of ultimate interest.

Explicating the Assessment Argument

"Person acting within situation" is the fundamental unit of analysis from an interactionist perspective (Chalhoub-Deville, 2003). Traditional assessment places the person in the foreground, in terms of theories of traits, although task design and response evaluation have always been integral to the enterprise. Viewing assessment in terms of interacting elements in an argument emphasizes their interconnectedness and co-equal status. Every element in an assessment argument and every relationship among elements can be viewed in terms of L/C/S models, to understand and guide the design and use of a test. Even though much of the machinery and methodology that evolved to serve assessment under the trait and behavioral perspectives can still be used, it can be reconceived in interactionist terms. It will not generally be feasible to comprehensively model all aspects of examinee capabilities, contextual features, and performances in full detail in practical assessment applications. This is as it should be, however, because models of perfect fidelity are not necessary for applied work at a higher level of analysis. As in any application of model-based reasoning, the question is not whether the model is a faithful representation of a phenomenon but whether the simpler modeled representation captures the right aspects for the purpose and under the constraints of the job at hand (Mislevy, 2009).

A claim in any assessment argument is based on observing a person act within a few particular situations, construed in a way meant to hold meaning beyond those situations. A claim cast in trait terms such as "control of grammar," "fluency," or "reading comprehension" foregrounds a characteristic of an individual, posited to characterize regularities in behavior over a range of situations (Messick, 1989) and hides the dependence on context. Reliability and generalizability studies first explore situations more or less like the testing situation and variations in examinees' actions across them (Cronbach, Gleser, Nanda, & Rajaratnam, 1972). Validity studies then examine intended use situations, which typically vary more widely, are more complex, and are not under the control of the examiner (Kane, 2006). Although context is in the background in the measurement tradition, analyses by practitioners and researchers to address both practical and theoretical problems address considerations that are important from an interactionist perspective; see, for example, Messick (1994) on design and validity in performance assessment and Bachman and Palmer's (1996) and Davidson and Lynch's (2002) analyses of task features.

Context

Task and test specifications address context to the extent that tasks exhibit relevant features, but they background the capabilities of persons to act in situations. L/C/S models connect the two and connect both to data concerning performances. *External* context refers to features of a situation as they are viewed from the outside by the assessor, through the lens of the relevant L/C/S models. The focus is on the L/C/S models in terms of which claims about examinee's capabilities are desired—that is, the features of the situation (some of which the assessment designer may have arranged, others of which arise through the examinee's interactions in the situation) that should activate appropriate actions on the part of the examinee.

Whether an observer will see such actions depends on the examinee's *internal* context, or the situation as she views it through the mental space she constructs (Wertsch, 1994). The examinee's actions are evaluated in terms of the targeted L/C/S models (e.g., appropriateness, effectiveness, fluency, correctness). The internal context the examinee constructed may or may not have incorporated the features that the assessor deems relevant, in terms of the targeted L/C/S models. Even when the examinee's situation model incorporates the salient features in targeted ways, the examinee might not act effectively or appropriately. Observable actions are imperfect indicators of the model that an examinee constructs in the task situation and are even more fallible as evidence about the situation model that the examinee might construct in a situation with different features.

Standard test analyses speak of examinees' capabilities in terms of how well they perform on some set of tasks and of task difficulties in terms of how well examinees do on them. These concepts serve well for sets of homogeneous context-lean tasks. Structured item response theory (IRT) analyses in these contexts add insight into the nature of proficiency by examining the features of tasks that make them difficult ("difficulty drivers") and the corresponding nature of capabilities that examinees are able to bring to bear on them. Such analyses examine task difficulties in terms of cognitively relevant features such as working memory load, number of steps required, and complexity of syntactic structures (Leighton & Gierl, 2007). This work exploits what Robinson's (2001) called "complexity factors" for reasoning in terms of a targeted set of L/C/S models: What features drive difficulty for examinees who act through these models?

Unidimensional analyses are less satisfactory for context-rich tasks that require a greater range of L/C/S models in coordinated use (Mislevy, Steinberg, & Almond, 2002). Tasks can differ in difficulty in the traditional sense (e.g., percents correct) for different reasons, but what makes a task difficult for one examinee may not be the same as what makes it difficult for another. Beyond complexity factors, another factor contributing to difficulty is whether a given examinee happens to have experience with and can activate relevant knowledge and actions. Robinson (2001) called these "difficulty factors." What makes medical knowledge tasks in German difficult for German medical students is the medical knowledge, but what makes them difficult for American doctors studying German is the German language. This variation, systematic though it is, constitutes noise or error through the lens of a unidimensional proficiency model.

Two ways that assessors can deal with complex tasks are design and analysis (Mislevy et al., 2002). Design strategies call for principled patterning of features in tasks. Analysis strategies use multivariate models to sort out different sources of difficulty among tasks and correspondingly different profiles of capabilities among examinees. We reiterate that exhaustive analysis of all features of task situations and all aspects of capabilities in terms of L/C/S models is not possible. The features to model are the ones that are most pertinent to the L/C/S models that are the focus of claims. We see next that many features of models need not be modeled in practice when task situations, use situations, and examinee characteristics are matched appropriately.

Conditional Inference

What makes medical knowledge tasks in German difficult is different for German medical students than for American doctors learning German, even when both groups face identical tasks with identical constellations of features. However, if the assessor knows that all of the examinees are American doctors studying German, she can rule out the alternative explanation of poor performance being caused by an examinee's lack of medical knowledge. Performance then grounds claims about these examinees in terms of German proficiency conditional on medical knowledge. If the assessor knows that examinees in another group are German medical students, the same tasks can ground claims about medical knowledge conditional on German proficiency. This simple example offers important insights:

- An assessor's prior knowledge about the relationship between the task demands and the capabilities of an examinee plays a role in an assessment argument.
- This information is not part of the task situations per se but a condition of the assessor's state of knowledge. Assessors with different knowledge (teachers vs. state school officers) would be able to draw different inferences from the same data and would be vulnerable to different alternative explanations.
- This knowledge does not appear in analytic models for assessment data, such as student variables in measurement models, yet it is integral to the variables' situated meanings.
- Tasks alone do not determine "what a test measures," but also the assessor's prior knowledge of capabilities that examinees are able bring to bear in what kinds of circumstances, on which they can condition inference.

The inferential burden of the examiner using complex tasks is simplified when it is known or can be arranged that certain demands of tasks, in terms of L/C/S models that are not the primary focus, are within the capabilities of an examinee. Even though the tasks may be demanding with respect to these capabilities, the examiner's knowledge allows inference to be conditional on their possession. Measurement models need not have student variables for these capabilities, although the meaning of the variables that *are* in the model is now conditional on them. Configurations 3 and 4, discussed later, take fuller advantage of conditional inference than Configuration 2.

Configuration 2, Continued: Lean Context, Predetermined Targets, for Broad Purposes

Consider again the configuration that produces, for example, language tests called reading, writing, speaking, and listening proficiency. Examinees use targeted language structures and strategies to achieve limited task goals, in lean contexts and with little interaction. The validity of the assessment use argument concerns the extent to which an examinee might bring similar language structures and strategies to bear in TLU situations. We can analyze this situation with Messick's (1994) conceptions of construct underrepresentation and construct-irrelevant variance, developed under a trait perspective but now viewed in terms of L/C/S models.

Construct underrepresentation occurs when "the test is too narrow and fails to include important dimensions or facets of the construct" (Messick, 1989, p. 34). This description comports with recognizing that task situations do not involve key features of TLU situations that would require a person to activate and act through relevant L/C/S models. That a person can activate and interact through appropriate models in the task situation does not guarantee that she will do so in the TLU situation. Conversely, decontextualization and abstraction in the task situation can fail to provide the cues that would activate targeted capabilities in the TLU situation. People struggle with proportional reasoning test items, yet carry out procedures that embody the same structures when they buy groceries (Lave, 1988). This is unsurprising from an interactionist perspective. It constitutes an alternative explanation in an assessment argument for success in a criterion TLU situation despite failure in simpler task situations that are formally equivalent.

Construct-irrelevant sources of variance arise from features of the task situation that are not reflected in the criterion situation. They can render success on tasks more likely or less likely than in the criterion situation, due, again, to mismatches in constellations of features across situations and the L/C/S models the tasks activate in examinees. Task features that make success more likely include familiarity with formats, cues, and social contextualization. Task features that make success less likely include demands for specialized L/C/S models not needed in criterion situations (e.g., a computer interface) and lack of context, motivation, interaction, meaningfulness, or feedback that a criterion situation would have.

The way forward, Chalhoub-Deville (2003) asserted, is examining which patterns of behavior are robust, both across and within persons. Which test situations call for L/C/S models and evoke performances that are likely to be similarly evoked in what kinds of criterion situations by which examinees? How does variation in criterion performance for a given individual vary with what kinds of task features (generalizability) and what kinds of criterion features (validity)?

Configuration 3: Rich Context, Predetermined Targets, for Focused Purposes

Tests of language for special purposes (LSP; Douglas, 1998, 2000) start from the desire to predict use of language in specific TLU situations: "If we want to know how well individuals can use language in specific contexts of use, we will require a measure that takes into account both their language knowledge and their background knowledge" (Douglas, 2000, p. 282). Thus, more is known about the features of the TLU situations in terms of required patterns of inter-action, genres and conventions, sociocultural considerations, and substantive knowledge. LSP tests intentionally include features that mirror those of TLU situations, to require the joint application of L/C/S models that are required in those situations. When language rules are addressed in these tests, they are in fact interlocked with a language user's knowledge of when, where, and with whom to use them, to paraphrase Rod Ellis (1985, p. 77).

As an example, the University of Maryland uses the ITAE (Maryland English Institute, 2008) to determine whether nonnative English-speaking grad-uate students can carry out the duties of a graduate teaching assistant. It includes an oral interview, a dictation listening test, and a 10-min "microteaching pre-sentation." Although the interview and dictation test are similar to broad pro-ficiency tests, the situations and topics concern the university teaching context and language use in that context. For the microteaching presentation,

> the examinee explains a principle or a central concept in the field in which s/he is most likely to teach. . . . The examinee selects the topic. The presentation should be delivered as though to a class of undergraduate students who have no substantial knowledge of the concept. In the final 2–3 minutes of the allotted time, evaluators and others ask questions related to the presentation. (Maryland English Institute, 2008).

Language for special purposes tests employ features that emulate the sit-uations and purposes with the aim of evoking the knowledge and interaction patterns of TLUs. In Toulmin's (1958) argument terminology, alternative ex-planations for both good and poor performance caused by mismatches of L/C/S demands are reduced and the argument from observed performance in the test situation to likely performance in the criterion situation is strengthened. In Messick's (1989) validity terminology, invalidity due to construct underrep-resentation is reduced. In interactionist terminology, the stronger similarities between the task situations and criterion situations make it more likely that an examinee will activate and act through targeted L/C/S models in both situations or will not do so in both situations.

This configuration illustrates a point concerning conditional inference. An LSP test requires capability to use language in a specified space of contexts, and demonstrating that capability jointly requires knowledge of substance, practices, conventions, and modes of interaction in those contexts. Deficiencies in any of these areas can lead to poor performance. The nature of the claims that can be made about an examinee from performance in LSP tests depends materially on the assessor's information about the examinee's capabilities with regard to these considerations—specifically, about the examinee's familiarity, through experience, with such contexts in respects other than the focal capabilities. For example, when the ITEA is used to qualify nonnative English speakers as graduate assistants, all of the examinees are known to have expertise in their substantive area. They are familiar with the contexts, mores, genres, and interactional patterns of academic situations, at least in the language in which they studied, including lectures of the type they are asked to present in their microteaching sessions. Choice of topic eliminates lack of substantive knowledge as an alternative explanation of poor performance. The claim is thus about using English to produce and deliver familiar academic material in a familiar situation. Both the assessment situation and the TLU situation are complex, but the examinees' capabilities with many of essential aspects of the situations are known a priori to the assessor and matched in the test design.

Configuration 4: Rich Context, Opportunistic Targets, to Support Learning

The final assessment configuration is using context-rich tasks in instructional settings, to support students' learning with individualized feedback. As an example, we consider task situations that are essentially equivalent to ITEA microteaching tasks, except employed in instructional sessions that help examinees who did not pass prepare for a retake. The same task situations, the same performances, and the same matchups among examinees' histories, test situations, and criterion situations remain in place.

Because the purposes and the claims they entail differ, the assessment arguments differ. They differ in a way that can be understood in terms of examinees' capabilities to instantiate and act through the L/C/S models that are appropriate to the task and criterion situations. When the microteaching task is used to screen graduate teaching assistants, only overall performance is reported. Because content expertise and situational familiarity were known a priori, it can be presumed that improving performance is not be a matter of, say, learning more about physics or criminology or the semiformal and minimally interactive lecture format. Rather the sources of poor performance could include incomprehensibility, particular distracting lexical or syntactic problems, or an inability to marshal resources in the lecture context. Any of these by themselves or in combination produce a failing ITEA score.

"Opportunistic targets" means that the claims of the assessment argument are constructed in response to each examinee's performance. What specifically leads to unsuccessful communication for this particular examinee in this particular performance? Are there problems with prosody or pacing? Is

there distracting use of tenses, such as "John eated the apple yesterday"? The examinee's particular difficulties in this performance determine feedback and instruction for that examinee. The student's attention will be called to those aspects of English usage, as it is used in these situations and how it helps shape meaning in them, where it appears that targeted experience will improve her capabilities. As such, this assessment configuration and use exemplifies the "focus-on-form" instructional strategy in second language acquisition (Long, 1988).

Conclusion

If language is a complex adaptive system, what is language assessment? Language assessment is gathering observable evidence to ground inferences about individuals' capabilities to use language in real-world, interactive, constructive situations, where the elements of the assessment argument are conceived, related to one another, and purposefully designed. This article sketches a way of thinking about language testing that is compatible with research on both language and on assessment. It provides a finer-grained and more situated understanding of the models and methods of the educational/psychological measurement tradition that guide practical applications. To flesh out the sketch, more detailed explication is required to connect the higher level, more coarsely grained narrative space of educational and psychological assessment with the lower level, finer-grained narrative space of the interactionist perspective. Worked-through examples with specific tests, in terms of specific linguistic/cultural/substantive models, are needed.

Revised version accepted 9 June 2009

Note

1 By substantive, we mean the knowledge and activity patterns related to the substance of an activity, such as cars, cooking, video games, interpersonal relationships, or any of the myriad domains in which people engage.

References

Bachman, L. F. (2003). Building and supporting a case for test use. *Language Assessment Quarterly. 2*, 1–34.
Bachman, L. F. (2007). What is the construct? The dialectic of abilities and contexts in defining constructs in language assessment. In J. Fox, M. Wesche, & D. Bayliss

(Eds.), *Language testing reconsidered* (pp. 41–71). Ottawa, Canada: University of Ottawa Press.

Bachman, L., & Palmer, A. S. (1996). *Language testing in practice: Designing and developing useful language tests.* Oxford: Oxford University Press.

Chalhoub-Deville, M. (2003). Second language interaction: Current perspectives and future trends. *Language Testing, 20,* 369–383.

Chapelle, C. (1998). Construct definition and validity inquiry in SLA research. In L. F. Bachman & A. D. Cohen (Eds.), *Interfaces between second language acquisition and language testing research* (pp. 32–70). New York: Cambridge University Press.

Cronbach, L. J., Gleser, G. C., Nanda, H., & Rajaratnam, N. (1972). *The dependability of behavioral measurements: Theory of generalizability for scores and profiles.* New York: Wiley.

Davidson, F., & Lynch, B. K. (2002). *Testcraft: A teacher's guide to writing and using language test specifications.* New Haven, CT: Yale University Press.

Douglas, D. (1998). Testing methods and context-based second language research. In L. F. Bachman & A. D. Cohen (Eds.), *Interfaces between second language acquisition and language testing research* (pp. 141–155). New York: Cambridge University Press.

Douglas, D. (2000). *Assessing language for specific purposes.* Cambridge: Cambridge University Press.

Ellis, R. (1985). *Understanding second language acquisition.* Oxford: Oxford University Press.

Fauconnier, G., & Turner, M. (2002). *The way we think.* New York: Basic Books.

Gee, J. P. (1992). *The social mind: Language, ideology, and social practice.* New York: Bergin & Garvey.

Greeno, J. G. (1998). The situativity of knowing, learning, and research. *American Psychologist, 53,* 5–26.

Kane, M. (2006). Validation. In R. J. Brennan (Ed.), *Educational measurement* (4th ed., pp. 18–64). Westport, CT: Praeger.

Kintsch, W. (1998). *Comprehension: A paradigm for cognition.* New York: Cambridge University Press.

Lave, J. (1988). *Cognition in practice.* New York: Cambridge University Press.

Leighton, J. P., & Gierl, M. J. (Eds.). (2007). *Cognitive diagnostic assessment: Theories and applications.* Cambridge: Cambridge University Press.

Long, M. H. (1988). Instructed interlanguage development. In L. M. Beebe (Ed.), *Issues in second language acquisition: Multiple perspectives* (pp. 115–141). Cambridge, MA: Newbury House/Harper and Row.

Maryland English Institute (2008). *ITA evaluation.* College Park, MD: Author. Retrieved July 2, 2008, from http://international.umd.edu/mei/572

Messick, S. (1989). Validity. In R.L. Linn (Ed.), *Educational measurement* (3rd ed., pp. 13–103). New York: American Council on Education/Macmillan.

Messick, S. J. (1994). The interplay of evidence and consequences in the validation of performance assessments. *Educational Researcher, 23*(2), 13–23.

Mislevy, R. J. (2003). Substance and structure in assessment arguments. *Law, Probability, and Risk, 2,* 237–258.

Mislevy, R. J. (2006). Cognitive psychology and educational assessment. In R. L. Brennan (Ed.), *Educational measurement* (4th ed., pp. 257–305). Westport, CT: American Council on Education/Praeger Publishers.

Mislevy, R. J. (2009). Validity from the perspective of model-based reasoning. In R. L. Lissitz (Ed.), *The concept of validity: Revisions, new directions and applications* (pp. 83–108). Charlotte, NC: Information Age Publishing.

Mislevy, R. J., Steinberg, L. S., & Almond, R. A. (2002). Design and analysis in task-based language assessment. *Language Assessment, 19,* 477–496.

Mislevy, R. J., Steinberg, L. S., & Almond, R. G. (2003). On the structure of educational assessments. *Measurement: Interdisciplinary Research and Perspectives, 1,* 3–67.

Robinson, P. (2001). Task complexity, task difficulty, and task production: Exploring interactions in a componential framework. *Applied Linguistics, 22,* 27–57.

Strauss, C., & Quinn, N. (1997). *A cognitive theory of cultural meaning.* Cambridge: Cambridge University Press.

Toulmin, S. E. (1958). *The uses of argument.* Cambridge: Cambridge University Press.

Wertsch, J. V. (1994). The primacy of mediated action in sociocultural studies. *Mind, Culture, and Activity, 1*(4), 202–208.

Young, R. F. (2000, March). *Interactional competence: Challenges for validity.* Paper presented at the annual meeting of the American Association for Applied Linguistics and the Language Testing Research Colloquium, Vancouver, BC, Canada.

Young, R. F. (2008). *Language and interaction: An advanced resource book.* New York: Routledge.

Subject Index

abstraction of regularity, 9, 92
action control, 233
acts of meaning, 206, 207,
    214, 223
adaptation, 18, 162, 164, 188-189,
    193-194, 199, 201, 239
adaptation of language, 188
adaptive structure, 187, 189, 202
adaptive variation, 213
affect, 1, 2, 13, 32, 49, 59, 86, 109,
    129, 137, 151, 192, 234, 235
agent, 13-15, 48, 51, 65, 70, 83-86,
    99, 163, 188, 230, 231, 236-238,
    240, 243-244
agent-based framework, 13,
    230-231, 243
agent-based model, 14, 51
analyzability, 33, 35, 38
apes, 162, 175-179
apparent design, 189, 199
appearance semantics, 118
appearance trials, 71, 72,
    74, 76
appraisal, 233, 234
aptitude complexes, 235
architectural constraint, 133
arcuate fasciculus, 172
argument structure
    construction, 70, 95
arguments, 31, 65, 67, 70-71, 78,
    80-83, 85, 87, 97, 241, 249-250,
    252, 258, 264
    assessment, 39, 249- 259,
        261-262, 264-265
    assessment use, 254, 255, 261
artificial language learning, 189
assessment configurations, 256
associative learning, 10, 92, 93, 99
asymmetry, 176

attention, 10-12, 16-17, 41, 60, 72,
    80, 93, 173, 178, 231, 234, 237,
    256, 265
    automaticity, 93
    blocking, 93
    transfer, 84, 93, 167
autonomy, 29, 34

basal ganglia, 177, 180
behavioral flexibility, 168
biological evolution, 163-164,
    188-189, 201-202
blended mental space see also
    situation model
bottleneck, 188, 197-200, 202
brain size, 18, 166-171, 173, 175, 180
brain stem, 179

categorization, 3, 7, 8, 11, 17, 27-32,
    34-35, 42, 65, 81, 91, 109, 115,
    219
category learning, 10, 95, 118
cause-effect relations, 239
cerebellum, 177, 178, 180
cerebral, 172, 177, 179
change, 2, 5, 7, 9, 11-18, 27-36, 38,
    42, 47-51, 58, 60-61, 163, 164,
    180, 195, 200, 202, 203, 209, 217,
    239-240, 242-243, 250-251
Chaos/complexity theory (CCT), 91
child language acquisition, 9, 18, 95
chunking, 17, 27-32, 42-43
chunks, 6, 30-31, 43, 109
cline of instantiation, 207, 208, 213
co-adaptation, 90-91, 95, 108-109,
    118, 162
coalescent tree, 193, 195
cognition, 2, 43, 90-91, 166,
    234-236, 239, 250

cognitive linguistics, 2, 11, 15, 48, 92
collexeme strength, 106, 108
community, 2, 9, 12-14, 48, 51, 53-61, 230-240, 251
competing influences, 28
competition, 13, 16, 189, 199
complex prepositions, 27, 29, 33, 36, 42, 43
complex recursion
  center-embedding, 126-130, 134-137, 146, 149, 152, 153
  cross-dependency, 126, 135-137
complexity theory, 238, 239
compositionality, 187, 192, 194, 196, 198, 200, 203
comprehension, 48, 64-69, 78, 83-85, 93, 99, 106, 107, 108, 129, 151, 177, 197, 251, 258
conceptual complexity, 162
conditional entropy, 196, 197
conditional inference, 261, 263
connectionism, 126
connectionist model, 110, 126, 131, 141
constituency, 27-29, 32, 38-43, 109, 132
constituent structure, 27-29, 31-33, 38, 41, 42
construals, 5, 10, 109
construct underrepresentation, 258, 261, 263
construct-irrelevant sources of variance, 262
construction, 5, 8, 10, 15, 64, 67-86, 90, 92, 93, 96-97, 99, 100, 102-113, 115, 118, 128, 147, 218, 224- 225, 251-252
construction archipelago, 90
construction learning, 67, 78, 86, 92
constructions (novel), 68
context, 3, 7, 8, 10, 28, 34, 38, 42, 48, 60, 69, 79, 93, 110-115, 130-136, 142, 158, 167, 174, 207-208, 213-214, 219-220, 224,

230-232, 236-239, 242- 243, 244, 252, 256-260, 262-264
  external, 110, 137, 144, 164, 181, 220, 222, 239, 251
  internal, 15-17, 27, 32-33, 38-40, 110-113, 115, 133, 171, 181, 222, 239, 251, 259
  lean, 256-259, 261
  rich, 18, 42, 91, 170, 181, 222, 260, 264
context of use-tenor, 207, 225
contingency of form-meaning-use mapping, 90
cooperative activity, 3, 4
coordination device, 4, 5
coordination problems, 4
corpus analysis, 3
corpus linguistics, 92, 93
cortex, 162, 170, 172-177, 179-180
  Area 10, 173
  association, 12, 33, 38, 41, 77, 99, 102, 106, 169, 170, 199
  Broca's, 172
  cingulate, 179
  dorsal stream, 175
  frontal, 171, 176
  occipital, 171, 175
  parietal, 171, 175
  planum temporale, 176
  prefrontal, 162, 172-174, 180
  premotor, 170
  primary auditory, 170, 175-176, 179
  primary motor, 170
  primary sensory, 170
  primary visual, 170, 175
  somatosensory, 170, 171
  temporal, 8, 110, 171-173, 175-176, 178-180, 221, 232
  ventral stream, 175
  Wernicke's, 172
criterion, 59, 254, 256, 257, 262, 263, 264
  features, 1, 2, 51, 69, 97, 99, 115, 171, 191, 194, 214, 218, 232,

250, 254, 256, 258-260, 262,
263
performance, 30, 64, 68, 70. 71,
73-77, 83, 126, 127, 129-130,
133-134, 136, 137, 149, 153,
157, 233, 250, 254, 256,
258-265
situations, 5, 9, 236, 237, 249, 251,
252, 254, 255, 256, 257, 258,
259, 260, 261, 262, 263, 264,
265
cross-linguistic influence, 10
cross-linguistic variation, 13
cultural change, 51, 164
cultural conventions, 50
cultural evolution, 9, 163, 165, 187,
188, 200
cultural transmission, 187, 200

depth of recursion, 129, 131, 137,
140, 142
design, 74, 76, 77, 200, 202, 242,
251, 258-260, 264
strategies, 219, 225, 231, 233, 234,
260-261
diachrony, 7
diffusion chains, 189
discursive practices, 251, 252
doing, 43, 164, 220, 233, 243. 257
dynamic interactions, 91, 110
dynamic system, 16, 28, 231, 233,
238, 239, 240, 241, 242, 243, 244
Dynamic systems theory (DST), 91

education, 40, 151, 218-223, 239,
257
educational assessment, 249
emergence, 2, 11, 36, 38, 54, 90, 92,
102, 106, 109, 110, 113, 115,
118-119, 188, 191, 196, 200, 202,
215
Emergentism, 238
emotion, 171, 234, 235
enabling, 217, 220, 225
encephalization quotient (EQ), 166

English, 124
evidentiary argument, 252
evolution, 1, 2, 3, 12, 17, 18, 47, 49,
54, 60, 118, 152, 162-181,
188-189, 193, 196, 201, 206, 217
brain, 17, 18, 91, 118, 162-181
co-evolution, 162
costs, 166, 256
cultural, 3, 9, 13, 18, 50, 51,
162-165, 187, 188, 200, 201,
236, 251, 252, 257, 265
language, 1-18, 27-30, 31, 32, 38,
42, 47-51, 53, 58-61, 65-68, 77,
78, 83, 84, 90-92, 93, 95-96,
99-100, 109-111, 115, 118,
126-127, 129, 131, 135, 149,
151, 152, 162-181, 187- 202,
206-209, 212-220, 222-225,
230-235, 238-244, 249-265
evolutionary model, 48
exemplar models, 31
exemplars, 7, 31, 67-72, 79, 86,
90-92, 95, 99, 106 109, 118
exploring, 86, 218, 220, 222, 225
expounding, 218, 220, 222, 225
expressivity, 191
extrapersonal patterns, 251

factors, 2, 3, 11, 15, 16, 27, 29, 32,
33, 42, 48, 56, 57, 65, 66, 75, 86,
90, 92, 93, 99, 109, 110, 115, 118,
181, 202, 231, 232, 235-240, 243,
244, 250, 251, 260
complexity, 11, 12, 18, 92, 131,
134, 135, 139, 140, 144,
149-151, 168, 174, 181, 206,
214, 225, 236, 237-240,
241-244, 260
difficulty, 53, 134, 135, 136, 237,
238, 260
first language acquisition, 86
fitness, 47, 49, 50, 61, 163
forced-choice, 64, 67
form-focus, 12

frequency, 5, 8, 10, 11, 15, 17, 30, 33, 49-81, 90-100, 102, 106-113, 118, 158, 193-195, 209
frequency distribution, 52, 81, 90, 92, 99, 100, 102, 106, 109, 113
type-token frequency, 101, 118
frontal lobe, 176

generality, 93, 106, 109, 118, 128
generalizability, 259, 262
generalization, 32, 36, 83, 91, 131, 132, 149, 252
generative linguistics, 188, 230
grammar, 5-8, 13, 14, 18, 27-28, 31, 42, 48, 65-66, 93, 110, 126, 127, 129, 131-139, 157, 170, 216, 219, 224, 252, 255-256, 258
grammatical prediction error (GPE), 134
grammaticality judgments, 149
grammaticality rating, 134, 135, 150, 153
grammaticalization, 3, 5, 7, 8, 18, 28, 32, 36
grounding, 111, 176
group size, 168

hemisphere (left, right), 172
higher cognitive function, 178
homonymy, 12
homologies/homologs, 165
human evolution, 167, 172, 173, 176, 180, 181

idiolect, 14, 15, 16
indeterminacy of communication, 5
individual difference factor, 243
inference, 8, 37, 252, 261
inherent variability, 214
innate, 9, 27, 65, 66, 83, 86, 127, 168, 189, 201
innate mapping theories, 83
integration, 151, 166, 171, 250, 251
interaction, 1-4, 9, 10, 15, 17, 18, 50-56, 59, 74, 76, 90-92, 106, 109,

133, 206, 214, 230, 232, 235, 237-241, 243-244, 251, 261, 262, 263
interactionism, 249, 250
interactor, 47, 49, 50, 53, 54, 57, 60-61
interactor selection, 49, 50, 53, 57, 60
intrapersonal, 250, 251
intrapersonal cognition, 251
intrinsic constraint, 126, 127, 153
intrinsic diversity, 15
islands, 90, 92, 97-99, 106-109, 115, 118
item response theory, 259
iterated learning, 187-189, 193, 200-202
iterative recursion
left-branching, 127, 128, 131, 142, 143, 152
right branching, 128

joint attention, 4, 15

language, 1-18, 27-32, 38, 42, 47-51, 53, 58-61, 65-68, 77-78, 83-84, 90-93, 95- 96, 99, 100, 109-118, 126-129, 131, 135, 149, 151-152, 162-181, 187-209, 212-214, 216-220, 222-225, 230-232, 235, 238-241, 243-244, 249, 250-265
language aptitude, 231, 232
Language Learning, 11, 77, 110, 200, 207, 213, 217, 219, 223, 225, 238, 244
language processing, 7, 127, 131, 149, 152, 171, 172, 177, 178, 180
language testing, 249-257, 265
learnability, 190-192, 214
learning, 10-12, 48, 64-70, 74, 77-80, 82- 86, 90-95, 99, 109-115, 118, 126, 127, 133, 149, 162, 163, 167, 168, 178, 188-193, 199-201, 206, 207, 214-225, 231-233, 237, 240, 242, 250, 251, 252, 254, 256, 257, 260, 264

learning biases, 201
learning error, 191
learning strategies, 231
learning styles, 231
lexicogrammatical resources, 215
limbic system, 171
lingueme, 13
linguistic conventions, 5
linguistic experience, 31, 126,
 127, 151
linking pattern, 64, 66, 78-80, 82-84
linking rules, 64-66, 67, 71, 77, 78,
 80-84
local leader, 60
localization, 170
locative-theme, 70, 78
longitudinal research, 242

making meaning, 207
mapping generalizations, 65, 66, 67
mapping trials, 71, 73-77
mathematical model, 12, 17, 47, 49,
 50, 60, 201
meaning element, 195, 196, 198,
 199, 200
meaning element variants, 196
meaning inference, 202
meaning potential, 206-209, 213,
 214, 217, 219, 223- 225
meaning space, 191
memory, 16, 18, 30, 48, 57-59, 68,
 127, 129, 137, 144, 149, 151, 165,
 173, 178, 250, 256, 260
memory limitations, 127, 129, 144
micro-discursive encounters, 91
midbrain, 178, 179
mixed methods research, 242
modeling, 2, 3, 7, 12, 13, 14, 15, 47,
 50, 51, 188, 209, 233, 240, 242,
 243
 computational, 3
 connectionist, 90, 92, 109,
  110, 115, 118, 126, 130, 131,
  136, 141, 142, 149, 151, 250,
  251

mathematical, 12, 13, 17, 47, 49,
 50, 53, 57, 60, 201, 242
Monte-Carlo analysis, 197
motivation, 231-240, 262
multilingual meaning
 potential, 223
multiple agents, 1, 2, 47, 250
multiword units/
 sequences, 29
mutual information, 6

natural selection, 14, 189, 201
neocortex, 169, 171, 178
nested structure, 30, 33
network, 5, 28, 31-34, 54-60, 92,
 110-112, 115, 130-137, 139, 142,
 152, 157, 174, 190, 251
network architecture, 32, 111
neural network, 234
neutral evolution
 (genetic drift), 47, 49
neutral interactor selection, 47, 50,
 51, 53, 56-59
new-dialect formation, 12, 59, 60

perception, 11, 12, 40, 48, 51,
 165, 178
perceptual saliency, 11
performance, 30, 64, 68- 77, 83, 126,
 127, 129-137, 149, 153, 157, 233,
 250, 254, 256, 258-260, 262, 264,
 265
phase transitions, 16, 17
phonological erosion, 12
phrase structure rules, 27, 32
phylogenetic descent, 193
pidgins and creoles, 11
population genetics, 61
possessive genitives, 131, 142, 144
preadaptation, 165
prefabricated sequence, 6
prepositional phrase (PP), 33
prestige, 49, 57-61
processing difficulty, 126, 136, 137,
 141-144, 146, 149, 151

production, 4, 15, 16, 48, 53, 60, 64,
65, 67, 78-85, 129, 151, 165,
177-179, 197, 199, 251
propagation, 49, 50, 53
prosody, 176, 264
protolanguage, 207, 214, 215
prototypicality, 90, 92, 93, 97, 102,
106, 109, 118
psycholinguistics, 2, 11, 93, 95, 128
purposes, 31, 92, 152, 225, 256, 262,
263, 264
broad, 18, 42, 108, 163, 166, 236,
237, 238, 250, 256, 263
focused, 41, 100, 188, 231, 256

qualitative research, 242
quantitative research, 241

random initial language, 191
randomness, 49
reanalysis, 27, 28, 29, 32, 33,
34, 38
recency, 10
recommending, 220
recreating, 220
recursion, 126-131, 134, 136-137,
141-143, 149, 151, 152, 165
recursive construction, 127, 130,
134-139, 151
recursive structure, 126, 127, 129,
137, 142, 149, 151
register, 212, 213, 219, 225
registerial repertoire, 213, 216, 217,
222, 223, 225
registerial variation, 213
regularity, 4, 189, 196, 200
relative clauses, 128, 129, 131, 151
reliability of form-meaning-use
mapping, 99
replication, 9, 48, 49, 50, 193,
194, 199
replicator, 47, 49, 50, 57, 61
replicator selection, 47, 49, 50, 61
reporting, 209, 212, 213, 220, 221,
225

salience, 10, 12, 16, 93, 199
schema, 90, 91, 92, 97, 102, 106,
115, 252
schematic meaning, 93, 102
school, 13, 15, 18, 124, 158, 216,
218, 220, 221, 222, 224, 225, 261
second language acquisition
(SLA), 10
selection, 6, 9, 47-50, 54, 57, 60,
164, 174, 177, 178, 199, 202,
209, 237
selection mechanisms, 49, 50, 57, 60
semantics, 18, 38, 39, 41, 42, 43,
65, 66, 68, 86, 97, 102, 106,
108-113, 118, 163, 170, 175,
176, 180, 216, 224
sentence processing, 126, 129-130,
131, 136, 137, 142, 144, 149
sequential learning, 13, 17, 30
sequential processing, 8
shared cognition, 3
shared cooperative action, 4
sharing, 16, 220, 245
signal segment, 196, 197, 199
signal segment variants, 196
simple recurrent network (SRN), 110
situated action, 250, 254
situations, 5, 9, 236, 237, 249-265
assessment, 39, 249-265
criterion, 59, 254, 256, 257,
262-264

target language usage (TLU), 255
task, 64, 67, 130, 131, 140, 167,
233, 234, 242, 250, 253,
256-264
use, 1, 2, 5, 7-16, 33, 34, 37-40,
49-50, 53, 54-57, 60, 61, 65, 69,
78, 79, 81, 85, 91, 92, 93, 97,
100-118, 126, 135, 139, 145,
152, 157, 165, 180, 188, 189,
196, 199, 207, 212-214, 218,
220, 233, 235, 238, 240, 244,
249-252, 254-257-265
skewed input, 69

social environment, 164, 235, 236,
    244
social identity, 9, 236
social interaction, 2, 3, 10, 15, 17, 18,
    92, 168, 173, 180, 235, 250
social motivations, 2, 237, 250
social network, 13, 14, 17, 50, 51, 57,
    231, 237
social network structure, 13, 14, 57,
    237
social status, 48, 202
sociality, 168, 180
sociolinguistics, 2, 11, 48
socio-semiotic process, 220
spatial, 171, 176, 178
speaker, 2, 4-6, 13-15, 28, 29, 37, 43,
    50-58, 92, 93, 100, 106, 230, 237,
    240, 250
speech, 1, 2, 4, 6, 7, 14, 41, 43, 48,
    51, 52, 60, 90, 92, 95, 96, 100,
    106, 107, 128, 133, 151, 171, 178,
    180, 224, 250, 254
speech community, 1, 4, 14, 48, 52,
    60, 92, 250
statistical mechanics, 51
syntactic bootstrapping, 65, 66
syntactic constituents, 29, 83
syntactic coordination, 95
syntactic tests, 39, 42
syntax, 18, 28, 29, 39, 65, 66, 68, 77,
    84, 86, 163, 173, 177, 180, 189
syntax-semantics mapping, 65, 77,
    84, 86
systematicity, 200
Systemic Functional Linguistics
    (SFL), 206
systemic memory, 212, 214

targets, 256, 257, 264
    inferential targets, 252
    opportunistic targets, 257
    pre-determined targets, 256
task, 64, 67, 130, 131, 140, 167,
    233-234, 242, 250, 253, 256,
    258-264

task demands, 261
task design, 253, 258
task processing, 233, 234
temporal lobe, 171, 175, 176,
    179, 180
test lag, 73, 75, 76
text score, 210
text unfolding, 207
thalamus, 177
theme-locative, 70, 78
thinking for speaking, 11
timing, 178
topicalized transitive, 85
Toulmin's schema
    alternative explanations, 84, 252,
        261, 263
    backing, 252
    data, 7, 9, 12-14, 27, 39, 40-42, 54,
        55, 59, 60, 64, 66, 67, 73, 75,
        78, 81-83, 86, 99, 102, 106, 108,
        112, 113, 126, 129, 130, 135,
        137, 147, 149, 151, 152, 172,
        173, 175, 179, 180, 188, 197,
        200, 241, 242, 245, 252, 254,
        256, 259, 261
    warrant, 252, 253
trait approach, 257
transitional probability, 41
transitive, 65, 71-76, 80-85, 99,
    131, 135, 138, 142,
    143, 147
transitive trials, 71, 72, 74
transmission bottleneck, 189, 191,
    199, 201

underspecification, 192, 194, 196
usage-based, 5, 7, 12, 13, 14, 48,
    49, 126, 127, 130, 133, 149, 151,
    152
    model, 4, 6, 12, 13, 14, 29, 31, 32,
        35, 42, 47-61, 109-113, 115,
        118, 126, 130, 131, 133, 135,
        136, 140-152, 157, 190, 206,
        225, 233, 241, 251, 252, 258,
        259, 260, 261

theory, 5, 12, 15, 18, 28, 40, 42,
  43, 57, 60, 86, 126, 127, 135,
  220, 236, 238, 241, 242, 251
Usage-based grammar, 260
utterance, 4, 6, 10, 48, 50, 80, 81, 82,
  93, 94, 96, 193, 194
Utterance Selection Model, 50

Verb-locative (VL), 90
validity, 249, 259, 261, 262,
  263
variant, 49- 61, 194, 195
variation, 2, 5, 9, 13, 14, 17, 48, 53,
  56, 58, 138, 164, 193, 199, 213,
216, 224, 230, 232, 234, 239, 240,
  251, 260, 262
verb-argument constructions
  (VACs), 90
vocal learning, 202
voter model, 51

weighted interactor selection, 47, 50,
  57, 60
white matter, 172, 173, 174, 175
word order, 11, 13, 69
word order bias, 11

Zipf's law, 95

LANGUAGE AS A COMPLEX ADAPTIVE SYSTEM

The Three Goals
David Budbill

The first goal is to see the thing clearly itself
in and for itself, to see it simply and clearly
for what it is.

      No symbolism, please.

The second goal is to see each individual thing
as unified, as one, with all the other
ten thousand things.

      In this regard, a little wine helps a lot.

The third goal is to grasp the first and second goals,
to see the universal and the particular,
simultaneously.

      Regarding this one, call me when you get it.

David Budbill, "The Three Goals" from *Moment to Moment: Poems of a Mountain Recluse*. Copyright © 1999 by David Budbill. Reprinted with the permission of Copper Canyon Press, www.coppercanyonpress.org.

15145972R00152

Made in the USA
Lexington, KY
20 May 2012